Claim Your Own Mental Fitness

Manage Your Mind

to Overcome

Addiction, Anxiety, Anger,
Grief, Trauma and Depression

and
Form Positive Relationships

REA ANNE SCOVILL, PHD

For my clients who have taught me so much.

Library of Congress Publication Data
Scovill, Rea Anne 1944

Claim your own mental fitness: manage your mind to overcome addiction, anxiety, grief, trauma and depression and form positive relationships. Includes bibliographical references and index.

ISBN-13: 978-1477507377
ISBN-10: 147750737X

1. Self-management
2. Resolving emotional problems
3. Relationships and parenting

Acknowledgments

First I want to acknowledge Alice Meehan, whose patient guidance of our young adolescent Sunday-school group led me to begin exploration of the Bible. I found in it inspiration for writing this book throughout the lengthy process; words such as "Everyone to whom much is given, of him will much be required" (Luke 12:48) helped prod me along. Our young, idealistic minister, Daniel Brand, told me that I had to look into my own heart to find the answers to my many questions. Warren Munro pressed me to develop strong writing skills in an English class at a high school where only 15 percent of the kids went to college and I never experienced an essay test. My parents sacrificed to send me to Swarthmore College, where Professors Thomas Blackburn and Harold Pagliaro wrote encouraging comments on my English literature papers. Their words helped me have the confidence to persevere through this work.

In the counseling psychology program at the University of Iowa, I was given an assistantship and living stipend. We studied numerous theories of personality along with the scientific basis for understanding human behavior. I was tasked to develop my own integrated therapy approach, combining what made the most sense to me from these. Robert Kurtz and Robert Stahman led their staff to provide wise, kind and well-devised training that has provided an excellent foundation for my thirty-five-year practice as a psychotherapist. The understanding I developed through the approach they taught has strengthened me personally and inspired me to keep growing professionally.

For the actual writing of the book, I must first recognize the enthusiastic support offered by my brother Jay, along with his thoughtful and diligent comments on the manuscript from start to finish. My son, Julian, has generously helped by providing the author photo, rendering the five figures and the front cover of the book and offering his insights. Numerous clients have read the book at various stages and offered comments that were especially helpful for the goal of making the book accessible to a wide variety of people. I must particularly thank my clients who had learning disabilities and struggled through the book, as they offered valuable insight into where my writing made it more difficult for them.

I've been blessed with the support of many dear people. My brother Pete offered his gentle feedback, knowing well my overly sensitive nature. Our friend Paul Hecker provided encouragement and support. My friend and fellow therapist Linda Herman shared with me the experience of writing as she crafted her book on parenting adult children while I wrote my book. She invited me to join Nancy Bartley's writing group, who listened to me read parts of my chapters. Nancy, a skilled journalist and writer, has offered many incisive suggestions. Linda Herman, Joan Breke, Sheila Ball, Liz Krantz, Barbara Harris, Maggie Ellis, Evelyn Huff, and Yvonne Waldbillig-Lutz have also given helpful feedback and lots of inspiration through their own writing.

My husband, John, has offered consistent encouragement and given up many hours of time with me over a four-year period. He's my computer guru who stepped in throughout the process to keep the machine humming and teach me new skills. He dropped everything to retrieve the book from backup when the computer crashed. He also thoughtfully edited the final version of the manuscript. He's been there for me in moments of doubt and times of exhaustion and taught me much about marriage up close and personal. Thank-you, John, my knight in shining armor.

Finally, I wouldn't have tackled a project like this if my clients hadn't shown me over the years that they needed more help than once-a-week therapy for a brief space in their lives. They taught me by their responses what ideas were useful to them, and those ideas became the focus of this book. Their sincere efforts to grow through our sessions and study on their own, their struggles with medication and frequent periods of inadequate help with debilitating emotional problems, and the fact that access for many was limited or denied for financial reasons inspired me to attempt a book like this.

I'd like to see many more books written from a broad perspective by experienced practitioners who know what actually helps clients grasp and hold on to what we teach. My clients taught me that they need us therapists to share our big picture view of what they need for mental fitness. They also need help to sort through the flood of self-help information available as they forge their own way of coping.

With the services available at CreateSpace, it's become easy and cost-effective to self-publish anything you want to share.. The writing support teams have offered valuable guidance in a process that respects me as a writer. I'd encourage other therapists to write about what they teach about mental fitness, describing the models they've found helpful and noting the references they'd recommend to clients. Our clients need more than what we can teach in our sessions to build and maintain mental fitness for life. This project has helped me clarify what I teach, and that's helped me grow too.

Contents

Contents

Addresses how inherited differences can affect your ability to manage your mind for mental fitness. Describes ways you can work around your own and others' limitations to improve your capacity to cope.

Describes how addiction works on many levels to derail your mental fitness. Offers tools that support sobriety and lasting self-esteem.

Describes how lifestyle and mental habits cause anxiety symptoms. Addresses short-term as well as more entrenched anxiety disorders. Offers a quick and powerful method to shut down a panic attack or other intense fight-or-flight reactions. Discusses medication issues for anxiety.

Describes how getting stuck in the angry stage of grief can undermine healing for a lifetime. Defines how to recognize and manage anger. Explains how to move through the grief process into stable mental fitness.

Demystifies dissociation, describing how it allows you to adapt and survive in a wide range of life situations. Describes trauma's impact on your mind and steps for re-associating traumatic memories. Identifies beliefs that cause avoidance of treatment and healing.

Describes how to overcome and prevent recurrence of depression. Addresses medication, heredity and relationship issues for depressed people. Briefly addresses bipolar-spectrum disorders and their special requirements.

Addresses how to stay on track by developing goals in key life categories. Suggests how to ensure that you hold beliefs and values that will maintain your mental fitness at good levels through stress for the rest of your life.

PART III: APPLICATIONS IN RELATIONSHIPS

Defines the elements of a relationship that allow it to deepen and grow over the years, as we hope our friendships will. Examines the beliefs that undermine friendship, and offers more flexible ways to look at friends. Describes how to cope when friendships wane.

Suggests how expectations for friendship should differ from those for acquaintance relationships. Explores how toxic beliefs can interfere with relationships at work, with neighbors and in community groups. Discusses issues unique to each of these areas.

Looks at how toxic beliefs can impact how you get along with your siblings, parents and extended families. Suggests using concepts for relating to friends and acquaintances to help define what's feasible with each relative.

Describes how toxic beliefs can interfere when you try to find an intimate partner. Suggests ways to use acquaintance skills to get to know a lot of prospects and friendship concepts to evaluate whether a prospect qualifies for a long-term relationship. Offers tips to help lead you away from especially negative prospects.

Describes the relationship between friendship and marriage. Explores how marriage can trigger beliefs that prevent intimacy, both sexual and emotional. Suggests ideas for how to create a home that supports mental fitness for both of you and your children.

Describes how to strengthen your mental fitness to help you meet the needs of your   developing children. Integrates concepts from previous chapters to help you manage your k i d s as unique individuals. Discusses the twelve toxic beliefs and how they can sabotage your   parenting. Offers techniques that can help you lead your kids into mental fitness and build your own along the way.

Challenges you to have courage and commitment to yourself as you work to develop the wise beliefs and expectations you need to enjoy the happy ending of mental fitness.

Appendices

List of Figures

Introduction

You're reading this book in search of something. How shall we define it? Shall we call it mental fitness, to be developed like an athlete builds his body for the triathlon of life? Shall we call it self-confidence, deeply rooted for all occasions? Or what about contentment that radiates out of feelings of fulfillment, both personally and in relationships? Each of you will likely define what you seek differently. Although you may come to this work because you suffer terrible anxiety or despair or you're worried about someone you love, bring along your capacity for wonder. New information about the human brain can inspire you to keep exploring how to manage your own mind for the rest of your life.

This book is offered as a guide and reference you can use to begin your work. Each chapter is designed to give you new things to try on your own or with occasional help from a therapist. Most of the work it takes to reach your potential must be done on your own, but you aren't given all the information you need to manage yourself well. Most of you can drive a car, use a computer or cell phone and cook if you have to. But you haven't been taught self-management 101. Here's an introductory course.

Introductory courses are broad but not superficial. I remember being enthralled with my intro-to-art course in college. I sensed the profound power of the works we studied. We didn't study all the artists of an era or all the works of each artist. But we got a sense for what was there for us to explore. You are the artist crafting your own life. You don't want to do it without knowing about the color blue or the feel of clay as you shape it or the way to create dimension in a drawing. You have all you need within you to craft a wonderful life. You just need to know how to access your strengths and manage the mind you have to carry you through.

This handbook is built on the principle that we can only learn in bite-sized pieces. Since mental fitness is not a simple goal, we'll begin with the most basic foundation concepts and move on to increasingly specific and personal functions. There are countless studies from many disciplines about how to learn. But you don't need them all for this introduction. I've selected just a few concepts and theories that work well to define the process. With these I've created an outline for your learning. Gradually you may develop a different organization that makes more sense to you as you find your unique ways of expressing your own mental fitness.

This book is organized in three parts, guiding you to build your mental fitness in order:

Part One: Learn how you can manage and care for your amazing human brain. Discover the basic principles of how your brain works and how it malfunctions to prevent mental fitness. Develop skills to help you identify and correct mental habits that would prevent your best functioning.

Part Two: Identify the obstacles you may encounter within yourself on your path to mental fitness. Natural variation in the human brain can cause difficulty. Human tendencies to avoid stress can get you caught up in an addiction that will stifle your growth. Emotional distress like anxiety, anger, grief or depression interferes with brain functioning and your ability to manage your mind. Explore ways to counter these obstacles and support continued growth in your mental fitness for life.

Part Three: Apply your new self-management skills in relationships. Since different kinds of relationships require different expectations, you'll need to recognize when you or others are taking the wrong approach. Learn concepts specific to each kind of relationship to improve your ability to handle all of them with confidence and success.

Throughout this study of mental fitness, you'll see that I've included the wisdom of others. Each chapter will offer some books or websites to help you explore more about the topics discussed. This book offers education, not therapy or medical treatment. If you have significant symptoms, you'll definitely need to seek counseling, medical advice and any other resource that can help you rebalance your mind. Times when you'd most likely need to get help are noted as we explore each problem area, but you should listen to your friends and family and your own sense of how you're doing to decide when to seek professional help. Your journey to mental fitness will definitely be shorter, more certain and less painful if you get help when you need it.

We're focusing on nonmedical approaches to mental health issues, but there are many physical problems that can contribute to insomnia, anxiety and depression. Brief mention will be made of these with each topic. It's important to get the best handle you can on any physical problems underlying your symptoms. Even a cold can reduce your ability to access new learning, and no amount of self-scrutiny will cure your depression if, for example, your thyroid is functioning poorly. Good mental self-care includes regular consultation with a primary-care doctor and any specialists recommended.

As you read you'll note that references to gender are alternated about every other paragraph. While this may be disconcerting at first, it is hoped that doing this will allow you to imagine examples of both men and women experiencing problems in similar ways in the situations described. We're working for a non-stereotypical understanding of yourself and your fellow humans.

Bring your curiosity along with your worries and enjoy this brief but pithy primer. Study the suggestions and seek help from a professional if you get stuck. This handbook won't conflict with what your therapist teaches you in most cases. It's built on guidance from a wide group of practitioners and researchers. Share it with people close to you so you can speak about your problems in the same language. Practice new mental habits until they become a part of you, overriding the old habits that pulled you down. You deserve to enjoy your life!

Introduction to
Part I:
Manage Your Mind for
Mental Fitness

art I offers an overview of how to manage your brain to build mental fitness. First I'll describe scientific principles to help keep your learning positive for you. Next we'll study a simple description of your three principal brain parts and how they can interact to cause emotional turmoil. Then we'll explore methods of calming and supporting your brain to prepare it for new learning.

We'll look at the ways you can observe how your different brain parts are functioning when you try to cope with stress. You'll learn a simple technique to calm yourself quickly and know why it works. Most importantly you'll discover the power of the brain part that lifts humans beyond the functioning of animals. We'll study key tools to help you keep this newly evolved, uniquely human, observing, organizing and coping brain part dominant. Step-by-step you'll build a program you can refer to daily to practice using these tools on your own.

How can you access what your mind holds secretly from your past that may interfere with your functioning and happiness? Through this program you'll get a handle on the parts of your brain responsible for your emotional reactions. You can know and understand these mysterious, ancient influences operating most often beneath your awareness. Gradually you can reprogram them to give you less worry and sadness, more contentment and confidence.

You'll learn how to maintain your new awareness of these ancient parts on a moment-to-moment basis, which will allow you to update them. Getting your whole brain connected with present reality is the key to functioning at your best each day. This can gradually bring you the self-control, self-esteem and resilient coping that you seek.

I:1

Learn Wisely to Learn Well

You may have felt overwhelmed if you've sought answers for your problems in the hundreds of books and articles available for self-help. I still laugh when I recall the time twenty years ago when I went to a bookstore to find books on improving sexual experience for couples. There weren't any in the self-help category, so I asked the young clerk where they might be. He blushed as he led me to the "how-to" section. When it really matters, people want to be sure they can find the answers without delay. It really matters that you find out how to understand and retrain your brain; both your relationships and sexual satisfaction will improve.

Let's zero in on *just what you need* to improve your situation. I'll refer you to others who've described the details in each problem area. How can you shut off a panic attack today? How can you stop letting that coworker irritate you now? How can you keep yourself motivated to complete tough projects? How can you stop getting anxious when you have to perform? How can you stop getting discouraged when you try hard but keep falling short of your goal? How can you manage your mind for stable mental fitness in the face of whatever life throws at you?

With this chapter you begin your study of how you can manage your mind to make yourself mentally fit. Let's start by helping you learn with comfort and efficiency. Through this lesson I hope you'll be able to enjoy this work more and suffer less frustration. To build your new learning, you must focus your inquiry. You need to study just one small cluster of concepts at a time to understand, practice and retain the memory of how they work. In this chapter we'll explore how to answer the following question: How can I learn to overcome uncomfortable and frustrating things about my mind with minimal discomfort and maximum speed?

Let's look at B. F. Skinner's work with simpler animals to identify the basics for what makes you tick. Skinner studied how rats and pigeons learn through experiments designed to isolate the key factors involved. He created a cage designed to guide and motivate these animals to learn. Called a Skinner box, this cage allowed him to try different rewards and punishments in a variety of ways to study how they learn. I'll just use the example of a pigeon. Skinner designed a way to deliver small amounts of food, like kernels of corn, through a chute into the cage if a pigeon pecked at a small disc nearby. The pigeon learned to peck the circle very quickly when he was rewarded each time he turned closer to the disc. Skinner called this rewarding "successive approximations" of the desired behavior and named this process "shaping."[1]

Skinner also studied the effects of punishment on learning with his Skinner box. For these experiments Skinner rigged an electric current to the wire mesh floor of the pigeon's cage. He discovered that punishment actually prevented the pigeon from learning to peck the disc; the pigeon became too distressed to learn anything. He went on to describe how for humans punishment also does not promote learning the new desired behavior. Instead people become fearful, avoidant, angry or even violent. Gradually, with more punishment, they lose interest in doing the things they used to enjoy, become irritable with others and lose their previous capacity to handle their responsibilities.[2]

How does Skinner's work with pigeons help answer our question? To reduce your discomfort as you try to learn new mental habits, you refrain from talking negatively to yourself when the work is disturbing or difficult. You don't shut down your efforts to learn by "shocking your feet" with punishing internal comments. To speed up your learning, note every time that you improve even a little when you practice a new habit or understand a new concept. Shape yourself with encouraging comments (and occasionally a chocolate candy) for your successive approximations of the new mental behavior. In this way you can comfortably build your new skills.

Shaping involves rewarding the change of one behavior at a time. This is why we'll study bite-sized pieces. You have to recognize when you've gotten something right so you can remember to do it that way again. If you give yourself a mental pat on the back, you hold on to the memory better. If you criticize yourself for not getting it perfectly, you chill your efforts.

Let's look at the story of Joe, who wanted to get himself to work out more to improve his mood and strengthen his muscles. Joe demanded a lot of himself at work and performed very well. Yet he reported that he constantly beat himself up for what he saw as his many failures. At home his many verbal shocks immobilized him like the pigeon. He spent his weekends and evenings on his couch eating crummy food and watching TV. He said he'd been depressed like this for months. He taunted himself for being weak-willed when he didn't keep his promise to go to the gym after work. He blamed himself for his lack of social relationships and for not knowing how to be happy. He tried to be honest with himself by focusing on his failures day after day. He told himself he was stupid, lazy, worthless, a loser and a social misfit.

Joe could recognize that he was feeling like the shocked pigeon. He set some goals to work out at the gym on a regular basis and to contact acquaintances to watch a game. Gradually Joe got himself to the gym more and more regularly. At first he learned to congratulate himself for going even once a week. He had berated himself for months because he stayed home. Now he had to refrain from that each night he didn't actually go. He tried different routines until he found one that would ease him into working out on his way home from work. Then he tried to be positive with himself about his success, rather than focusing on how out of shape he'd gotten or how he wasn't going even more often.

Joe began to give himself a pat on the back each time he made a call to a friend. He tried to stop finding fault with himself when he didn't get assurance that the other person really liked him. He tried to remind himself that if he was kind, polite and had a genuine interest in others, he could feel good about himself regardless of what another person thought. He tried to stop his usual punishing worry about what he might have done wrong.

Joe and I analyzed his new social experiences to help him identify what he was doing right each time to ensure that he kept doing those things. We briefly noted any missteps to help him avoid doing them but also to help him learn more supportive self-talk when he made what he considered an error. Joe gradually became more actively engaged and less depressed. He felt he was making progress toward learning how to be happy and was committed to keep working on it.

It will take some creative effort to design your own Skinner box for reaching your goals. You don't have a rewarding corn dispenser set up for you. You'll have to discover what steps to take to build your new habit or skill and what rewards will keep you working. Remind yourself that rewards, both in your self-talk and during your daily routines, are what you *must have* to guide, inspire and sustain your progress. Dwelling on your mistakes is powerful self-sabotage and is a habit you need to notice and cut short. You only need to note your mistakes long enough to stop them; that's all that punishment is good for. You should feel (a little) foolish—not virtuous—if you beat yourself up.

To help you set up your personal box of conditions for learning, I've gathered from the work of Skinner and other writers just what is necessary for developing mental fitness. Each of them addresses other issues we'll ignore and shut out of this box. Gradually you'll develop the ability to select for yourself what you need to grow and ignore what isn't helpful. To maintain and further develop your skills, begin a computer file or a notebook where you write in your own words what helps you hold on to each concept or skill as you progress through this book and long afterwards. Eventually you'll master these mental habits, and they'll become natural for you.

When you encounter new stressors, like recovering from an accident or coping with a new baby, you can resume your focused shaping techniques if you need new mental habits to cope with these. Skinner offered the phrase "thematic prompt" for reminding yourself of what you've just begun to learn.[3] Once you understand a concept and have practiced it a little, create a thematic prompt to help you access it the next time you need it. Skinner indicates these only work if you already know the concept. When you need to redirect your thinking, use short phrases as thematic prompts to cut off your negative self-talk patterns quickly and substitute positive comments instead. Watch for quotes that you can post on your bathroom mirror or in your phone to help recondition your brain.

Look at your phrase-prompts often and practice them until they reside in your own mind. Instead of saying, "To be honest, I really haven't done my best here," try phrases like these and make up prompts that especially speak to you:

- What kernel of corn can I give myself now?

- Oops! That's shocking my feet again.

- Enough of the self-abuse!

- My goal in this is to…

- What would be a good first step?

- At least I tried it and got a couple of things right.

- What should I work on the next time?

- What little rewards can help keep me on track today?

To learn wisely and learn well, remember these four steps:

1. Focus to define your new skill in bite-sized pieces.

2. Develop it by using positive self-talk and other rewards.

3. Practice it deliberately and often.

4. Be patient with yourself and avoid negative self-talk that discourages you.

Notes

1. B. F. Skinner, *Science and Human Behavior* (1953; repr., New York: The Free Press, 1965), 91–98.
2. Ibid., 172–178.
3. Ibid., 214.

I : 2

Prepare Your Brain

Mental fitness requires a healthy brain. Even an otherwise functional brain becomes impaired when it's not allowed to recover each day. Are you forgetful, irritable, having problems with concentration and not following through with things? Are you feeling like you are on your very last nerve, at the end of your rope or losing it too often? You're very likely sleep-deprived. Before you try to evaluate what new habits to develop for improved mental fitness, give your brain some rest. You'll find the learning process much easier and you'll have fewer and milder emotional symptoms after just a few days of adequate sleep.

Focus on how you can give your brain and body a good night's sleep. You may not be allowing yourself the eight or nine hours most people need to sleep. Ask for your family's support and change your work schedule to allow enough time for sleep at the same time each night as often as possible. If you function well on six or seven hours, be sure to plan for that much time nightly. But don't think you can enjoy stable mental fitness or develop new skills in managing your life if you're chronically denying your brain enough time to recover.

Perhaps you're allowing enough time for sleep but find yourself unable to get restorative sleep during that time. Do you feel like you're sleeping but wake up feeling tired? Medication, sleep apnea or some other physical problem may be interfering with your quality of sleep. Consult with your primary-care doctor to improve your condition as much as possible. Avoid medication to help you sleep until you've tried the techniques described below, if possible, because it can prevent you from getting quality sleep.

You may be one of the many people who allow themselves time to sleep but often lie awake too much of that time wishing they could sleep. This wish can become desperate and frustrating when the problem gets worse and you dread how awful you're going to feel the next day or how poorly you'll function due to your exhaustion. Rubin Naiman has researched intensively to discover what can interfere with your getting the sleep you need and what you can do to improve the quality of your sleep.[1] His suggestions are included below.

As you work on preparing your brain for mental fitness, remember to stay positive with yourself. Guide yourself into your new sleep habits one step at a time. As you keep trying, you'll gradually get into a calmer, more sleep-friendly state of mind, even if you can't get all the sleep you'd like. It's a vicious circle; you're so tired you can't manage yourself well, and that upsets you so much that you can't sleep. Be gentle and stay positive with your sleep-deprived self as you try to make these changes, despite having a less functional brain. You may even need to ask your spouse or a counselor to help you remember to make a doctor's appointment or follow through with a particular step until you're better rested. Here are the steps to build new mental habits that support a good night's sleep:

1. Develop good sleep hygiene.
    A. Go to sleep and get up at the same time seven days a week as much as possible; this consistency is especially important when you're just beginning to establish your improved pattern. Allow for eight to nine hours of sleep during a one-block time period each day.
    B. Sleep in a cool, quiet, dark room. Sleep quality is better when you stay comfortably cool. Your brain won't make the melatonin you need for sleeping all night unless the room is totally dark. Naiman's studies indicate that even a night-light or turning on a light briefly can interfere with production of melatonin for the entire night. Install room-darkening shades or use an eye mask if it's too light. Earplugs help if noise can't be avoided.
    C. Develop a pre-sleep routine. Don't eat a meal, drink or exercise within at least two hours of going to bed. However,

a light, non-liquid snack like a piece of toast may improve brain chemistry for sleep. Avoid emotional stimulation from television or relationships before bed. Ask for cooperation from others in your life to address issues much earlier in the day if possible. Naiman stresses the need to reduce the amount of light you have in the hours immediately preceding sleep, because lower light signals the brain to prepare itself for sleep. Before artificial light was developed, that's what nature provided.

2. Prepare your thoughts for restorative sleep.
   A. At least one hour before bed, take fifteen minutes to sit down with a pen and paper and think through your day. Ask yourself, "What might bother me when I try to sleep?" Identify any worrisome thought, interpersonal encounter or frustrating task that you experienced. Briefly list each of these.
   B. Review the list. You're engaging your waking brain to handle some of your issues before your overactive night brain takes over and tries to solve them. You won't eliminate all the problems but you can greatly reduce them, leaving your night brain less disturbed and with less to process. You'll see that your list breaks out into three categories:
      a. Items that you can solve right now just by giving yourself some time to think them through outside the pressures and distractions of the day. Cross these off your list.
      b. Items that can be addressed tomorrow or at some future time. Make a second list for these and note when you can get to them. Create a plan for your next day, including some of these. Cross them off your first list.
      c. Items that will be on your list for a longer time; these are your ongoing stressors, like health or financial concerns you can't handle quickly. It may help to consider what steps you've already taken—like working with your doctor—to reassure your night brain that things are not too scary. You may be able to think of some additional tasks for a second "to do later" list to reduce these worries further.

4. Take steps to manage your stress better. In the chapters ahead you'll study new skills to help reduce your reactivity to problems. Consider seeking a therapist if you're struggling. She can offer ideas your tired brain might not think of and encouragement (kernels of corn) you might not be able to provide yourself yet. You can add "ask my counselor" to the "plan" side of your list for items that seem to defy any solution. This idea of help might soothe your night brain a little.

5. Carefully consider medication. For some stressful times medication may help you be less anxious or depressed during the day and sleep better at night. Naiman indicates that since most medications for sleep are habit-forming and prevent quality sleep, they should be used as little as possible. He describes the widespread social damage caused by an epidemic of reliance on sleep-inducing drugs. He indicates that most drugs, including over-the-counter sleep aids, prevent dreaming and create a fake sleep that leaves you deeply fatigued. Further he notes there's a rebound of miserable insomnia when you try to stop taking sleep medication. This tends to make you resume taking the drugs. He describes how dreaming increases after you take drugs that suppress it and may temporarily cause problems during the day.

Try to develop the above-described sleep habits before you seek medication. Naiman suggests valerian, 5-HTP and tryptophan for short-term insomnia, rather than dream-suppressing antidepressants or addictive tranquilizers. Melatonin taken in no more than three-milligram doses (more can cause insomnia) and herbal formulas like Sleep MD help some people and may not cause dependency or interfere with the quality of sleep. Work with your doctor and your therapist to find the best formula for you with the goal of using medication as briefly as possible.

You must be sure you have been evaluated for obstructive sleep apnea before you start taking medication to help you sleep. You can find user-friendly discussions about how to recognize this and its impact on your health at MedicineNet.com.[2] Symptoms include memory and concentration problems, fatigue, headaches, irritability and snoring. If you have obstructive sleep apnea you have three times the risk of being in a car accident than the general population. Untreated it leads to high blood pressure within four years, congestive heart failure, atrial fibrillation and insulin resistance which can lead to diabetes. Four per cent of men in the United States have this problem and two per cent of women. Obesity makes it worse. It is estimated that only ten per cent of those who have this disorder receive treatment. I've had two men referred to me in the past year for treatment of anxiety, irritability, headaches or concentration problems. Both had obstructive sleep apnea. Treatment eliminates symptoms and may reverse medical complications. Treatment varies, but most people overcome even the awkwardness of a sleep machine when they start to feel so much better every day.

If you aren't diagnosed with sleep apnea, consider medication. Observe the effects of any medication on how you function the next day. Memory problems, irritability and fatigue indicate you haven't found the answer yet. Some people feel better the next day after having slept poorly than after sleeping with the help of medication. Keep track of what you've tried and what the effects have been in your mental fitness notebook or computer file. Some of the most troubling cases I've seen are people who've taken sleep medication for years and no longer can get the benefits of any medication. They become very desperate and may lose their ability to function. It seems as though the medication has created permanently the problem it was prescribed to cure.

For some mental health problems, like bipolar disorder, medication that addresses the disorder and also ensures sleep is not optional and must usually be used indefinitely. Sleep deprivation can quickly and seriously destabilize many people with bipolar disorder. Medications to treat clinical depression and severe anxiety usually help prevent insomnia, although they also impact the quality of sleep, according to Naiman. Despite their drawbacks they offer much-needed support for these conditions when used appropriately. Treatment and medication for these problems will be further discussed in Part II.

Careful use of medication can be very helpful. Your insomnia may have left you so exhausted that even medication-impaired sleep is better than nothing for a while. Be sure your doctors do a thorough evaluation, follow up with you the entire time you're medicated and listen to your feedback respectfully. Change doctors if you find yours is impatient with your concerns and complaints. You're experimenting with your brain in ways that are still poorly understood and you deserve the most thoughtful guidance.

Additional guidance for understanding sleep, dreams and how to get more restorative sleep is offered in Alex Lukeman's book *Sleep Well, Sleep Deep: How Sleeping Well Can Change Your Life.*[3]

Notes

1. Rubin R. Naiman, *Healing Night: The Science and Spirit of Sleeping, Dreaming and Awakening* (Minneapolis: Syren Book Co., 2006).
2. MedicineNet, wwwmedicinenet.com/sleep apnea. Accessed June 9, 2012.
3. Alex Lukeman, *Sleep Well, Sleep Deep: How Sleeping Well Can Change Your Life* (New York: M. Evans & Co., 1999).

I : 3

Keep Your Cool

We have many styles for losing our cool. We get anxious or angry, hurt or irritated. We each express these feelings in our own way. We may yell, withdraw, distract, throw things, curse, spew out words, avoid or even suppress our feelings in an effort to deny we've lost it. This can happen during an otherwise peaceful day when we've felt calm and enjoyed pleasant activities. Where do these explosions of feeling come from? How can we prevent or interrupt them? We feel embarrassed or just frustrated when we lose our cool, and this distracts us from what we're trying to do. We'll often blame ourselves rather than learn from the situation, shocking our feet (like Skinner's pigeon) and shutting ourselves down.

Why is it so hard for us to keep our cool? There are lots of reasons. In this chapter we'll study how our three-part brains set us up to have trouble. We're using a greatly simplified model of the brain to focus on a basic problem with how we're wired. This model was described by Louis Cozolino in a 2008 article for professionals.[1] We're wired to lose our cool and have to work hard to stop overreacting to events we experience. We deserve to know how these problems begin with our own brains.

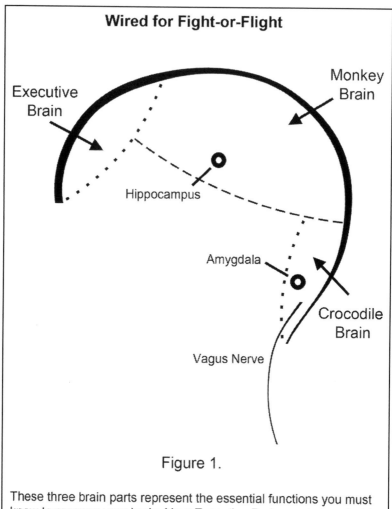

Wired for Fight-or-Flight

Figure 1.

These three brain parts represent the essential functions you must know to manage your brain. Your Executive Brain must stay alert to keep your Monkey Brain from signalling your Crocodile Brain to put your body into fight-or-flight.

Where Do You Lose Your Cool?

Let's look at figure 1, which offers a side-view model of the brain. It shows three primary brain parts: the neo-cortex, the mammalian and the reptilian brains. Each of these is very complex, comprised of many parts that perform a multitude of functions. An excellent source if you want to understand your brain and how it works with more accurate detail is John B. Arden's 2010 book *Rewire Your Brain*.[2] You don't need to study the brain in this complexity to keep your cool. Here's what you need to know:

1. The neo-cortex is the most recently evolved part of the brain, hence "neo" for "new." It's the part that most dramatically separates humans from other animals. It's called the *executive brain* because it organizes, evaluates and carries out your plans. Like an internal manager, it can observe you as you go through your days and direct you to change your thoughts and behaviors.

2. The next brain area is called the ancient mammalian, because it formed in mammals like monkeys thousands of years ago. Your *monkey brain* sorts, connects, stores and interprets incoming information from the senses, the body and the executive brain. Its focus is to recognize any incoming data that could threaten your survival.[3] It quickly notifies your reptilian brain if there seems to be a threat.

3. The reptilian brain is so named because it very closely resembles the brain of a crocodile and other reptiles. For our purposes you can think of it as your *on-off switch* that is under the control of your monkey brain. When your monkey brain interprets incoming data to be threatening, the *crocodile brain* switch goes to "on" and your Vagus nerve alerts your body to prepare for running away or fighting to protect you and save your life. This is called *the fight-or-flight response.*

How Do You Lose Your Cool?

You lose your cool when your ancient brain parts overwhelm your executive brain. Consider how the other two parts are oriented. Your monkey brain is designed to respond very quickly to any possible danger. Since it often can't tell whether a danger is life-threatening or simply unpleasant, it errs on the side of caution and signals your crocodile brain to switch into fight-or-flight mode too frequently. Your crocodile brain's main function is to respond to messages from the monkey brain without question and trigger your body into fight-or-flight immediately.

Your executive brain evaluates your life situation to decide which of many responses would be best. When you're delayed in traffic, lose your keys, lose your job, cope with an injury to your child, forget an appointment or suffer rejection by a lover, it's up to your executive brain to recognize quickly that your life isn't threatened even though you feel upset. Next it must tell your monkey brain *not* to signal your crocodile brain into action. If your executive brain fails to do this clearly and quickly, your monkey brain will interpret these situations as life-threatening and immediately involve your body through your crocodile brain. This is how you lose your cool.

A Huge Misunderstanding

Unfortunately your executive brain is not generally trained to recognize or communicate that the situation isn't actually life-threatening. Instead it focuses intensely on each problem, big or small, making false conclusions and extravagant statements about how terrible this is for you. You'll say repeatedly, "This is killing me" or "I just can't take this anymore" or "This is unbearable." You don't naturally say, "This is terrible, but it won't kill me" or "I hate being in traffic, but I can stand to wait if I have to" or "It's incredibly unfair, but unfairness must be tolerated." These false statements often put your crocodile brain into action several times a day to save your life, though in reality your life is actually threatened only once every ten years if that. The one time your life truly might be threatened is when you're riding in your car, where impulsive fight-or-flight is clearly not helpful.

Input from your monkey brain keeps your poorly trained executive brain confused. Since 80 percent of the nerve fibers from the Vagus nerve flow from the body to the brain,[4] your executive brain gets overwhelmed quickly once fight-or-flight is signaled. Your monkey brain frequently misinterprets your executive brain's comments. If you're running late, your stomach may knot up or your head begins to ache. Unless you're late getting out of a burning building, these are inappropriate reactions. But your monkey brain notices the intensity of your executive brain's concern and concludes you're in danger. This must have been a valuable connection when humans were constantly threatened by predators or earthquakes in the early stages of our evolution. It may be helpful in war zones today. But in your usual daily life, it's an annoying and unnecessary throwback to ancient times that needs to be recognized for what it is.

Here's an example that illustrates how your executive brain can set off a misunderstanding even when you're not that concerned about something. In my mid-thirties I had a new job that kept me at a desk all day for the first time in my life. I felt that I was losing my body tone and told myself over a period of months that I needed to get more exercise. I wasn't really worried, because I hadn't changed my exercise habits. I just observed now and then, "I'm getting out of shape, and it's not good for me."

One night I awoke from a sound sleep in a panicky state, my heart racing, my breathing labored and my stomach clenched. I'd been dreaming that I was running as fast as I could to catch up with my sister to inform her that she had a life-threatening disease. This disease was causing her body to distort into the shape of a child's toy figure—a rubbery, flattened Gumby doll character. She would glare over her shoulder as she kept ahead of me, telling me to leave her alone. Next I was also chasing my brother, who had the same affliction. In the dream I *knew* that if they didn't get immediate treatment they would die, but they wouldn't listen to me.

As I gasped for breath and shook with the memory of this nightmare, I (using my executive brain) applied my dream-interpretation techniques to crack it. I had no idea where it came from. I wasn't sick, I don't have a sister and my brothers were healthy. Frederick Perls' Gestalt psychology gave me my first technique, which was to consider each part of the dream as a projected part of myself and my feelings.[5] I realized I was chasing my male and female parts. But why? I turned to my second dream-interpretation technique to survey what worrisome thoughts I might have had in the previous day or two that my oh-so-helpful monkey brain might be trying to process.

After a bit of musing and trying to calm myself, I got the connection. I'd been telling myself that I was out of shape for months. Finally my monkey brain became alarmed and played out the problem in its melodramatic style in this dream. The main point here is just how overblown the reaction was. Fortunately it takes more than a few months of a sedentary lifestyle to kill us. My executive brain was fully aware of that fact as it observed that I was out of shape. I wasn't particularly upset, and my executive brain didn't actually perceive any danger, but my monkey brain listened each time I said that and concluded it needed to take over, warning me in a nightmare to save my life.

Flip Your Fight-or-Flight Switch to "Off"

Keep your cool by talking more carefully to your monkey brain to keep it from engaging your crocodile brain in fight-or-flight. Think about this from the point of view of a crocodile. When a crocodile is startled, it doesn't ask why; it just slides into the swamp or attacks. It doesn't do this because of something that might happen in an hour or a week; it's only reactive to immediate danger. When your executive brain worries too often about non-life-threatening things, your monkey brain may interpret this frequent signaling to mean that the situation is immediately dangerous.

Therefore, if your body feels tense, override all the confusion by stating clearly, "This won't kill me," "I won't die from any of these worries" or "I hate when this happens but I can get through it." I learned to say to my stomach, "I get to worry about this without *you* getting involved." Talk simply and with conviction, as though you were trying to reassure a frightened four-year-old child. Get your monkey brain to turn your fight-or-flight switch to "off."

Remember that even the smartest monkey isn't worrying about next week or even tonight. Only your executive brain has the ability to know that future events *aren't* an immediate threat that calls for your body to get into fight-or-flight mode. Your body can't solve many of your problems at all. Your executive brain must speak clearly to your monkey and crocodile brains on a continual basis to keep your cool. Body reactions can remind your executive brain that it's time for a clarifying word.

Begin to keep track of the self-talk that triggers your particular system into action. Practice noticing what you said to yourself before your body had an uncomfortable reaction. I've described some triggering phrases. Watch out for more subtle ones that are just below your awareness. For example, you may think it's unfair that you didn't get a raise, but your body may not get triggered until you say you "can't stand" this unfairness. Other similar phrases are that you "can't bear" it or it's "intolerable." One client noticed that when she said it was "unacceptable" that her husband did something, that's when she'd really explode. "I've had it" has similar power for many.

Calm Yourself with the Truth

As you isolate and combat these overblown phrases from your thoughts, find truthful and more calming statements to replace them with. Your monkey brain can tell when you're giving it false reassurance. Try phrases like "I hate that I have to bear this but I can," "I'm really upset about this but I can deal with it" or "I don't want to stand it but I can." As I struggled to overcome panic attacks years ago, I often told myself, "Just stick to the truth; don't rile yourself up with a bunch of lies about what you can't stand." I found I could say I hated something or that I was furious or sad as much as I wanted to without getting panicky. I just couldn't tell myself that I "couldn't stand" feeling those things. Look for your own triggering phrases and revise them.

Once you begin this process, you'll realize you've been able to stand these upsetting things many times before and will likely have to deal with such annoyances again, like losing your phone, finding your children have made a mess, overdrawing your bank account and all the other repeated aggravations of your daily life. It just gets you more frustrated to engage your body by telling it you can't stand them. Perhaps your monkey brain translates these words literally and prepares your body quickly to help you avoid being crushed. If you take flight and quit trying to cope, you haven't solved the problem. If you fight by yelling or throwing things, you may create even more of what you already felt you couldn't stand.

Even when they only get partly hooked, your body systems are stressed and through your Vagus nerve interfere with your executive brain's capacity to sort out the situation. Of course habitual, unnecessary arousal of your body does cause fatigue and eventually damages the heart, nerves and glandular systems. This stress won't kill you any time soon though. You don't have to focus on your rapid heart rate and scare yourself about your body's reactions as many do. You have time to learn better coping skills.

If you have trouble sleeping after you've done the writing exercise in chapter 2, add "It won't kill me" after each worry on your list. This gives your monkey brain a clear signal that all these worries aren't issues it needs to dramatize in your dreams. Try to make a workable plan or even a first step for each worry. When you can't find a plan for a serious worry, note that it won't kill you *tomorrow* and you might get some sleep. Your on-off switch is only relevant for *immediate* danger.

Another way your brain gets confused and moves into fight-or-flight is when you punish yourself with negative self-talk about your own behavior. In chapter 1 we discussed B. F. Skinner's observations that punishment creates the feelings and bodily reactions of fear, avoidance and potentially violent rage. These reactions happen because your monkey and crocodile brains signal your Vagus nerve to prepare for fight-or-flight. Realize that you need to avoid punishing treatment of yourself for this reason as well. You've learned that you can't build new behavior with punishment. Now you're learning that you can't keep your cool if you practice it either.

The three-part design of your brain sets you up to switch into fight-or-flight too quickly. You must sharpen your executive brain at the same time you reprogram your monkey and crocodile brains to be less reactive. In the next chapter I'll walk you through a process that will help you do both. Gradually you'll be prepared to unravel more complicated reaction patterns in Part II, like anxiety, depression or addiction. These also make it hard to keep your executive brain in charge and keep your cool. Finally you'll be ready to tackle keeping your cool in relationships when you study them in Part III.

Here are some self-talk thematic prompts to help remind you of these concepts and stay calm:

- I hate this but it won't kill me.

- This may seem unbearable but people, including me, can bear a lot.

- I don't want to do this but I can stand it.

- Looking around, I can see that I'm in no immediate danger.

- This person is annoying and offensive but not dangerous.

- I've got this handled; my body doesn't need to get involved.

- It won't help to get myself all upset.

- I screwed up but I'm in no danger because of it.

- This is more like a chess game than a battle for survival.

Notes

1. Louis Cozolino, "How Evolved Are We? The Triune Brain in the Consulting Room," *Psychotherapy Networker*, September/October 2008, 20-27.
2. John B. Arden, *Rewire Your Brain: Think Your Way to a Better Life* (Hoboken: John Wiley, 2010).
3. Douglas Fox, "The Private Life of the Brain," *New Scientist*, November 2008, 28-31.
4. Bessell A. van der Kolk, "New Frontiers in Trauma Treatment," workshop by The Institute for the Advancement of Human Behavior, 2007.
5. Erving and Miriam Polster, *Gestalt Therapy Integrated: Contours of Theory and Practice* (New York: Vintage Books, 1974).

I : 4

Meet and Reprogram Your Inner family

The focus in Part I is to teach you the keys for how to manage your mind for mental fitness. Chapter 1 described some learning strategies from B. F. Skinner. Chapter 2 discussed how to prepare your brain for its best functioning by getting enough sleep. Chapter 3 defined how to manage your most extreme reactions by limiting your brain's fight-or-flight responses. This chapter will incorporate these ideas to show you how to reprogram your brain permanently for mental fitness. You'll learn a way of thinking about your brain that will allow you to manage it intuitively as you go through your days. Then you'll learn research-based techniques for how to reprogram it for easier management indefinitely. Chapter 5 will describe behavioral things you can do to keep yourself comfortable and happy as you begin to apply these principles in parts 2 and 3.

Before scientists could observe the brain in action with modern brain-imaging techniques, therapists tried to describe what they thought was happening in their clients' brains. They based their theories on what clients reported about their feelings and their behavior. In the early twentieth century, Sigmund Freud named what we're calling the executive brain the "conscious" mind. He grouped our monkey and crocodile brains into functions called the "unconscious." Freud also divided the unconscious into the "superego" and "id," which he described over decades of writing in similar language not designed for use by nonprofessionals.[1]

An Intuitive Model of Your Mind

In the mid-twentieth century, Eric Berne renamed these parts and redefined them to help the average person manage his own mind in his book *Games People Play: The Psychology of Human Relationships.*[2] He named our personality parts Adult, Parent and Child. Although the Adult part does correspond to the executive brain described in chapter 3 and figure 1, the Parent and Child parts don't really line up with the monkey and crocodile brain parts and are very much intertwined. In chapter 3 I noted how quickly a worry in your Adult mind could set them off together into fight-or-flight.

Because of this connection, I'll use the term "inner family" to talk about the combined activities of your Parent and Child parts when it's not useful to identify them separately. You may wonder if the inner family would correspond to Freud's concept of the unconscious. Since I've found that Freud's word choice is often confusing for clients, we'll study the inner family only in terms that help teach you how to understand and manage it.

Your goal is to manage your mind as you encounter your life. For years I've found that Eric Berne's model gives clients a quick grasp of what they're dealing with. When Joe in chapter 1 came in feeling stuck and down on himself, he could identify some with Skinner's pigeon with the shocked feet. But he could really recognize his Child part's feelings of rebellion and hurt. He could easily see that his Parent was beating his Child up, then he could join me more comfortably in an Adult-to-Adult discussion about how to turn this around after sorting out his Child and Parent parts.

I'll borrow from Berne's model because it defines aspects of your mind that feel familiar to you immediately. You can begin at once to manage and redesign your brain with these intuitive concepts. Let's look briefly at each one.

Your Child

Your Child is the creative, personal part of you that expresses your energy. You can tell when your Child is triggered into fight-or-flight by the types of feelings that are expressed in your body through crying, yelling, stomach pain, muscles tensing or dizziness. Your Child expresses lots of positive feelings through your body, too, with a lightened feeling, a laugh, a wink, singing or a quiet contentment. Your Child holds your sense of yourself and your feelings of love, hate, joy, sorrow, pride and shame. It holds beliefs about your self-worth, security and what you deserve. Its beliefs about itself and what it anticipates from others develop as it interacts with others.

Your young inner Child is like a three- to eleven-year-old in its need for approval and in its feelings of vulnerability. You can access it easily by thinking about how you felt and how the world looked to you during your childhood. Remember first grade? The playground? The teacher, the alphabet posted in your classroom, other kids? How about your neighborhood and the kids you played with? What did your first bike look like, and how did you learn how to ride it? You felt vulnerable and wanted to depend on your parents for your care and security as a young child. You accepted their guidance, because your brain was designed to admire and trust them out of your need to receive their help in order to survive.

Your adolescent Child is like a twelve- to eighteen-year-old in its demands for recognition and its anger when it's thwarted. By this time your brain has developed enough to make you seek gradual independence from your parents' guidance and control, because you need them less for your survival. You increasingly seek to define your own beliefs, looking more to your friends than your parents for ideas about who you want to be. This adolescent part also holds the Child energy and creativity of your system, though they are expressed in more grown-up ways. It has strong positive and negative feelings about your worth and what you should be entitled to do. It's more rebellious than your young Child part, ambivalent about depending on your parents and more frequently angry.

You can observe either of these Child parts when you laugh at a joke, cry over a sad story or feel indignant over someone's hypocrisy. You express your Child when you create a project, share your feelings with another person or clap your hands with enthusiasm at a play. Below I'll describe how your Parent parts impact your Child's sense of who you are as they try to manage its feelings and behavior. Create a file in your computer or a file case to hold what you discover about your Child and fill it with color, humor and wise quotes. You'll get some sense of its nature and what it needs from this chapter. Chapter 5 will offer ideas for how to support your Child's growth, along with activities that will encourage your Child's creativity, confidence and contentment. The more comfortable your Child is, the more your Adult will be able to focus on managing the world outside yourself.

Your Parent

Your Parent sorts, interprets and stores incoming information. Its ways of doing this are rooted in your culture and your experience growing up with your own parents. The Parent holds the beliefs you've formed about what to expect in life, how you should evaluate your experience and what kind of person you are. These beliefs form a network for sorting new experiences that can bias your interpretation of new events. The Parent can be harsh and critical, indulgent and supportive, wise or ignorant. Discussion of your Parent is divided into three parts: Critical, Indulgent and Wise. Create a file to collect your insights about your Parent to grow as you do and remind you in the future.

Your Parent holds beliefs about rules and what you *should* do or be. Your Parent functions to restrict or nurture your Child part, impacting your feelings of self-worth and security. Your Parent expresses beliefs absorbed from your parents, teachers and other social influences. If your parents held reality-based beliefs as you developed, your Parent will probably treat your Child kindly. If not, unless you've had some healing input, your Parent's faulty interpretations will make your Child feel bad unfairly. Later I'll discuss how your Adult can reprogram your Parent to help you overcome toxic influences from the past.

You can recognize your Parent when you find yourself pointing at someone and scolding him. Your Parent is active when you comfort a friend with soothing words or talk with them about how you think things should be. Your parent gives your Child permission to relax, have fun or spend money. It can also scold your Child for having too much fun or failing to get something done. And your Parent can comfort your Child when it is hurt, lonely, frustrated or disappointed.

You can also recognize when your Parent is communicating beliefs to your Child by noticing when there's a shift in your feelings. If you were driving around feeling peaceful and suddenly felt a pang of anxiety in the pit of your stomach, your Parent told your Child something that made it afraid. What did your Parent say? You may be able to identify this quickly at times or you may have to explore your Parent more deeply to figure it out. As your Adult works to bring your Parent up-to-date, it becomes kinder, more reasonable and less prone to set off fight-or-flight reactions.

Your Adult

Your Adult functions separately from your Child and Parent parts, but the reactions of the latter two can overwhelm your Adult at times. In chapter 3 I discussed how your executive brain is in charge of helping you keep your cool and manages the fight-or-flight tendencies of your other brain parts. I call your executive brain your Adult throughout this book. Adult is a good name for this part, because it can only be fully expressed when your brain capacity has reached maturity at about age twenty-five in adulthood.

Your Adult observes, evaluates and modifies your behavior and attitudes. It's responsible for managing and harmonizing your Parent and Child parts for effective functioning. It's your reasoning, non-emotional brain part. Your Adult is also charged with managing how you relate to the outer world. Only your Adult can plan how to keep you fed, clothed and sheltered, organize your activities with other people to meet your social needs and provide for the education you need to find meaningful work. To accomplish these things, your Adult has to motivate your inner family to follow through with the goals it sets.

Your Adult has the life experience to recognize errors in Child and Parent beliefs but can't hold an independent perspective until it can fend off inner family influences. As I noted earlier, your inner family holds beliefs from your childhood. Some beliefs formed when you were very young and believed that your parents knew everything about you and life. Some beliefs developed as you interacted with other kids, teachers and neighbors. You picked up some expectations as you watched people interacting on television or in videos.

While you watched and participated, your Parent and Child parts formulated beliefs about the rules for living. Your Adult will operate as if these rules are true for your present circumstances until it can examine them. For example, you might expect your boss to be unfair if your mother was or assume that it's your fault if a friend gets mad at you. Your Adult choices for a reaction will be inappropriate if its judgment is skewed by Parent-Child influences.

Your Adult must handle your inner and outer worlds with flexibility in order to balance the demands of each. Only a strong, independent Adult can possibly perform all the Adult responsibilities well. Remember to keep your Adult ready to learn by following the guidelines I've already defined: keep yourself rested, use positive feedback much more than negative and keep your cool by shutting down extreme fight-or-flight reactions quickly.

I've noted a fourth requirement for learning: take it in bite-sized pieces. Below I describe a process and some concepts that will help your Adult organize your personal Skinner box to manage your new learning step by step. After introducing some new concepts, I'll discuss how you can use them to hold your learning together after you've grasped each one. Using key phrases to prompt your memory, you'll soon be able to practice these concepts in your daily life.

Tools to Help Your Adult Take Charge: Cognitive-Behavioral Therapy

Therapists have developed tools to help your Adult manage its responsibilities more effectively. In the 1950s Albert Ellis defined a process for maintaining Adult awareness of Parent-Child activity, calling it rational-emotive therapy.[3] Gradually therapists evolved his and other practitioners' discoveries into what is now called cognitive-behavioral therapy. This process describes how to recognize when you overreact and to identify specific self-talk that caused the extreme reaction. Why is self-talk so important? It reveals to your Adult the beliefs from the past that your Parent and Child parts use to interpret your present experience; it's your window into your inner world.

Once your Adult knows the beliefs creating your overreactions, you can modify the beliefs and your behavior. For example, in chapter 3 we changed "I can't stand it" to "I hate this but I *can* stand it" to reduce fight-or-flight tendencies. Fight-or-flight reactions are of course disturbing. As cognitive-behavioral therapy (CBT) allows you to become more aware of all your reactions and identify the beliefs triggering them, you may find that you're struggling to keep your Adult perspective.

If that happens you must seek out a CBT therapist to help you revise the disturbing beliefs that are causing your Child to get so upset. After clients learn how to use CBT, many return to therapy for brief tune-ups, managing well with their own tools in the meantime. They seek help when increased reactivity indicates there's a belief that they need to revise but can't identify or combat on their own or when life events overwhelm their Adult capacities.

Cognition is just a fancy word for thought or belief. CBT is a system that allows your Adult to manage your inner family. When you struggle with overreactions in your inner family, you can't always change your life circumstances or your feelings about them. But your Parent and Child both have beliefs and expectations you *can* uncover and evaluate. By examining these exposed beliefs with your Adult, you can find ways to revise them and take a different approach to your problems. Let's look at the key elements of CBT to equip your Adult for its work.

Toxic beliefs: CBT allows you to recognize beliefs programmed in during childhood that routinely override evidence from your actual experience. In fact, by third grade most people without this programming would evaluate situations more accurately. Your tainted interpretation of experiences leads you into disappointment, hurt and anger. Probably some of your beliefs are unique to Western culture, while others are more universally human. I'll focus on twelve of the most common ones, but you'll discover additional toxic beliefs as you practice CBT over the years.

Combating a belief: This work is the core of CBT. To change a belief, your Adult identifies it and then finds ways to correct it to reprogram your Child and Parent parts. Since literally hundreds of books and countless therapy hours have been expended in this work, it would be a disservice to suggest you can fully develop your skills in this effort here. However, we can get you started. Throughout these chapters there are examples for how to combat common beliefs. Related books that continue this process are referenced in each chapter.

Self-talk: In this process, talking to yourself (aloud or not) helps maintain Adult control of how your beliefs are influencing your reactions. As I noted in chapter 3, your inner family brain parts are designed to operate protectively for your survival, without Adult interference. They use your old beliefs to determine quickly when to switch your body into fight-or-flight mode. While this was good for survival in primitive times, it's bad for nuanced functioning in modern times.

Self-talk is like the switch to manual pilot when autopilot isn't working. When your Adult observes bodily reactions that indicate your Parent is using a false belief with your Child, it must take over. Then your Adult must switch off the false belief and switch on a valid and more positive belief to pull your body back from a fight-or-flight reaction. Your Adult uses self-talk to make this switch.

Monitoring: This is a technique of self-observation that allows your Adult to discover when an old toxic belief is impacting your reactions during the day. You can begin by noting what feelings are occurring in your body. Then assign your overall feeling a number from one to ten, with ten for the best you can feel and one for the worst, each time your Adult checks in. Do this about every two hours. When you note a significant drop, like from a seven to a four, review the preceding two hours to identify when the drop occurred. Perhaps you had a disturbing conversation or realized you forgot something important. Then ask yourself, "What is my belief about this event? What expectation did I have?" Monitoring is like peddling a bicycle. Your Adult must keep monitoring to balance your Child and Parent parts.

CBT Basics: Eight Steps to Identify and Combat Toxic Beliefs

1. Monitor your feelings every two hours. Choose a number between one and ten that reflects your general sense of well-being, with ten being the best and one being the worst you can feel.

2. Note dips in your mood by comparing your numbers.

3. If your number drops, review the two-hour period for a disturbing event or thought.

4. Ask about the situation: "What did I believe it meant?" or "What expectations did I have?"

5. Challenge these beliefs or expectations. Substitute more realistic, comforting and valid concepts, reflecting what *your own* experience has taught you to expect, rather than what your programming says *should* happen.

6. Note especially tendencies to say "I can't stand it" or "why me?" These set off the most painful episodes of despair or anxiety with their fight-or-flight signals.

7. Practice and be alert for similar situations triggering unrealistic expectations and their associated hurt and disappointment; you'll find you have just a few tough ones. Study memories of your parents' beliefs and teachings for the roots of these.

8. Make time for this process; it often uses a lot of energy. Note even the smallest improvements and insights to build upon and avoid staying with discouraging thoughts when change comes slowly. Remember that some anger or disappointment is often appropriate. Your goal is just to reduce the intensity of reactions that disable you, not eliminate all negative feelings.

Twelve Toxic Beliefs

When you have in mind the twelve toxic beliefs, your Adult can recognize what's triggering your reaction more easily. Quickly you'll discover which of these beliefs are the most likely to upset you unnecessarily. Here are common beliefs to memorize for quick recognition as you monitor your feelings throughout your day:

1. You must have the approval or love of one particular person or most other people.

2. You can feel proud of your efforts only if you perform better than someone else.

3. People (including you) should be blamed or punished when they don't measure up to the standards you set.

4. If something threatening might happen, it's helpful to worry about it frequently.

5. One's past is responsible for most of one's present behavior and emotional adjustment.

6. A kind and compassionate person must get very upset over other people's problems.

7. It's unbearable when you work hard for something and you don't get it.

8. Happiness depends on what life gives to you.

9. It's more comfortable to avoid than to face problems or responsibilities.

10. If you love others, you have a right to be very dependent upon them and they on you.

11. If you're very talented or attractive, you're entitled to recognition and an easier path.

12. If you're very clever, you can find shortcuts around the frustrating rules in society.

How Long Will This Process Take?

How do you get from having only the false belief, to having the new belief, to having easy access to the new belief, to finally having the new belief replace the old one? This is the main task of CBT. The list of twelve toxic beliefs is a shortcut for your Adult. You can select a belief instead of trying to define one yourself for what caused the strong reaction. Now you have a name for the toxic belief. Next your Adult must combat it and suggest a new valid and positive belief instead. This self-talk develops the manual pilot so that it can redirect you.

B. F. Skinner identified a special kind of self-talk that's most helpful for recalling a new mental habit and named it a thematic prompt, as noted in chapter 3.[4] However, he also indicated that this only works if the new mental habit is well established. You may think this could create a real hitch in your practice, leaving you to fumble along, mired in your old beliefs for a long time. But there's a strategy to help you get around this dilemma.

Let's consider the case of the teacher, Bonnie, who repeatedly became upset when others were upset at work. She connected this reaction to the sixth belief, that she had to join other people's pain or she would be a cold and uncaring person. She combated this belief by recognizing that she had limited energy that she must use carefully in order to be helpful to others. She couldn't help all those who were upset, nor could she help anyone if she got as upset as they were. She formed a new belief, which was that it would be more helpful to listen and just offer what help she could without getting so upset. To remind herself of all this reasoning, she came up with the catchy prompt "somebody has a problem here, but it's not me." She used it in her head each time she felt herself getting drawn into another person's drama. She said it made her feel much better immediately each time.

This example illustrates the effects of some other principles of Skinner that were noted in chapter 1.[5] Bonnie focused on one type of situation and one belief to practice, creating a kind of Skinner box for her learning. She imitated the conditions for the pigeon that learned how to peck a disc and got rewarded. She identified a comforting belief that would serve as a reward if she remembered to practice shutting down toxic belief #6. She knew where the situations were likely to occur—in the teacher's lounge; this would be like the pigeon knowing which end of the cage to go to. Then she just had to zero in on the triggering situation, like the pigeon to his disc, and do the new mental behavior.

Each time, Bonnie was rewarded by feeling much better, just as the pigeon was rewarded with a kernel of corn. She didn't scold herself when she forgot to remind herself, just as the pigeon didn't get a shock when it went to the wrong end of the cage. Using all these principles, she quickly learned to embrace and apply her new belief, "It's better to listen and just offer what help I can without getting so upset."

There are so many toxic beliefs for countless situations; how can you tackle them all? Your brain is designed to learn what you practice. It's also designed to forget what you don't. Skinner observed that "doing something else," like substituting a new belief, results in "extinction.[6] He noted that this doesn't create the problems for learning that punishment does.[7]

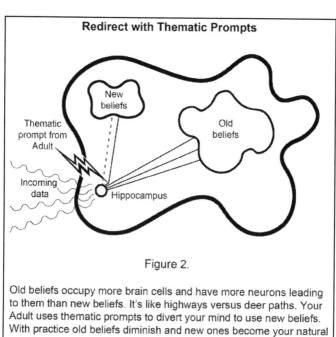

Redirect with Thematic Prompts

Figure 2.

Old beliefs occupy more brain cells and have more neurons leading to them than new beliefs. It's like highways versus deer paths. Your Adult uses thematic prompts to divert your mind to use new beliefs. With practice old beliefs diminish and new ones become your natural reaction.

Let's look at figure 2 for a model of how your brain substitutes a new belief for an old one. Your hippocampus is like a clearinghouse for incoming data, such as what you see or hear and self-talk from your Adult. It sorts this data out into your memory centers for processing. Electrochemical pathways to your old beliefs are like freeways in your brain. Paths to your new beliefs are like faint deer tracks and only grow with repeated access. Bonnie had a revised belief she'd just begun to practice. She used a thematic prompt—"somebody has a problem here, but it's not me"—to redirect her to use her new belief when the hippocampus was about pull from the old one.

As you practice you'll gradually build a freeway to each new belief. Then your hippocampus will connect more readily to your new belief. How can you make yourself get enough practice to strengthen the new belief? You've already heard how your Adult struggles even to stay awake. We can all identify with Joe in chapter 1; he fought with himself about going to the gym to build his body up to a desirable level of fitness. Bonnie's experience demonstrates the secret. You feel better immediately when you effectively shut off a toxic belief, and the relief can last for hours. You feel better when you exercise too, but you have to get suited up and go there. Your Adult, Parent and Child are always with you. Using a prompt to practice a new belief brings results in seconds, not after a half hour of sweating. You feel more comfortable, but not sore, sweaty and tired. You don't need to shower and wash your hair each time. You can practice in your pajamas, so you're more likely to want to practice often and can learn fast.

Getting to Know Your Inner Family

We've been studying how you can effectively tackle one toxic belief at a time. You are understandably daunted by having twelve to remember and apply in various situations. If you scan the twelve beliefs, you'll discover that you aren't bothered by all of them. In fact, as you monitor your feelings, you'll find that the same ones crop up time and again in similar triggering situations. You can focus on these without too much trouble.

To ensure that you can carry your new learning into the rest of your life, it will be helpful for you to group these beliefs. Since toxic beliefs originate in your Parent and Child Parts, you'll look there for how to group them. Once you do this, you can anticipate your reactions in new situations based on your knowledge of your own inner family's typical beliefs. This awareness prepares your Adult to redirect your brain to a new belief more easily. But first let's discuss some ideas for how your Adult can expand its ability to cope with all the new information.

Some Organizing Tips for Your Adult

Since the focus of this book is to help your Adult stay in charge, the message is addressed to your Adult. When you practice CBT as you go through your day, you're deliberately using your Adult functions to observe your inner family and identify problem areas to correct. This practice is already expanding your Adult capacity to learn comfortably and efficiently. Your Adult can only stay in charge if it develops a strong habit of monitoring. To balance your Child and Parent parts, your Adult must keep peddling.

I'll continually draw attention to how this work can grow your Adult with each concept I bring up in this book. You'll aid your Adult if you create files in your computer or file case to access when you need reminders. You can use a notebook but you may end up having sloppy notes that interfere with your continued learning. Sticky notes are fine for thematic prompts of learning you've really got, but they don't help you find the lesson behind the prompt if you forget it. A smartphone can connect you to your computer any time you need a reminder for the thematic prompt you've put in it. This book is organized to provide your Adult with the basic lessons and prompts to get you started. Your Adult will need to add its own prompts and creative ideas for managing your Child and Parent parts over time.

Your Inner family: The Interaction

Keep a file on what your Adult observes about the interaction between your Parent and Child parts. I've divided the Parent into Critical, Indulgent and Wise types, and you'll find that you have aspects of all three of these. Each Parent is described through a dialogue between it and its Child to illustrate the type of interaction each would create. The twelve toxic beliefs are split up, as the first six relate mostly to the Critical Parent and the next six most often relate to the Indulgent Parent. Next I'll describe revisions of all twelve to illustrate the impact of a Wise Parent on its Child. Many of the toxic beliefs can be used by either your Critical or Indulgent Parent. Throughout the remainder of the book, we'll study many examples of how to cope with these beliefs of either Parent. After the dialogue I've provided for each of the three Parents types, I've summarized what your Child would be like if this parent were dominant in managing it.

Your Critical Parent speaks to your Child in extremes, blaming and criticizing it unfairly when things go wrong, and saying things like "you always screw up," "you'll never learn," "you should have known," "you're a jerk," "you're stupid," "you're ugly," etc. This dialogue between the Critical Parent and Child illustrates their interaction for the first six toxic beliefs.

1. P: You must have the approval of significant people, or even most people.

   C: I'm worthless if someone doesn't like (respect, admire, validate) me.

2. P: You're only worthwhile if you outperform someone else.

   C: I'm ashamed that I didn't do better.

3. P: If you make a mistake, you deserve to be blamed and punished. No one else should make that kind of mistake, and if they do they must be held responsible.

   C: I always screw up, no matter how hard I try. I hate Alvin; he doesn't even try.

4. P: If something might be dangerous, you've got to worry constantly until it's over.

C: It'll be my fault if I don't keep thinking about it and it happens.

5. P: You'll never amount to anything because of your bad childhood.

   C: There's something wrong with me that keeps me from getting what I need.

6. P: When you care about someone, you have to get as upset as they are if something goes wrong for them or you're being selfish.

   C: I feel really guilty for feeling this way, but I'm tired of listening to Susan and trying to help her.

You can tell that you have some Critical-Parent messages if your Child feels worthless, ashamed, incompetent, defective or guilty very often. As you go through your days, note when these feelings occur and see if one of these Critical Parent beliefs isn't playing in your head. Begin to combat these by recalling the wisdom of Skinner discussed earlier: only kernels of corn guide you to better thinking.

Self-punishing words shut down or distort your Child energy like the shocks to Skinner's pigeon. You can't succeed without rewards when you try to learn something. When Critical-Parent messages prevail, your Child feels anxious, depressed and miserable much of the time. Sometimes you're likely to vent some of your Child's deep hurt and anger by turning your Critical Parent on someone else.

Your Indulgent Parent expects too little of your Child, conveying the belief that your Child is deserving but helpless through such messages as "you'll be taken care of," "don't stress yourself," "let other people worry about it," "you're special," "you're fine just the way you are," "you deserve to be happy no matter what." This dialogue between the Indulgent Parent and Child illustrates their interaction for the second half of the twelve toxic beliefs.

7. P: You should expect to be rewarded whenever you work for something.

    C: I'm quitting; it's just not fair that he got promoted and I didn't.

8. P: It's not your fault that you're unhappy; life keeps letting you down.

    C: Why me? When is it my turn to get a break?

9. P: If you don't feel like doing something, just put it off and you'll have a better day.

    C: I can't stand to do things when I'm not in the mood.

10. P: When someone really loves you, they'll always be there for you and let you depend on them.

    C: It's so unfair! Everybody always lets me down; I'm there for them, but they reject me.

11. P: You're very special and shouldn't really have to work that hard.

    C: I just want to have fun; I don't need to stress myself out.

12. P: The rules are for people who aren't as smart as you.

    C: Nobody can tell me what to do; I can always find a way around it.

You can tell that you have some Indulgent-Parent messages if you feel betrayed, cheated, frustrated or unlucky very often. When Indulgent-Parent messages prevail, your Child often feels out of control and helpless when things go wrong. It has a pervasive sense of being treated unfairly when it doesn't get what it wants and blames others for its problems. It tends to have extreme ups when it's getting its way and downs when it's thwarted. It has trouble cooperating to learn new mental habits or new life skills because it believes others must provide for its happiness.

These messages encourage your Child to expect a lot for very little effort. Your Child may come to feel entitled to a lifestyle or recognition that other people feel they have to earn. This sets your Child up to be angry and easily discouraged when it's coping with real life.

Your Wise Parent has learned to modify these widely held beliefs. It's either grown up with wise and caring parents or it's learned to correct toxic beliefs through painful experience. The Child of a Wise Parent has a more stable existence due to its realistic expectations about what hard work, relationships, and life experience will bring. It has the energy and confidence to persist at difficult tasks because it receives little rewards along the way from its encouraging Wise Parent. The following interactions between the Wise Parent and Child demonstrate how the beliefs of the Critical and Indulgent Parents can be altered to be more reasonable and fair.

Critical-Parent Beliefs Modified by a Wise Parent

1. P: It's great to have someone else's approval, but you have to judge for yourself how well you're doing. You don't need their approval, but try to learn from what they say.

    C: I'm proud of my efforts, but maybe they have a suggestion that would help me.

2. P: Work to express your own unique talents; you can't be compared to anyone else. It's fun to excel, but you don't need to win a competition to feel good about yourself.

    C: Bob feels like he's better than me now, but I'm proud of how I've done.

3. P: You're going to make mistakes, but blaming yourself won't teach you anything. Notice what you did right and try to do it better the next time. Others need encouragement too.

    C: It's hard not to be upset over losing my time and efforts with my mistakes, but I want to keep working on it, so I'll try to stay positive.

4. P: If you anticipate a serious problem, try your best to prepare for it, but scaring yourself with how bad it could turn out may deplete the energy you'll need if it happens.

    C: It's hard not to think about how bad it could be, but it feels better to focus on what I *can* do.

5. P: It's frustrating when past problems make it harder for you to have a fresh outlook on new situations, but you can learn to discriminate the past from the present with practice.

    C: When I realize how I'm safer now that I'm a capable adult than I was in a similar situation as a child, I feel calmer.

6. P: Another person's pain may tempt you to get too involved in trying to help them; you'll allow them to feel competent and keep yourself from getting overwhelmed if you set some limits.

    C: It's hard not to feel guilty taking time to enjoy myself when Alice is suffering so much, but I want to be refreshed when she really needs me again.

Indulgent-Parent Beliefs Modified by a Wise Parent

7. P: When you work hard in a situation, the only guaranteed reward is your pride in yourself; the chance for other rewards is increased by your efforts, but not guaranteed.

C: It feels unfair that people have to work so hard and have so much disappointment, but it's a comfort to feel good about how I tried and what I learned.

8. P: When you don't get what you want in life, you can choose to blame others, but that won't improve things. You must create your own contentment, regardless of what comes your way.

    C: I feel stronger when I can improve my mood or make myself accept things better, but it's not always easy.

9. P: When a problem seems too hard to tackle, avoiding it won't make it go away. You may escape it for a while, but it will loom larger if you dread it than if you get right to it.

    C: If I can make myself get it done, I'll feel free to do what I want afterwards.

10. P: You can't expect another person always to be available to support you, and you can't do that for anyone else either. Life demands that we focus on our own issues at times. Dependable relationships require people to be responsible for meeting their own needs.

    C: I guess I'm the one who knows best what I need, so I can take care of that and enjoy sharing wants with other people.

11. P: You're unique and special, but not more so than anyone else. You have the same responsibility for yourself as others do and just as much power to make your life good.

    C: When people praise me, I feel special, but I can't forget that I still have to do my part.

12. P: You feel lucky when you break a rule and no one notices, but don't get the idea that you can ignore the rules and get away with it. Ask yourself what would happen if everybody did that.

C: I'm glad I didn't get caught, but I don't want everyone to lie (cheat, steal, speed). It would leave chaos, and I wouldn't feel safe, so I'll try not to do that again.

Recognize which group of beliefs best describes your Inner family. If you know you tend to have more Critical-parent messages, you can focus on those beliefs to get more balance and calm. If your Indulgent-Parent messages win out, work on them first. Gradually, Wise-Parent messages will allow your Child to be calm and confident, which will enable your Adult to manage your life more easily.

Watch Out for Three Child-Brain Habits

As your Adult monitors, you may notice habits of thinking that don't seem connected to a Parent belief. These may be carryovers from your smaller, simpler child brain which will remain until you reprogram them. These will be discussed further in parts 2 and 3.

1. **Black-and-white thinking**: A young child's brain simplifies when it tries to organize its intake of data. Young children naturally think things are either bad or good, always or never, happy or sad, fun or boring, big or little, black or white. Your Adult must recognize when you've slipped into this habit. Then you can explore the range of options that's actually available to consider.

2. **Overgeneralizing**: Again, the simpler child brain often fails to recognize or accept the difference between two similar situations. A child may be fearful of a situation that reminds him of a traumatic experience, like going in the water if he got water up his nose once. Your Adult must recognize when it hears your Child saying, "This is just like that time when I almost drowned!" and help it identify how the present situation is different and less threatening. This habit also can occur when a good thing happens, like winning big at the casino. Your Adult must study the numerous factors to consider in the situation before letting your Child have a hundred dollars to blow.

There's nothing your Child can do to make the next time just like the time of the big win.

3. **Over-connection to others**: Young children naturally believe they are the center of attention and also feel like they cause what happens around them. They assume that others, especially their parents, can read their minds and that they know what their parent is thinking or feeling. A two-year-old can easily have a tantrum because his mother didn't know what he needed and has to be helped as he develops to express himself so he can be understood. Your Adult must note when you *assume* someone else will understand you and must make the correction before your Critical Parent accuses that person of not caring about you or not listening. Your Adult must also help you avoid assuming you understand another person before you've clarified the communication.

Young kids feel responsible if things go wrong and sometimes when things go well. Children born on the Fourth of July often think the fireworks are for them until they're four or five. It takes Wise-Parent guidance and years of experience for people to realize how little power they actually have over events and other people. Your Adult can relieve your Child of much self-consciousness by reminding it that other people are also focused on themselves. Your Adult also can relieve your Child of much guilt by helping it realize that it doesn't have the power to make others feel or do very much.

These immature brain habits don't automatically disappear as you get older and can remain to confuse your thinking indefinitely. Your Adult must identify these errors and work with your Wise Parent to retrain your Child for more complex functioning. These mental habits represent only three of many; they have been chosen because they seem to occur most often and the others usually get handled when CBT is practiced on the beliefs. When your Adult recognizes that your Child is howling that it "can't stand," "can't take" or "won't tolerate" something, it can correct most Child-brain errors quickly.

Here are some references you might enjoy if you want to explore some of these concepts in more depth. David M. Clark and Christopher G. Fairburn give a thorough description of cognitive-behavioral therapy in their book *The Science and Practice of Cognitive-Behavioral Therapy*.[8] If you want to learn about research-defined brain functions in more detail, you can check out the work of Jodie A. Trafton, William P. Gordon and Supriya Misra, who describe their professionally oriented CBT approach in their book *Training Your Brain to Adopt Healthful Habits: Mastering the Five Brain Challenges*.[9] Roy F. Baumeister and John Tierney offer additional cutting-edge research about recently identified brain-based interference for several Adult functions in their book *Willpower: Rediscovering the Greatest Human Strength*.[10]

Take Your Learning with You

Keep a copy of the twelve toxic beliefs, the three child-brain errors and the eight steps for self-monitoring to remind you of how to do this process all day, every day. They are listed in appendix A for easy reference. Add the list of helpful hints below. Develop your own personal files to keep your insights where you can review them in the future if you get out of balance. Gradually you'll find your Child and Parent are not as reactive as they were and you'll know they've been reprogrammed.

1. Be alert for self-talk that quickly triggers your inner family, such as "I can't stand it when…" or "It's unbearable" or "I can't take it anymore!" These comments send your inner family into fight-or-flight mode and make it very hard for your Adult to stay in charge.

2. Find thematic prompts (brief phrases) to trigger recall of your replacement beliefs. Repeat these when problem situations occur to shut off each old belief and replace it before you get upset, like Bonnie with "somebody has a problem here, but it's not me." When you know these beliefs by heart, it's easier to identify one as you go through your day, much like a multiple-choice problem instead of an essay test.

3. Create emotional space for this work by taking brief breaks to monitor your feelings more often if you're having trouble hanging onto your Adult control. If you get upset in spite of your efforts, focus on something else (reading a novel, studying a calming picture, working a crossword puzzle) or take a brief walk to soothe and distract your Parent-Child activity, allowing your Adult to step in again. More of these ideas are coming in chapter 5.

4. Be aware that even after you've had success for months rerouting to your new beliefs, the old beliefs are still well established in your memory (as in figure 2). They will tend to reassert themselves when you get tired, sick or overloaded. Just grab your manual-pilot self-talk prompts to redirect your mind again to the new beliefs.

You're getting to know your Parent and Child parts and have begun a process to help your Adult reprogram them. This process follows a logical formula to reach the deepest levels of your emotional, illogical being. You may have experienced some emotional (Child) reactions even as you read about Child and Parent beliefs and recognized some of yours. How your Adult can provide you with the support you need for this work will be discussed in chapter 5.

Below are some of the healthy beliefs and feelings you'll begin to experience as you build your mental fitness.

Wise Parent to Child:

- You get to be human; you don't have to be perfect.

- You deserve your space in the sun.

- Try your best to be fair and kind to others; you deserve that for yourself.

- You have all the gifts you need to make your life good.

- You can learn from all your experiences and become stronger.

- You can heal from your traumas and disappointments if you work at it.

- You can know love and joy all through your life.

- Be careful and thoughtful, or you'll give and receive more hurt.

- Be patient and thorough, or you'll waste your efforts.

- Recognize your limits, or you'll get overwhelmed.

- Set your goals, or you'll have more regret.

- Consider others' feedback, or you'll be alone.

- Discipline your body, or you'll suffer more pain and illness.

- Face your problems, or you'll be ashamed.

Child to Parent and Adult:

- I want to explore freely what I find.

- I want to laugh and play with others.

- I want to express my gifts to sing, dance, write or build.

- I want to love my friends, my dog and cat, my family.

- I want to be loved and cherished throughout my life.

- I need guidance and encouragement.

- I need to have the chance to be myself.

- I need to live without fear and shame.

Adult to Parent and Child:

- Let's look at the facts.

- Let's look at the big picture.

- What's best in the long run?

- No need for fight-or-flight just now.

- We can take our time to get it right.

- We have to compromise to keep our balance.

- We can work it out together.

- I'll "keep peddling" by monitoring to always be there for you.

Notes

1. Sigmund Freud, ed. Peter Gay, *The Freud Reader* (New York: W. W. Norton, 1989).
2. Eric Berne, *Games People Play: The Psychology of Human Relationships* (1964; rev. ed., New York: Ballantine Books, 1992).
3. Albert Ellis and Robert Harper, *A Guide to Rational Living* (Hollywood: Wilshire Books Co., 1977).
4. B. F. Skinner, *Science and Human Behavior* (1953; repr., New York: The Free Press, 1965), 214.
5. Ibid., 91–98.
6. Ibid., 239–240.

7. Ibid., 69–72.

8. David M. Clark and Christopher G. Fairburn, *The Science and Practice of Cognitive-Behavioral Therapy* (New York: Oxford Press, 1997).

9. Jodie A. Trafton, William P. Gordon and Supriya Misra, *Training Your Brain to Adopt Healthful Habits: Mastering the Five Brain Challenges* (Los Altos: Institute for Brain Potential, 2011). See also Institute for Brain Potential online, last accessed June 8, 2012.

10. Roy F. Baumeister and John Tierney, *Willpower: Rediscovering the Greatest Human Strength* (New York: Penguin Press, 2011).

I : 5

Self-Care, Self-Control and Self-Esteem

Looking over the list of toxic beliefs, you can see that many involve your connection with others. With the first you're dependent on others' approval, with the second you need to win out over someone else, with the third you require others or yourself to measure up to some standard, with the sixth you feel guilty if you're not upset enough about a loved one's problems, with the seventh you depend on others to recognize and reward your efforts and with the tenth you can't feel loved unless you're heavily dependent on someone else. How can you have self-esteem on any stable basis when you have to count so much on others? You can't. That's one reason these beliefs are toxic.

You can take better care of your inner Child than anyone else. Only your Adult can know when your Child needs something from moment to moment. Only your Wise Parent can always be there for it. This chapter describes how to combat toxic beliefs that keep your Child insecure and needy. Through this process you can gradually reduce the influence of your Critical and Indulgent Parents and strengthen your Wise Parent. When you practice this process, your Adult capacity to observe your inner family and manage it grows stronger. We'll also study activities that your Wise Parent can provide to comfort and reassure your Child frequently. Appendix A repeats the description of the cognitive-behavioral process and the twelve toxic beliefs described in the previous chapter for easy reference.

Is a Cat Worthy? Finding Self-Esteem on Your Own

The eighth toxic belief, which is that happiness is controlled by life circumstances, has set you up to think that you have a right to expect that others should keep you comfortable and happy. Giving that up releases energy to discover how to give yourself what you really need. This is not an easy thing to do. You may feel lost and betrayed when you first realize that you have to rely primarily on yourself to get through your life. Many people have to grieve the loss of this toxic belief to get beyond it.

Our whole society teaches that we have to depend on something outside ourselves to be happy—cars, perfume, soap, beer, etc. And we're usually raised to feel we can't really manage without someone else looking out for us or being there for us. It's true that you need relationships with others to have a fulfilling life. It's also true that you can't be healthy in relationships if you have unrealistic beliefs about what another person is supposed to do for you. You must learn how to manage in your own mind what *only you* can control.

How do you achieve self-esteem or self-worth on your own? Since that's the only way you can have it on a dependable basis, it must be possible. Your inner family can't relax until it trusts that your Adult has this handled. Your inner family needs to feel secure that others cannot inflict the kind of damage that would make you very depressed or destroy your self-esteem. It's responsible for keeping you at a survival level of functioning. For you to experience more than that, your Adult must reach higher without threatening that basic security. As long as your inner family worries about this, it will try to control every interaction you have and every decision you make in your life and relationships. Your Adult doesn't have a chance of staying in charge with this kind of pressure. You have to create a deep well of reassurance within yourself.

Some of you may feel so unworthy that it's hard for you to invest in this work. I've often suggested that people in this quandary consider a more basic concept of worth. For example, is your cat or dog worthy? What about a sunflower? Could we agree that you have worth because you exist as a living creature? People who have religious faith often have less difficulty with this, unless their faith teaches them to expect too much of themselves, which creates shame. Most agree that God wouldn't make someone entirely worthless. I encourage you to look at life as a journey; you make choices all along the way that either get you stuck, damage you or move you forward. When you can keep your Adult in charge, you can make the best choices for a journey on which your sense of worth or self-esteem can grow.

Self-Punishment and Low Self-Esteem

The third toxic belief, which is that people must be blamed and punished if they fail to measure up, invites your Critical Parent to torment your Child when you make a mistake. This leaves your Child with chronic feelings of low self-esteem. Let's revisit Joe from chapter 1 to see how this happens. Joe was often immobilized after periods when he beat himself up for not accomplishing what he set out to do. He'd come home after work and just sit on his couch and watch television to blot out the bad feelings his Critical Parent created in his Child. As I noted in chapter 1, punishment doesn't often build new positive behavior or attitudes.

Joe's Indulgent Parent tempted his Child with the ninth toxic belief, which is that avoidance is easier than facing difficult problems. On the one hand, Joe was procrastinating about working out, eating right and making social contacts because he believed this was easier. On the other hand, he strongly believed that he had to face up to this avoidance in order to respect himself. He told himself that to be honest with himself, he had to focus on everything he was doing wrong. While it's potentially effective to face ourselves honestly, we have to examine what "honest" means. Is it really true that all we should do when we evaluate our efforts is to look at our mistakes? Doesn't honesty include the whole picture? Where's the Wise-Parent solution?

The answer to this question might be clearer if we look at how a young child was evaluated with this cultural negative bias about honesty. While I was working with a home for abused boys, I found an evaluation of an eleven-year-old in which the examiner noted that he was not cooperative with her testing. She proceeded with it anyway and concluded that while it was really a shame to have to say this about an eleven-year-old, he really had no positive traits and faced a grim future no matter what was done with him. Now when you hear this, hopefully you're outraged that she would draw this conclusion about an-eleven-year old child. Surely a thorough and accurate evaluation would find some positive traits in anyone. When you think you're being honest by focusing only on your faults and errors, you 're making the same mistake.

The third toxic belief—that we should blame ourselves when we make a mistake—combined with a belief that being honest with ourselves involves focusing only on the negative is a recipe for low self-esteem. Store this realization in your Wise Parent as your Adult probes your inner family to discover your own toxic beliefs and how they impact you. Your Critical Parent may otherwise be quick to pounce on your Child for being stupid, dishonest, careless, etc. To build new beliefs in your Wise Parent, you must try to give yourself credit for every wise moment and diligent behavior from now on. To keep your Child motivated and protect your self-esteem, you must also stop blaming and begin rewarding yourself through your self-talk and your self-care.

How Your Adult Can Manage Your Inner Family

You strengthen your Adult every time you monitor, since this involves practicing the thoughtful self-observation skills unique to human beings. As you scan yourself to determine what number from one to ten describes your present state, you're checking in with your Child part. Any time you note bodily reactions, you're observing your Child part's response to your situation, filtered through your Parent beliefs about it. When your Adult manages your Parent parts carefully, your Child feels a steady current of confidence and self-worth. You feel comfortable.

Here's an example of how an alert Adult can work out an inner conflict. Despite all my efforts, I still (rarely, of course) make an error in scheduling my clients that results in their coming for a session I can't provide. On one such occasion a few years ago, I fought back against the gut-wrenching (Child) guilt that could ruin my peace of mind for days.

Critical-Parent message: "You have no right to do that to someone, especially someone who's counting on your help! You always screw things up!"

Adult correction: "That's the third toxic belief again- 'you should be blamed and punished if you aren't perfect.' We've been over this many times before, and you know it's unreasonable to think you'll never make a mistake, even one that lets another person down."

Wise-Parent message: "You always *try* to get it right and you forgive your clients when they screw up an appointment. You don't deserve to suffer like this."

Adult negotiation: "How about if you get to forgive yourself once for every ten times you forgive your clients for a botched appointment?"

My Child calmed down quickly with this deal, and my Critical Parent was well readjusted. I haven't tortured myself over that kind of error since, although I've needed to remind myself of the deal my Adult made to keep my Critical Parent in check.

A weak Adult can leave your inner family in turmoil. When your Critical parent restricts your Child too long, the Child becomes vulnerable to temptation and unenlightened friends. It may finally break away, taking refuge in any Indulgent Parent support it can find, and in the ninth toxic belief that it can worry about today's problems tomorrow. Eventually, there's a bitter and painful confrontation when the Critical Parent wakes up to view the wreckage. Those credit cards you ran up, the friends you told off when you drank too much or the promises to your children that you broke give your Critical Parent ammunition to beat up your Child severely. Your still-fragile Wise Parent can't easily counter so much acting up. Your self-esteem gets battered, and your growing confidence that you can build a meaningful life gets crushed. If this becomes a pattern, you may take flight into an addiction, which will be discussed in Part II.

In recent years the society that has often created so many problems also has generated some new ways to support your Adult. You can use your handy phone to plan your day and schedule your week. If you form good habits for using this and other technological supports, your Adult can begin to organize more carefully. It can draw from your Wise Parent to plan for breaks for your Child and avoid letting it impulsively overcommit you. You'll have less opportunity for your Critical Parent to pounce if you don't stand people up or forget an important responsibility. Of course, your Adult also must observe your involvement with these delightful devices to be sure you don't use them too often for play at the expense of your responsibilities.

By revising your beliefs, your Adult can gradually bring peace to your inner family and build your Wise Parent. This process requires your Adult to strengthen its ability to observe your Child reactions quickly by consistent monitoring. This sounds like hard work, and it is. But each time your Adult relieves your Child's feelings of hurt, fear or sadness, you're rewarded with happier feelings and you'll feel inspired to keep working. How can your Adult know what to do when it tunes in to your Child's feelings?

Revising Your Critical Parent

For the hurt and sad Child, the Adult must correct Critical-Parent beliefs. The most frequent problem belief of your Critical Parent is the third one, which is that people, including you, should be blamed when they don't measure up. You can't be perfect, and punishment disrupts your learning and your energy for it, just like shocks to the pigeon's feet. You can't build anything with it. Your Adult must train your Wise Parent to defend your Child, reminding your Critical Parent that you deserve fair and kind treatment just like anyone else. Finally, your Adult should note that positive input is the only thing that works to guide an errant Child. You must have kernels of corn to grow.

You can find ideas for what other Critical-Parent beliefs might be pressuring your Child by studying the twelve toxic beliefs in chapter 4 and appendix A. You can get other ideas from remembering what your parents said when they criticized or corrected you. What do you say when you're upset with yourself? For example, you might say "I always screw up," "Nobody really cares about me," "I'm ugly (fat, skinny, too short, too tall)," "I'm stupid," etc. Once your Adult identifies these Child beliefs, it can challenge your Critical Parent about them.

Your Adult can begin to alter your Critical Parent to be more fair and reasonable. The cognitive-behavioral system you're learning gradually creates a Wise Parent who's not abusive and hurtful to your

Child's self-esteem, confidence and enthusiasm. With revised beliefs your Wise Parent can set fair limits and offer useful warnings to your Child. As this happens your Child will feel more secure and have fewer very sad or angry feelings. Your Wise Parent might say, "Be careful," "Prepare first," "Look before you leap," "Don't forget what you promised." These messages guide and protect the Child, reducing impulsive mistakes and interpersonal problems. Without these your Child could plunge into excessive behaviors that alienate healthy friends or lead to an addiction, which would impair your Adult function.

Sleuth Out Your Indulgent Parent

We've looked at how your Adult can revise your Critical-Parent messages, transforming them into the reasonable limits of your Wise Parent. Your Adult must also revise the corrupting messages of your Indulgent Parent to stabilize your Child. The Indulgent Parent sets your Child up for trouble in both your inner and outer worlds. While even a cat has worth, most of us expect more of ourselves than we do of our pets, and other humans also require more of us.

Your Child brings its own unique ideas about what it likes to do and what inspires it to try hard to develop your talents. Your Indulgent Parent can sabotage your success and self-esteem by telling your Child it deserves the good life without having to work for it. Your Adult can also identify Indulgent-Parent messages from what your parents said to you and what you can guess they said to themselves. Refrain from bringing in your Critical Parent as you study others and yourself to maintain your best Adult functioning.

The Indulgent Parent is quieter than the Critical Parent, so your Adult must often look at a person's behavior to recognize when it's operating. What excesses do you note in others? Are they very overweight, do they drink too much or use drugs inappropriately? Do they have trouble accomplishing basic adult chores, like cleaning, organizing, paying bills, filing taxes, cooking healthy meals, getting to doctor's appointments or keeping a job? They may have one or more of the problems we'll discuss in Part II that prevent good Adult function.

It's also likely that they have Indulgent-Parent messages that set them up for their dysfunction and the discomfort they experience.

What are you saying to yourself when you procrastinate, ignore Wise-Parent warnings, take a shortcut around a rule or fail to follow through on a promise? Your Adult needs to identify your Indulgent-Parent messages in order to challenge and revise them. Your Adult can help you get things done in a timely manner, manage your things and take care of your needs once it builds your Wise Parent. As humans we never lose our Indulgent or Critical Parents; we can only reduce their influence.

Cultivate Your Wise Parent

Strengthening your Wise Parent is one of the richest and most rewarding experiences you will ever have. As you learn new fair, truthful and positive beliefs about yourself, your growth unfolds easily. To recognize your Wise Parent, note what you say to yourself when you feel proud, content, capable, joyful, etc. If you suffer from addiction, depression or anxiety, you have a weak Parent. When you exercise your Adult by revising your Parent messages, you also strengthen your Wise Parent. I'll describe how to combat these problems specifically in Part II.

You can also grow your Wise Parent through rewarding experiences that help you form healthier beliefs; these are the kernels of corn to guide and encourage you. When I suffered panic attacks and depression in the early 1970s, I worked intensively on my inadequate Wise Parent. I still remember a poster depicting a large oak tree after a sleet storm, its icy branches lit up by the sun. Under the picture was the phrase, "In the depths of winter, I finally learned that within me there lay an invincible summer."[1] Tears welled up in my Child as I said to myself, "I don't believe that yet but I think I can learn to believe it."

You can find new Wise-Parent messages anywhere, whether it's from a character in a book you read, a picture in a magazine or talking with a friend. Your monitoring Adult can notice your Child's reaction through your body's emotional signals (tears, laughter) when you encounter a message you especially need. Write it down and put it where you can see it often. You may also have treasured items that comfort or inspire your Child. Take a moment to contemplate these thoughts frequently, and they will join your Wise Parent for life.

I still love to buy myself a card that has a picture or phrase that urges me to grow a new message in my Wise Parent. Recently I found a card with a drawing of a little girl hugging her teddy bear and beaming with contentment. When I saw that, I thought, "I need to feel like that more often," so I posted it on my Wise-Parent bulletin board. This card reminds me to listen more to my Wise-Parent messages to slow down and let my Child simply enjoy a moment. I tend to get too focused on accomplishing things due to Critical-Parent messages that I should always keep my life in perfect order at a high rate of productivity.

The bulletin board in my office demonstrates how clients can begin to program new positive messages into their Wise Parents. Posted on it are animals I made to hang in a mobile over my son's crib forty years ago, some great quotes, cards reminding me of inspiring places, artists' works that lift me and pictures of my pets and family. These can all draw me into moments where my Wise Parent is free to encourage my creative Child to be hopeful about what will come next.

Happy Spots Lead You Out of Turmoil

Through diligent self-observation, your Adult can discover what beliefs are upsetting your Child and work to embrace more realistic and fair beliefs. However, reassuring new self-talk is necessary but not sufficient for creating security and confidence deep within yourself. Your inner family must experience positive and comforting feelings frequently in order to install your new, more encouraging beliefs. It's a creative task for your Adult to find activities and situations where you feel safe and comfortable. Very gradually, with your consistent effort, the new beliefs and self-talk will become your "natural" response to new situations.

Create what one of my clients named "happy spots" every day to help you sample the feelings that you're working for. Our minds are wired to shift channels with amazing speed. Notice how fast your mood can change in response to daily life events. It can also shift due to inner events. You can find ways to shift out of a worried, angry, irritated or overwhelmed state into a calmer mood. Just as you would comfort a young child, distract yourself with some activity that grabs your attention. Read a chapter in a novel you like, gaze at a picture of a loved one, look outside at a beautiful tree or even a cloudy sky, talk about something pleasant with another person, walk your dog, research a question or stretch and touch your toes a few times.

It takes commitment to plan for these distractions at first and to use them quickly when you need to calm your Child. Each time you do this, your Adult functioning grows stronger and your Child relaxes a little. You will feel this in the easing of your tight stomach, jaw, shoulders or anywhere else your body holds onto anxiety. These happy spots are at least as powerful as self-talk changes to improve your basic confidence that you can make your own life worth living.

Meditate to Soothe Your Inner Family

I noted in chapter 4 that you can only have lasting confidence and security when your past-encumbered Parent and Child parts become connected with present reality. In present reality you aren't a vulnerable child and you have many resources to protect yourself from harm. You don't need fight-or-flight responses often at all. As your Adult works to update and reprogram your Child and Parent beliefs, you can take breaks from their influence systematically. These breaks are possible when your Adult focuses your attention intensely upon the present. Above I mentioned brief activities that allow this. Longer times of focus on the present can increase your Adult functioning and reduce inner-family conflicts that create anxiety and depression.

There's a huge body of work devoted to creating these longer periods of focus on the present. Meditation, mindfulness, yoga and other Buddhist practices all focus on improving your awareness of the connection between your body's expression of feeling and your mind. Regular practice in one of these disciplines greatly increases your ability to keep your Adult in charge. Combined with cognitive-behavioral principles, these studies can really speed you on your journey.

I first learned hatha yoga from Jess Stearn's *Yoga, Youth and Reincarnation*[2] in 1975, when I still fought panic attacks and stomach-clenching anxiety over the smallest errors. I was stunned by how slowing everything down for just a few minutes could transport me to a much better place. Meditation reminds you of how you could feel if you weren't distracted by managing your life. With gradual practice your Adult can deliberately insert moments of this feeling into your busy days. These moments can draw your Child body and mind to peace and away from tension.

I often introduce highly anxious clients to this feeling by having them practice Herbert Benson's technique described in *The Relaxation Response*.[3] He derived the technique from studying Buddhist monks and then modifying what they did to suit Western hyperactive minds. His technique involves repeating a calming phrase over and over for about fifteen minutes as you sit or lie down in a darkened, quiet place. He suggests "love and peace" or "the Lord is my shepherd;" clients have used many others, like "the mind is a parachute" or "music is soothing." You can choose your own phrase or phrases. Keep them short, pronounceable and clearly comforting. Say your phrase out loud so you can remember to keep saying it.

If you try this you'll find that your mind tries to overrun the phrase with all sorts of thoughts. As Benson teaches, you just let them wash through you as you keep saying your phrase. If you're fairly calm when you try this, you'll discover that after a few minutes your mind supplies fewer distracting phrases. You slip into a different state of mind where the last minutes go by rapidly. If you're very anxious, that shift may not occur. In either case, you'll find you're much calmer than you were fifteen minutes before. Sometimes you'll even experience a creative insight following this exercise, especially if you were trying to solve some problem prior to doing it. Benson notes that with regular practice, you can reduce your general anxiety and find this creative state of mind more readily.

Carolyn Hobbs expands these ideas in *Joy No Matter What*,[4] guiding you to observe your bodily reactions as a way to maintain your present focus. Jeffrey Brantley and Wendy Millstine offer ideas for comforting moments in *Five Good Minutes in the Evening*.[5] Paul Roland's *Meditation Solutions* includes coping methods for numerous issues.[6] Daniel Siegel offers case histories to illustrate the power of meditation to change the mind neurologically in *Mindsight: The New Science of Personal Transformation*.[7] Finally, The Motivation Store on the Internet lists numerous other avenues to help you stay connected to the present through any modality you wish.[8]

Define Who You Are and How You Want to Be with Others

We've been working on beliefs about your worth that threaten to shut you down before you even try a relaxation exercise. If you try to relax into the present moment before you've strengthened your Adult and contained your Critical Parent, you may encounter difficulty. Let's turn again to the task of defining what makes a person worthwhile. Who do you like and admire? List a few of these people and then brainstorm the traits you value in them, such as honesty, courage, kindness, humility, a sense of humor, generosity, creativity, persistence, commitment and loyalty. I find people are surprised by how down-to-earth and accessible the traits they really value are.

You don't need to envy people who have these, because you can choose to develop them too. People also admire talent, intelligence and good looks, but not as much, because these are just gifts. Of course, it's admirable when people work to develop their gifts. Let's consider what your gifts are. A self-esteem worksheet is offered in appendix B. See which traits you've already developed and which you need to work on. You'll probably find that some of the traits you admire in others are ones you've also begun to develop in yourself.

You may note that the traits that are listed above as those most often admired are expressed when relating to others. If you doubt your worth, it may be due to disappointment in the quality of your relationships. I've mentioned that most of the twelve toxic beliefs involve misconceptions about what we should expect from ourselves and other people. Study these and monitor your thoughts and feelings, combating the ones that set you up to get angry or disappointed in dealing with others. Get some help from a cognitive-behavioral therapist if you get stumped. Meanwhile, keep in mind that learning to rely on yourself for basic contentment prepares you to have more positive relationships.

Others aren't drawn to someone who tries to control them in a relationship or who easily gets deeply wounded. When you understand that you *want*—rather than *need*—friends, they will appear. When you're expecting good from others, rather than hurt and rejection, they won't have to walk on eggshells to be around you. Be patient with the process you're learning and don't expect to find your most important new relationships right away. Your increasingly capable Adult mind and improved inner balance will gradually take you where you want to go.

How Do Your Gifts Mesh with Others in the Larger World?

If you're disappointed about what you've been able to achieve thus far on your journey, perhaps you need to find a different direction in work or gain some new skills. There's a remarkable instrument that can give you some valid direction for exploration. It's a forty-five-minute test called the Strong Vocational Interest Inventory,[9] which you may have taken in high school without realizing its power. It asks questions like, "Have you ever considered being an airline pilot?" or "Would you rather go to a party or read a book?" It's not obvious how these questions could discover anything important about a person.

However, decades of research and follow-up have proven that if your pattern of scores on the Strong Vocational Interest Inventory is very similar to the pattern of scores of people in some occupational field, you'll be very satisfied in that line of work. If your scores are very dissimilar or moderately similar, you'll indeed be very to moderately dissatisfied. This test is not only useful for career decisions; it's also helpful to get ideas for volunteer work and hobbies. It helps you discover how your gifts interface with the world around you. Take it, explore and begin to plan for a future where you can feel more satisfied with your achievements and enjoy the journey too. Some community colleges have counselors who will help you take and interpret the Strong Vocational Interest Inventory for under a hundred dollars.

Self-Control and Self-Esteem through Patient Self-Care

Our Adult can exercise what we call "self-control" only when our inner family is fairly comfortable and secure. We've just begun to explore ways to provide the self-care needed to accomplish this. Patience with yourself is a key aspect of improving your self-care skills. If you're more impulsive, controlling, anxious, needy, thin-skinned and frustrated than you wish, you're just not that skilled at handling your inner family yet. Don't stop practicing your meditation, monitoring and belief work. I'll introduce concepts and examples ahead that will make more sense if you keep working. Journal occasionally about what you observe in your struggles. Build your files of new Parent messages. It's great to look back at where you were after about three months of this program. Glen Schiraldi's *Self-Esteem Workbook* offers guidance that employs some of the concepts described here, if you want to focus on building your self-esteem.[10]

Strengthen your Wise Parent with messages that give you a chance to maintain your Adult self-awareness at a high level, such as "I'm feeling overwhelmed, confused, etc., and I need to sort things out," "I deserve to take some time for myself" or "There's no need to hurry my decision." In Part II I'll discuss some individual differences that make this work more difficult for some people than others. Be especially patient with yourself when you're sick, even if it's just a little cold. I've noticed repeatedly over the years that people can't hang on to their new self-care skills when they get sick. You'll recover your improved functioning quickly when you feel better. And keep finding those key phrases that prompt you to remember your newly revised beliefs during your day.

Keep your Critical Parent in check with these messages:

- I don't *need* any particular person's approval, though I may *want* it.

- I don't need to have everyone like me.

- Another person's success is not a threat to me.

- Concern is good; worry is a waste of energy.

- Past problems don't predict my future.

- I screwed that up, but I can do better next time.

- I do have some good traits and skills already, like...

Limit your Indulgent Parent with these messages:

- People can care without getting totally upset over my problems.

- Hard work just improves my chances; it doesn't guarantee success.

- I can still feel okay even if I'm having a tough day.

- I'll feel better even if I take just one step to change.

- I can learn to feel confident on my own.

- I want others to respect me for doing my share.

- I want others to trust me because I follow the rules.

Affirm your Wise Parent with these messages:

- If a cat has worth, so do I.

- I can overcome my extreme fight-or-flight reactions.

- I'm anxious because I don't know how to relax yet, not because I'm in danger.

- Even tough experiences may offer some wisdom.

- I can take time to build my inner strength.

- There is help when I get stuck or confused.

- Managing my inner family will give me peace and self-respect.

Notes

1. Albert Camus and Philip Thody, *Return to Tipasa, Lyrical and Critical Essays* (New York: Vintage Books, 1970), 169.
2. Jess Stearn, *Yoga, Youth and Reincarnation* (New York: Bantam Books, 1965).
3. Herbert Benson, *The Relaxation Response* (New York: William Morrow, 1975).
4. Carolyn Hobbs, *Joy No Matter What* (York Beach: Conari Press, 2005).
5. Jeffrey Brantley and Wendy Millstine, *Five Good Minutes in the Evening* (New York: MJF Books, 2006).
6. Paul Roland, *Meditation Solutions* (London: Octopus Publishing Group, 2002).
7. Daniel J. Siegel, *Mindsight: The New Science of Personal Transformation* (New York: Bantam Books, 2010).
8. The Motivation Store, accessed May 23, 2012, http://www.getmotivation.com/store.
9. Strong Vocational Interest Inventory, https://www.cpp.com/products/strong/index.aspx, accessed November 10, 2012.
10. Glen R. Schiraldi, *The Self-Esteem Workbook* (Oakland: New Harbinger, 2001).

Introduction to
Part II:
Obstacles to Mental Fitness

We've explored how your Adult mind can be strengthened to manage your inner and outer worlds more effectively. The monitoring, belief work and self-care described in Part I can reduce some inner-family fight-or-flight pressures on your Adult. In Part II we'll study specific problems you may encounter that can interfere with your Adult's function and look at how to prevent or overcome them. Chapter one describes specific *inherited differences* that can make Adult control more difficult for some people. Chapter two explains how any *addiction* can prevent your Adult mind from coping well with your inner family and your daily life.

Chapter three tells how *anxiety* can escalate to cause very disturbing fight-or-flight symptoms and how your Adult can make immediate adjustments to reduce it. We'll examine the beliefs that trigger anxiety and the specific self-talk and self-care to reprogram yourself for a calmer future. Chapter four explains how your Adult can use concepts of the *grief* process to manage unrelenting *anger* and resolve any blocks to your progress.

A special kind of grieving occurs following *trauma* that can permanently impair the functioning of your Adult. Chapter five describes how this happens when your inner family uses dissociation to protect your ability to survive and what needs to occur for the resolution of trauma. Next we'll explore *depression*, where your Adult capacities are reduced due to stressors from within and without that overwhelm your functioning. I'll help you sort these out and find ways your Adult can resume control. Finally chapter seven describes how your Adult can strengthen your Wise Parent to *maintain your balance in the future* as you face outer-world stressors. We'll look at methods other people have used to maintain themselves through study, contemplation and group support. An increased understanding of how human beings must struggle to keep their Adult in charge can help you form more satisfying relationships. We'll explore the challenges these bring to your Adult functioning in Part III.

II:1

Individual Differences

Once your Adult is free from inner confusion and false beliefs, you can observe the real world with more clarity. One insight that will help you keep your expectations realistic is that people are really different from you and each other. By kindergarten you were able to recognize that the kids in your class differed in countless ways. You could see it on the playground, during nap time, while you colored and when you read or wrote your first letters. Some learned numbers fast, some couldn't spell, some were good at drawing, some were shy, some were leaders, some could run faster, etc.

By the time you were in high school, you may have lost much of this awareness. Instead you probably began to embrace the third toxic belief—that people should be blamed if they don't measure up. Who should make this judgment—you, your friends, your parents, your teachers? And measure up how? The third toxic belief is based on the assumption that everyone's really alike somehow and can be judged with one measuring stick. By junior high you may have had no problem blaming and punishing other kids or even your teachers if they weren't as honest, hard-working, attractive, mature or socially adept as you thought they should be.

How could you have lost your earlier clarity? Your parents may have subscribed to many toxic beliefs, including the third one. It's taboo for teachers to discuss differences between children openly in their classes. In a misguided effort to protect children's self-esteem, teachers may tell kids "everyone can do anything, if they try hard enough." Perhaps the religious idea that we're all equal in the eyes of

God gets confused with the idea that we're equally able to function. This belief sets us up to judge others without knowing anything about them. We also judge ourselves without realizing our own difference from others.

We Differ in Our Ability to Put Our Adult in Charge

Your ability to put your Adult in charge and rebalance your inner family also differs from others' in ways you may not realize at all. I find that many clients get a boost to their Wise Parent when they realize what handicaps them. Rather than being dismayed or losing self-esteem, most are relieved to discover they've done very well considering what they've had to overcome. Their Child feels like it's getting more fair treatment and its mood lifts. Feeling pride instead of shame helps them be more patient with themselves and frees their Adult to learn. The therapy experience becomes more a collaborative study between two Adults than a Parent-to-Child interaction, where clients have the "sick" Child and the therapist has the only Wise Parent.

Each person comes in with a different set of obstacles for learning how to put his Adult in charge. Some people can't self-observe or monitor in any stable, consistent way. Some can't access the Child feelings that could help their Adult discover negative Parent messages. Some have basic Adult capacity but are too exhausted or emotionally distraught to focus and follow through. You need to cut yourself some slack as you begin this process. And you should let go of blaming others while you're at it, just to reclaim some of your energy. After all, what may be preventing them from doing their best? You may know even less about their handicaps than you do about your own.

Comparing Apples to Oranges: Shaking the Second Toxic Belief

What if you feel you're less than someone else—less attractive, intelligent, popular or capable? It's hard to be tolerant of others if you feel smaller when they're around. To begin, have faith that you can eventually discover your own strengths, even if you can't see all of them yet. The second toxic belief—that to be worthwhile you have to compete and win over anyone else in a given field—keeps you uncomfortable when others do well. When it is added to the third belief (that you should be blamed if you don't measure up), the second belief can fill you with envy and shame. Grade rankings in school and competition in sports, music or other talent areas combine to give you an artificial system for measuring your worth. Wise and caring parents and teachers may try to tell a child that he is much more than any competition could ever measure, but their encouragement is overwhelmed by the general social message. My teenage son once said to me, "Of course *you* think I'm a good artist; you're my *mother*."

How many people give up trying in their youth when they see others who seem to have so much talent? I quit writing poetry for years after I read John Keats's brilliant work in college and learned he died at age twenty-three. How many people are stuck with the junior-high notion that the only way they can succeed is by competing against someone else? Competition between confident people in a specific situation is stimulating and constructive; competition with others for your feeling of worth creates confusion and needless hurt. It's comparing apples to oranges. Since we're all unique in countless ways, we can explore how to discover our own and other people's special package of gifts. Only then can we all combine our talents for the best community.

Not Everyone Has a High IQ

Let's consider some traits that, when combined with these two beliefs, create confusion that can derail your Adult. People with high IQs can usually learn monitoring and belief-revising skills easily. However, the belief that we're all alike often sets them up to expect that others can do as well as they can. Many I've worked with expressed hurt and anger about how others don't seem to try or to cooperate with them. They must consider how few people have a high IQ and what that often means for the learning capacity for those with lower IQs. Then, instead of being angry or hurt, they can respond by trying to be good leaders and remain patient while they share their better understanding.

Once people with high IQs realize another person may feel defensive after his experience growing up as a C student, they're usually willing to reach out with more sensitivity. When they also come to appreciate that intelligence is not the only worthwhile trait, they can develop genuine appreciation for others. Genuine interest in one's fellow man is what Dale Carnegie found to be the key for how to win friends and influence people in his famous book by that name.[1] We need our brightest people to become inspiring leaders, not snobs who isolate themselves with other high IQ folks. We could have many more very bright leaders if we'd teach children the truth about differences between people when they're young. I've never heard of any program to explain to kids who are grouped homogeneously what this grouping means or how they'll have to adjust their expectations when they get out in the real world.

Some of Us Are Wired to Be More Reactive or Sensitive

Apart from academic intelligence, there are other differences that impact people's ability to keep their Adult functioning. Elaine Aron indicates that her highly sensitive person (HSP) trait affects 15–20 percent of mammals.[2] Her website, HSPerson.com, offers a self-test you can use to see if you're in this group. This website also includes her free quarterly newsletter, *Comfort Zone*, which describes research and offers support for HSPs. I've worked extensively with HSPs for about ten years and have given Aron's self-test to over two hundred clients. The following comments reflect my observations rather than Aron's research, unless her work is specified. I've noted that sensitivity cuts both ways, bringing both joy and pain to the affected person. Many HSPs have to work harder to keep their Adult functioning while they build stronger Wise Parents to manage their higher reactivity. Fortunately, since HSPs tend to be very conscientious and analytical, they usually practice their lessons faithfully to reduce their reactivity.

HSPs have normally functioning Adult brains that get overwhelmed by Parent-Child tendencies to jump into fight-or-flight too quickly. I've noted that HSPs scoring in the upper half of Aron's self-test are prone to debilitating anxiety symptoms when they get overly stressed. Their inner family is especially prone to triggering fight-or-flight reactions leading to obsessive-compulsive fixations, panic attacks, insomnia or long-term general feelings of dread. These problems will be discussed at length in the chapter on anxiety issues, which appears later in Part II. For HSPs scoring in the lower half, the Adult loses its ability to calm the inner family for shorter periods less often. Many HSPs from both sectors of the scale struggle to maintain the dependable, compassionate behavior they believe they should always express. Their Adult's effort to manage their trigger-happy inner family is tiring.

The ongoing struggle to keep the HSP Critical Parent from jumping on its Child when it acts up crying, yelling or whining with fatigue can be very frustrating. Elaine Aron asserts that 70 percent of HSPs are introverts. I'd suggest that may be due in part to how exhausting it is for their diligent, functional Adults to manage their overly reactive inner families when they engage with other people. For some it's just over-stimulating to be with other people, even when the interactions are positive. Aron also notes that HSPs are more prone to depression than non-HSPs. I've seen many people whose struggles to cope became too frustrating and led to withdrawal from others. These people over-analyze each encounter, allowing their Critical Parent to attack their Child or find fault with the other person. Too much withdrawal from others often leads to depression.

Sensitivity can also lead to positive life experiences. Aron's self-test inquires about sensitivity to art, music, flavor or fragrance. Many HSPs become artists, poets or musicians. Others can learn to take soothing breaks while they savor a novel, a favorite singer or the sweet scent of a wooded place after it rains. Aron's test also inquires about sensitivity to the needs of others and a wish to improve things for them. An HSP whose Adult is managing its inner family well can offer generous, thoughtful empathy to others. When HSPs fail to do this, they usually know it and feel bad about themselves. They can learn to make amends and forgive themselves rather than withdraw.

HSPs are conscientious and usually cautious. These traits can make them excellent employees who will stick with a difficult job and do it to the best of their ability for years. They can be counted on in organizations to follow through with the tedious behind-the-scenes work. They will be there for their friends. However, they tend to get upset when their diligence and faithfulness are not reciprocated. HSPs in counseling often describe their feelings of betrayal in friendships and work situations when others don't reciprocate what they feel they've sacrificed or given too much to provide. They can be helped to realize that blaming others for not performing saps their own energy and doesn't change things. Moreover, this adherence to the third toxic belief boomerangs when their Critical Parent nails their Child for mistakes.

HSPs benefit from recognizing that their perfectionistic wiring, not a higher moral position, leads to many of their "sacrifices." If Abby goes out of her way to organize a program for her group, spending hours preparing material to keep everything in order during the activity, she may be doing more than is required because it helps her feel less anxious to put everything in perfect order. Others won't care so much about keeping things in order and may resent—not appreciate—her efforts to control everything. HSPs must evaluate how much of their effort is done simply because they feel driven to do it to reduce their anxiety. Then they can possibly see how others without this anxiety might not feel the need to perform at the same level, even though they may also be very committed to a project.

One client recognized that sending thoughtful notes to a friend who never sends notes put pressure on her friend and created unnecessary stress in their relationship. Insight into the need to accept others at the level we find them helped her let go of hurt and anger in her relationships. HSPs can benefit from empathizing with their coworkers and bosses who struggle with their own weaknesses as they cope in the workplace. But HSPs also need to respect their own needs and remove themselves from relationships or job situations which make them work too hard to keep their Adult in charge. When the effort becomes too difficult, it feels like a sacrifice, which can leave the HSP Child feeling used, angry and bitter. HSPs generally need more time to recover and recharge than non-HSPs. They need extra time to rest and repair their inner-family harmony every day.

ADD and Learning Disabilities Make Life Harder

Attention deficit disorder (ADD)[3] and its associated problems, like attention deficit/hyperactivity disorder (ADHD) and numerous learning disabilities (like dyslexia), are thought to affect 10 percent of men and at least 5 percent of women.[4] Thomas Brown noted that ADD and ADHD are 91 percent inherited but whether an affected parent has a child who is ADD or ADHD varies unpredictably.[5] Brown indicated that while hyperactivity tends to diminish as children mature, attention and organizing deficits persist into adulthood and continue to impair executive (Adult) function.

In elementary school some kids with ADHD are identified because they're disruptive in their classes. Others are identified because they're bright in some areas and much less capable in others, which may be evidence of one or more learning disabilities. Those who have ADD without hyperactivity (often girls) are frequently overlooked and may spend years struggling with lower self-esteem and less respect from others. Terms assigning blame are often used to describe those with ADHD, such as lazy, irresponsible, impulsive, immature, unreliable and disappointing underachievers. Your Adult must be aware that this harsh, moralistic evaluation may be based on factual error. If you have ADD, your Adult needs to get its Critical Parent off your Child's back and the backs of anyone else it condemns unfairly as well.

People with ADD often have learning disabilities involving memory, communication and processing deficits. These also interfere with their Adult's capacity to function. People with dyslexia can't read adequately to discover information their Adult needs to navigate in the outer world. People with visual or auditory memory problems can't remember what they see or what they hear accurately or for very long. People with certain processing problems can learn well but can't communicate their understanding, because they can't write or speak what they want to express. People with ADD and learning disabilities need a stronger-than-average Wise Parent and Adult to overcome their difficulties and cope with their embarrassment and frustration. But their Adult brains are frequently asleep or groggy and are less capable of managing their inner family or coping with demands from the outer world.

Daniel Amen has studied ADD through thousands of brain scans[6] and worked to make people more aware of why people with ADD often can't function as others expect them to. Brain scans made it obvious why stimulant drugs—often the only way to diagnose ADD in the past (if you had ADD, they worked)—usually have such a dramatic effect. Brain scans showed that the Adult brain area of people with ADD was often very inactive compared to non-ADD brains. Amen has also offered guidance for managing ADD in close relationships.[7]

Amen demonstrates how stimulants activate the Adult brain, allowing some people to become more focused, organized and responsible within a few days. Thomas Brown, noted above, also cites research that shows how the correct doses of the appropriate stimulant medication greatly improve a child's ability to function and protect his self-esteem. He compares it to providing someone with glasses, not medicine. He encourages the use of medication adjusted for the specific needs of the individual. I've seen adults successfully manage their dosage to keep the medication level low (which reduces side effects) on an as-needed basis.

People with ADD can be very intelligent and capable. Imagine the frustration you'd have if you couldn't keep your Adult on track due to your own brain's dysfunction, performing like a C student when you understand like someone with a higher IQ. Not surprisingly, some are embittered and have a chip on their shoulders by the time they're adults. However, many people with ADD have a generous and forgiving nature and a happy and easygoing manner that's very engaging. I wonder how much is wired in and how much is due to wisdom acquired as they struggled to survive their childhood. I've seen this wisdom appear in people with ADD, irrespective of their IQs.

Denial of Differences Is Cruel, Damaging and Common

Today there's lots of research and guidance for children and adults with ADD once they're identified, but many schools don't want to identify them. In one local area, teachers have been told that they can't suggest to a parent that their child may have ADD "because they aren't medically qualified." The truth is that the schools aren't adequately funded to serve all the children who could benefit from extra help. When parents sue for extra services, the extra money to provide for their child's needs could prevent many other children from getting what they need.

One of my clients illustrates the consequences of ignorance about ADD. "Sharon" came in shortly after retiring and said she was feeling lost and somewhat depressed. She described her history, where her learning disabilities were severe enough to be identified, but her ADHD hadn't been recognized. In fourth grade she was placed in a special class for the retarded where she was treated kindly but received little help for her reading and spelling deficits. She described struggling when put into regular classes in high school during the 1960s because she couldn't read well. She only received her diploma when she paid for extra help after she got a job. She worked her way into a good job and performed well for her entire adult life. At one point in her thirties, she sought an evaluation to find out why she had such trouble reading. She was diagnosed with dyslexia, but not ADD.

Sharon is also an HSP and was very conscientious with her monitoring homework, but she kept having episodes of depression where she felt confused, foolish and very lonely. She described waking up with "a cloud in the front of her brain." She was leery of any medication but willing to go for evaluation by a doctor specializing in adult ADD. He established that she was very much affected and prescribed Adderall, which stimulates the Adult brain areas to function more normally. He also gave her some handouts about ADD. She was stunned to realize what the diagnosis has meant for her and upset not to have known what she was dealing with. She discovered *Ten Simple Solutions to Adult ADD* by Stephanie M. Sarkis[8] and implemented the practical guidance offered.

Sharon is finally able to feel comfortable in her own skin after a lifetime of social anxiety. Being an HSP with ADD can be a double burden interpersonally. ADD makes you impulsive or inattentive, and the HSP trait makes you self-critical when you, for example, interrupt or lose track of the conversation. Sharon's Wise Parent finally became stronger than her Critical Parent and her Child was able to begin experiencing a lot of joy. Due to side effects, she chose not to take medication, though while on Adderall she reported being able to read a book in two weeks instead of two months. But she hasn't lost all the benefits and can still read better, even without Adderall.

Despite being misunderstood often throughout her life, Sharon has never become bitter. Somehow her Adult was able to realize early in life that, as she explained it, "there wasn't any benefit in bitterness." Sharon is clearly very intelligent and wise. She has a remarkable sense of humor and tolerance for others. She could have started living a happier life many years ago with appropriate diagnosis.

Personality Disorders Invite Judgment and Harsh Treatment

During a powerful workshop in 2004, Gregory Lester presented the essence of what he'd learned in twenty years of working with people diagnosed with personality disorders.[9] Lester noted that while people have sympathy for those suffering from anxiety or depression, they have little for those with personality disorders. Such people are considered "bad." He indicated that these people's behavior is organized to keep themselves and others unaware of their deficits. He noted that in long-term therapy with them, he was able to uncover brief glimpses of the terrible pain they suffered when they recognized how they were different.

In 2011 Brian King offered a workshop where he described the essential features of people who have personality disorders and whose brain abnormalities make them function very differently from most people.[10] He estimates that these people may comprise 10–15 percent of the population. Their brain dysfunction varies, but they all have deficits in their Adult brain functioning.

You can recognize that a person may have a personality disorder when you find he consistently lacks the ability to walk in your shoes or empathize. This doesn't mean he can't sympathize or care; it just means he can't do the cognitive task required for feeling your feelings. In order to empathize, you must be able to simultaneously perform the following tasks: accurately observe the other person's expressions of feeling, imagine how you'd feel in his situation, adjust for any differences you're aware of between his probable reaction and yours and then respond in an appropriately sympathetic manner. Empathy is truly a shortcut in social relating for those capable of it. One client commented that it would be "like science fiction" to be able to imagine how someone else feels.

If you have trouble interpreting others' reactions, imagining how they might feel or doing all these things at once, then you can't empathize easily during a social interaction. You could learn to think about it later and do some of these tasks sequentially. You could also ask the other person to clarify his feelings if you're aware that you may have misinterpreted them. You can develop skill in how to offer appropriate sympathy. These compensating behaviors must be learned and can only be practiced when your Adult is not over-whelmed with feelings of fight-or-flight due to past hurt and frustration. Identifying personality disorders in children would allow for them to get help in compensating. Early help might reduce for many the attitudes that lead them to alienate others or withdraw from them for the rest of their lives.

Most of us have known examples of people with personality disorders whom we would call "bad" because their behavior is very hurtful and they exhibit little or no remorse. These include people diagnosed as sociopaths, who make up the majority of the inmates in our prisons. Look at *The Sociopath Next Door* by Martha Stout for more insight.[11] Jon Ronson offers a glimpse into these people's minds in his book *The Psychopath Test: A Journey Through the Madness Industry*.[12] Another type is the borderline personality; with these people, their Adult inability to manage their feelings is obvious when they unload their rage. *Stop Walking on Eggshells* by Paul T. Mason and Randi Kreger has been helpful to many who try to cope with people having this disorder.[13] Richard Moskovitz's *Lost in the Mirror* gives insight into what it feels like to have a borderline personality.[14] And people who alienate others with their unrelenting focus on themselves and how they can shine have a narcissistic personality. *Help! I'm in Love With a Narcissist* by Steven Carter and Julie Sokol may help you identify and understand people with this problem.[15]

Since the remaining disorders Brian King described have an inhibiting effect on people, they're less often identified except in extreme cases. One is the paranoid personality, whose immediate reaction to others is distrust. These people can get into trouble with the law due to their isolation and tendency to build up anger. Those with obsessive-compulsive personalities try to control everyone and everything in their vicinity. When people have obsessive personality disorder, their entire capacity for empathy and functioning is affected. When people just have obsessive-compulsive disorder, they can have the normal capacity to empathize and function except for some particular specific situations. In these cases their brain focuses too intensely and they can't let go of their worry, for example, about being poisoned or forgetting something (this will be discussed further in the chapter on anxiety issues).

Two other personality disorder groups have similar names but very different problems; they are schizoid and schizotypal. Adults diagnosed with a schizoid personality had Asperger's syndrome as children, according to Brian King. These people, mostly men, may be very bright and capable in their careers but inept in their social relationships. Many avoid close relationships due to feelings of embarrassment and having been ridiculed growing up. Working with them in therapy, I find they're often willing to try hard to compensate for their inability to empathize with others in order to maintain their marriages. With understanding from their wives, schizoid men can often learn to participate meaningfully in their families. Sometimes they have a child who inherits similar problems. David Finch, who has Asperger's syndrome, wrote *The Journal of Best Practices: A Memoir of Marriage, Asperger Syndrome, and One Man's Quest to Be a Better Husband.*[16] Many of his ideas are good for any marriage.

Asperger's has been related to autism, where people's Adults are overwhelmed by their inability to process sensory and interpersonal stimulation. Brian King rated Asperger's and autism along a spectrum from less to more impaired. At one end of the spectrum, autistic people can barely function due to being confused and overwhelmed. Their confusion and frustration can lead them to have violent tantrums or be very difficult to manage. Temple Grandin describes her struggle with autism in her book, *The Way I See It: A Personal Look at Autism and Asperger's,*[17] which was made into the movie *Temple Grandin.*[18]

Asperger's syndrome is at the less-impaired end of the autism spectrum. These people have trouble interpreting social cues like facial expressions and make awkward or embarrassing social errors. They lack the ability to empathize on the spot but can learn to offer compassion. They can also have anger or anxiety problems due to frustration with their inability to cope, especially in social situations. In some cases schizoid people seem to lack interest in relationships, but unless you get to know them well, you couldn't be sure it's as simple as that.

A colleague of mine indicates that kids with Asperger's really want to have relationships and suffer when their problems prevent them from connecting with others. Tony Attwood offers a comprehensive view in his book *The Complete Guide to Asperger's Syndrome.*[19]

The schizoid/Asperger personality disorder group is the only one where diagnosis and treatment have begun extensively with children. Many are being helped with early intervention to improve the function of their brains. Counseling also helps them learn to accept and compensate for their deficits without feeling the humiliation that could derail their Adult. At present, diagnosticians have prohibited the diagnosis of other personality disorders until people are eighteen. This is likely to change as new learning about the brain gives more insight into how personality disorders develop. It would be better if anyone who has a brain dysfunction that will be recognized as a personality disorder at eighteen could get help very young. I've known families with sociopathic and borderline personality-disordered kids who would have welcomed more appropriate help beginning with their kids' earliest years. To learn more about these and other personality disorders, see Duane L.Dobbert's *Understanding Personality Disorders: an Introduction.*[20]

People with schizotypal personality disorder comprise our next group. These people have eccentric thought processes and often find relationships difficult. Some actually become schizophrenic, but many just live on the fringes of society, in some cases becoming homeless due to their inability to cope. Kim T. Muser and Susan Gingerich in their book *The Complete Family Guide to Schizophrenia: Helping Your Loved One Get the Most Out of Life*[21] describe a spectrum of disorders where those diagnosed schizotypal have less severe symptoms than those diagnosed with schizophrenia.

This discussion would not be complete without addressing schizophrenia, a complex disorder affecting about one per cent of the population. Muser and Gingerich indicate that it presents itself between the ages of sixteen and thirty, with some people being well-adjusted and some poorly adjusted before they develop symptoms. Much more than a personality disorder, this mental illness has been studied and theorized about probably more than any other. They emphasize the importance of diagnosis as early as possible for a disease which masquerades as many other problems. People with schizophrenia may have problems with concentration and impulse control like Attention Deficit Disorder, mania and delusions as with bipolar disorder, depression and anxiety. Generally they are impaired with deficits in their capacity to engage their Adult to manage their life due to poorly understood problems in their brains.   Muser and Gingerich explain that each person afflicted has a unique combination of these problems occurring with differing levels of intensity at any given time, making diagnosis difficult. However, with the right diagnosis, a combination of medication, social support and therapy can help prevent escalation of symptoms and gradual stabilization of most people with schizophrenia. Without this many will be hospitalized with extreme symptoms; they comprise most of the patients in state mental hospitals. These authors describe how families can understand and cope with this disease which is considered at least partly genetically based. New research and treatment programs have begun to make even this daunting and long-mysterious source of Adult dysfunction more manageable. Milt Greek offers an inside view of what it feels like to have schizophrenia in his book about his own struggles, *Schizophrenia: A Blueprint for Recovery*.[22]

It's hoped that with increased understanding of what causes disabling interpersonal deficits, children can be helped to avoid shame and anxiety because of deficits they were born with. There's been some progress in general acceptance and support of people with physical disabilities, but we have a long way to go with some of these mental disabilities. It feels like science fiction to contemplate how different these people could be if they weren't shamed and judged throughout their childhoods for behavior they can't help.

There are some movements afoot to make changes in how we teach our children about what people are really like. In the *Monitor on Psychology*, December 2009, Michael Price described a conference where psychologists, neuroscientists, educators and Buddhist leaders planned for ways to teach children compassion and self-understanding.[23] In the *Monitor on Psychology* October 2009 Amy Novotny described two broad studies where Martin Seligman revealed the impact of teaching these things to school kids, and the result was that *all* the students' academic and social skills were improved. There were also fewer discipline problems and fewer reports of depression among the kids.[24]

Anxiety and Depression Reduce the Ability of Our Adult When We Need it Most

Emotional problems are more widely shared and better understood and accepted than the brain-based individual differences described above. It's important to recognize that anxiety, depression and other emotional imbalances also temporarily impair the functioning of your Adult in ways that will be discussed in later chapters. It's best if your Adult can stay alert and notice when you're impacted by emotional distress early in the problem, so you can make some accommodation and get help if you need it. When you contemplate all the possible obstacles to keeping your Adult in charge, it becomes obvious how really inappropriate blaming or punishing yourself can be. You should just be applauded for keeping your Adult functioning whenever you can as a struggling human being.

Try to identify when others may be suffering from anxiety or depression and modify your expectations, rather than blaming them. Responding with hurt or anger because you take personally their impaired behavior doesn't foster better functioning in them or you. When they behave badly, bring your Wise Parent on board quickly to be gentle with them and reassuring to your own Child. When you can do that, you're helping compensate for the inadequate Parent that's causing their distress, much like a therapist does. Often you can soothe their Child, and their Adult can struggle back into control; then they'll respond with less hostility. If this doesn't work, your Wise Parent must assure your Child that you did the best you could. As Bonnie, the depressed HSP teacher coping with workplace stress, reminded herself, "Somebody has a problem here, but it's not me."

Self-Knowledge Can Set You Free

These examples represent some of the medically recognized individual differences our Adult must consider as it scans our outer world. When you identify someone behaving like her Critical Parent or hurt and angry Child is in control, it's wise to change your expectations. You can always be pleasantly surprised if her Adult reemerges sooner than you'd expected. The genuinely respectful and fair approach of your Adult and Wise Parent may allow the other person to control a defensive Child more quickly.

If you have any of these challenges yourself, it's good Wise-Parenting to educate yourself like Sharon did to find deep self-acceptance that others may not always support. You'll relieve some anger about who you "should have been." You'll be more able to fend off the criticism of people who have no idea how hard you've had to work and how easy they've had it in many cases. It can feel good to be the bigger person, especially with others who've ignorantly tried to make you feel small. Your self-knowledge can set you free.

I'd like to emphasize that, in the words of Brian King, "we are in the infancy of understanding" individual differences in our brains.[25] In 1956 when I was twelve, I babysat with a family whose older son was autistic. I learned that his parents had been told with great authority by a famous child psychologist in Chicago that his problems were due to his mother's cold, rejecting behavior toward him. This very loving and committed mother and father helped their son gain some quality of life despite his "help" and the ignorant arrogance of many professionals in those years.

It's refreshing to hear now how professionals are actually being professional and acknowledging more often the limits of their knowledge. Any amateur can sound off about his opinion on a topic. As a consumer, you need to be wary of "professionals" who state they have firm knowledge about individual differences. Just look at how confusing the labels remain: Asperger's and schizoid, schizoid and schizotypal, obsessive-compulsive personality disorder and obsessive-compulsive disorder. These reflect both the early misunderstanding of these problems and the continued dysfunction in the professional ranks as we try to incorporate new learning about the brain into the old frameworks for looking at people.

Here are some self-talk phrases that can help you keep your Adult in charge:

- Somebody has a problem here, but it's not me.

- It's not politically correct to admit that people aren't equal in their coping abilities, but it's honest and fair.

- I have what I need for a fulfilling journey through life.

- Only I have the necessary information to evaluate my efforts.

- Some people sure need to work on the third toxic belief.

- I'm guided on my journey by my weaknesses as well as by my strengths.

- My suffering gives me more compassion for others with tough differences.

- Consider the source, then use your own judgment.

Notes

1. Dale Carnegie, *How to Win Friends and Influence People* (1936; rev. ed., New York: Simon & Schuster, 1981).
2. Elaine N. Aron, *The Highly Sensitive Person: How to Thrive When the World Overwhelms You* (New York: Broadway Books, 1997); see also http://www. HSPerson.com, accessed June 7, 2012.
3. Edward M. Hallowell and John J. Ratey, *Delivered from Distraction: Getting the Most Out of Life with Attention Deficit Disorder* (New York: Ballantine Books, 2006).
4. American Psychiatric Association, *Diagnostic and Statistical Manual of Mental Disorders,* DSMIV-TR (2000); see also http://www.Allpsych.com/disorders/dsm.
5. Thomas E. Brown, *Recognizing ADHD: Neurobiology, Symptoms and Treatment* (Chicago: Pragmaton, 2001).
6. Daniel G. Amen, *Healing ADD* (New York: Berkley Books, 2001).
7. Daniel G. Amen, *ADD in Intimate Relationships* (Newport Beach: Mindworks Press, 2005).
8. Stephanie Moulton Sarkis, *Ten Simple Solutions to Adult ADD* (Oakland: New Harbinger, 2005).
9. Gregory Lester, *Personality Disorders in Social Work and Health Care* (Nashville: Cross Country Education, 2004).

10. Brian E. King, *Understanding Personality Disorders* (Haddonfield: Institute for Brain Potential, 2011).

11. Martha Stout, *The Sociopath Next Door* (New York: Broadway Books, 2005).

12. Jon Ronson, *The Psychopath Test: A Journey Through the Madness Industry* (New York: Riverhead Books, 2011).

13. Paul T. Mason and Randi Kreger, *Stop Walking on Eggshells: Taking Your Life Back When Someone You Care About Has Borderline Personality Disorder* (Oakland: New Harbinger Publications, 1998).

14. Richard Maskovitz, *Lost in the Mirror: An Inside Look at Borderline Personality Disorder* (New York: Taylor Trade Publishing, 2001).

15. Steven Carter and Julie Sokol, *Help! I'm in Love with a Narcissist* (New York: Evans Publishing Group, 2005).

16. David Finch, *The Journal of Best Practices: A Memoir of Marriage, Asperger Syndrome, and One Man's Quest to Be a Better Husband* (New York: Scribner, 2012).

17. Temple Grandin and Ruth Sullivan, *The Way I See It: A Personal Look at Autism and Asperger's* (Arlington: Future Horizons, 2008).

18. *Temple Grandin* (made-for-television biopic), Ruby Films, Gerson Saines Production, HBO Films (USA, 2010).

19. Tony Attwood, *The Complete Guide to Asperger's Syndrome* (Philadelphia: Jessica Kingsley Publishers, 2007).

20. Duane L. Dobbert, *Understanding Personality Disorders: An Introduction* (Westport: Greenwood Publishing Group, 2007).

21. Kim T. Mueser and Susan Gingerich, *The Complete Family Guide to Schizophrenia: Helping Your Loved One Get the Most Out of Life* (New York: The Guilford Press, 2006).

22. Milt Greek, *Schizophrenia: A Blueprint for Recovery* (Athens: Milt Greek, 2008, rev. ed., 2012).

23. Michael Price, "More Compassion, Less Competition," http//:monitor on psychology.com, Col. 40, December, 2009.

24. Amy Novotny, "Resilient Kids Learn Better," http//:monitor on psychology. com, Vol. 40, October 2009.

25. King, *Understanding Personality Disorders*.

II : 2

Addiction: Tootle and the Field of Flowers

A favorite old children's story features a charming, fun-loving young train engine named Tootle.[1] He admired the older, more capable engines and wanted to grow up to be just like them. But at one point he tired of the strict limits of the track and jumped off to cavort in a field with the flowers, the birds and the butterflies. Everyone can relate to that feeling. Haven't we all envied our dog or cat for their easy enjoyment of the present, free of human concerns about the future? But the older engines were worried about Tootle; they knew he couldn't stay on track if he kept jumping it.

You can't keep derailing your Adult and travel your journey well. You'll rust in the field right along with Tootle. Stanton Peele and Archie Brodsky wrote that it's not an inherited flaw but rather our human nature that makes us all want to take breaks from our human awareness. It's when you block your Adult too much that you develop an addiction.[2] Addictions prevent your Adult from gaining skills to balance the inner family and handle stress. The darkest secret of addiction is that it short-circuits your growth. Addictions "spoil" your Child, teaching instant gratification instead of the patience needed for security and growth. There's no reworking of a faulty belief or new strength for your Wise Parent.

Your Indulgent Parent's beliefs dominate when addictions take over. It agrees with your Child that it's catastrophically unfair when you try hard and fail to get rewarded for your efforts (the seventh toxic belief). It encourages your Child to rely on outside support (from the addiction) for feelings of comfort and happiness (the eighth toxic belief). It supports procrastination and avoidance when facing problems (the ninth toxic belief). It deems it unbearable if someone lets you down and supports unhealthy involvement with others who encourage the addiction (the tenth toxic belief). It allows your Child to indulge in feelings of being "special" in its need for extra excitement or support (the eleventh toxic belief) or "clever" in its ability to score the addictive high (the twelfth toxic belief).

Of course, once the addiction spree is over, the Critical Parent crushes your Child, ultimately setting off another round of self-indulgence. Critical-Parent attacks intensify with every addictive episode, provoking more demands for quick relief by the Child. With a weakened Adult and inadequate Wise Parent, your inner family becomes a seesaw between the Critical Parent and the Child, where the only stabilizing force is the addiction. The roller coaster ride of the outer family of an alcoholic is legendary.

Chemical Addictions and the Brain

Referring to the inner family to describe addiction has merit for your ongoing work to build your mental fitness. The concepts are simple enough to carry around with you during the day as you try to keep your Adult in charge. To empower your Adult to cope with your demanding Child and inadequate Parent parts, you need more information. Scientific understanding of the brain remains in its early stages, but you don't need additional information to avoid getting addicted. Sadly, a lot more information is needed to cure addictions in the wide variety of people affected. Let's look at some of what is now understood about how your brain is impacted when you take the shortcut to peace or ecstasy through addiction to non-prescribed drugs. Prescription drug addiction will be discussed in chapter three on anxiety and chapter six on depression.

Daniel Amen describes the impact on the brain of different chemical addictions, illustrating short- and long-term damage in pictures taken from brains scans.[3] All of them damage the Adult brain as well as other brain areas. He expresses great concern for the increasing social denial of the real brain damage caused by marijuana use and the move to legalize it. His brain scan of a sixteen-year-old who used pot daily for two years should chill anyone who argues for making marijuana more available. To keep your Adult in charge, you must overcome widespread socially programmed denial about just what addiction does to your brain. Chemical addictions directly prevent the functioning of the Adult mind. If your goal is to keep your Adult in charge, you can't destroy your physical ability to do it.

Addicted Parents and Their Kids' Risk of Addiction

Brown et al. note that when parents abuse drugs and alcohol, their kids are more likely to abuse drugs and alcohol before age sixteen.[4] They indicate addicted parents lead their kids to early addiction in two ways: they provide poor models for how to cope with stress and fail to supervise their kids to keep them away from alcohol. Brown et al. describe how early abuse of drugs and alcohol leads to addiction by age thirty. They offer a detailed comparison of the difference between normal adolescent development and drug-impacted development, specifically noting how damage to the adolescent brain prevents and distorts development.

Brown et al. emphasize that addicted parents also teach their children beliefs that lead them to minimize the problems of substance abuse, despite experience with their parents' abuse. What kind of beliefs? Beliefs of the Indulgent Parent that lead the Child into self-talk like, "I can't take it," "I need this to cope," "There isn't really anything else to help me enough" and "It's unfair to expect me to do this on my own." These messages and self-talk dominate the thinking of people dependent on substances to function. They reveal how little Adult and Wise-Parent input they have for coping. Claudia Black's book *It Will Never Happen to Me* is written for adult children of alcoholics who often do let it happen to them because of how they were raised.[5] This book describes thoroughly the impact of alcoholic parents' damaged capacity for close relationships on their kids' ability to feel comfortable with intimacy. Weaker relationships make addiction more likely in their future. Clients with alcoholic parents are frequently stunned to find their deepest feelings identified in Black's book. It helps their Adult begin to connect with their hurt and withdrawn Child.

Nonchemical Addictions and the Brain

New brain research examining the impact of nonchemical addictions on the brain is beginning to find disturbing parallels with chemical addictions. Jon Grant and Marc Potenza report similarities in brain reactions between pathological gamblers and cocaine addicts.[6] Let's consider these nonchemical addictions and what we can already observe about their impact. A person with an eating disorder is as preoccupied with thoughts of food as the alcoholic is with the next drink. Though lacking a chemical addiction, the person becomes dependent on the food obsession and often has a lifetime of struggle to give it up.

The dynamic in the inner family of a person with such an obsession is just like that of the alcoholic: a needy Child who presses for instant pleasure, the harsh Critical Parent who beats the Child up, the weak Wise Parent who has little credible positive feedback to give and the Adult who's overwhelmed by the chaos and pressures within. In this state the Adult often makes poor decisions that create even more chaos and pressure to take comfort in the obsession. I've seen people who depend on exercise to handle their moods plunge into depression when they're injured. They remain depressed if they can't physically keep up their addictive level of activity. There's an alarming growth in the number of people who neglect everything in their lives in order to play computer games or even work on their computers.

How do addictions get their hold on you? Lance Dodes describes how to focus on the moment you make the choice to pursue an addictive behavior in order to begin uncovering the source of your drive for it.[7] He argues that the most powerful feeling that motivates addiction is helplessness. His very clear and focused approach encompasses cognitive-behavioral therapy (CBT) concepts, though he does not identify it as CBT. The Child too quickly decides it's helpless because of the entrenched Parental messages discussed in Part I. Dodes urges you to focus (using your Adult) with a monitoring-type approach to begin controlling your addiction. Then he describes with many clear examples how to change your thought processes and beliefs to manage addictive urges.

The intense focus of an addiction rewards you with relief from Critical-Parent pressure. When you obsessively plan for what you can eat, when you can drink, when you can get on the computer or when you can have sex, you forget about internal and external problems even before you engage in the addiction. With nonchemical addictions you retain the ability to figure out how to maintain the addictive activity indefinitely. You remain sharp mentally and can win at the computer game or develop an eating ritual. Your Child is then totally free to pursue the food, the gaming or the contacts without any concern for the consequences until your Critical Parent catches it again.

Cognitive-Behavioral Therapy and Addiction

If you're hooked on any addiction, you can't make progress with cognitive-behavioral therapy alone. CBT requires self-observation and intricate processing your weak Adult couldn't do consistently. You wouldn't have the patience to set aside your quick fix in order to work for a process that only promises rewards in the long run. There are rewards along the way, but there is not the reliable relief the addiction offers. The problem is that you need *some* patience to begin to build more. If you've been hooked longer, it will be even harder to believe you can learn new ways to cope that can bring genuine and lasting satisfaction.

Our society hawks the message that only immediate gratification is important. All the ads insist you need the hamburger, the car, the new tech device *now*. With the Child seduced from all sides, only a very strong Adult-Wise-Parent team can set effective limits. Only a powerful Wise Parent can keep your Child hopeful and confident that it has the capacity to overcome its addiction and learn better ways to cope.

Consider Sophie, who came in determined to take off fifty pounds before her wedding. She had embraced the ninth toxic belief, which enabled her to avoid the problem of her weight gain for many years. She described how she liked to indulge herself by going to two McDonald's drive-throughs and loading up at each with two Super-Sized meals and a shake. She explained that she didn't want either server to know she would eat that much. Her clever Child peeked out with a conspiratorial grin as she confessed. Since she had some Adult monitoring skills, we identified her (Child) belief that she had a right to enjoy herself, which was supported by her Indulgent Parent's twelfth toxic belief, that she was really too clever to have to follow the usual rules.

We discussed having Sophie explore some other ways of nurturing herself (for Wise-Parent growth), and she had begun doing some reading and puzzles for fun. Yet her Child still believed strongly that the best way to feel good was to binge. I challenged her to practice self-observation (using her Adult) and note *all* her feelings just as she took her first bite of the next Big Mac. The next week she came in and exclaimed, with a mixture of petulance and excitement, "You ruined it!" She went on to describe how doing this had made her aware of the anxious guilt that accompanied her pleasure. She went on to lose her excess weight quite rapidly, as her McDonald's adventure was no longer the pure fun she'd imagined it to be.

Would Sophie maintain her present level of Adult and Wise-Parent control? She moved soon after she lost her weight, and if she didn't stay in treatment, the chances of her holding on to this with so little practice were not good. It takes a long time to convince your Child that a pleasure it has come to love is bad for it. What happens when you take away a little child's favorite blankie? I've helped parents get their teenage sons away from their computer after daily gaming for two to four years in the safety of their own homes. The computer had to be locked up, the family had to deal with abusive tantrums and it took years for the youth to get back into a normal school and work pattern with nongaming friendships when our work was successful.

Feeding the Hungry Heart: the Experience of Compulsive Eating, written by Geneen Roth in 1982,[8] described in personal terms the intense pain of the Child that can be expressed in eating addictions. She offers a workbook, *Why Weight? A Guide to Ending Compulsive Eating*,[9] to help identify the beliefs that trigger binges and ideas for how to heal a wounded Child.

Judith Beck has developed a five-step CBT program to overcome overeating in her book *The Beck Diet Solution: Train Your Brain to Think Like a Thin Person*.[10] She focused on preparing her clients with changes in their self-talk before they began to change any behavioral habits. Only after they could define and revise the Child self-talk that accompanied their overeating were they allowed to begin exercise and diet plans. Once clients developed improved eating and exercising habits, they learned tools for maintaining their new self-talk and behavioral habits. They learned how to plan for times they'd be especially tempted, like holidays and parties. Finally, they'd learn how to stay on track with realistic expectations and supportive self-talk.

Patrick Carnes offers research and wisdom to help those struggling with a sexual addiction at his website GentlePath.com. See also the latest edition of his groundbreaking book *Out of the Shadows: Understanding Sexual Addiction.*[11] Like alcohol or food, sexual interest and behavior are not an addiction until they interfere with one's personal or work life. The billion-dollar pornography industry, now easily accessed on home computers, is leading many into this addiction that destroys marriages and lives. It confuses the Adult enough that some addicts become predators who can even rationalize sexual abuse of very young children.

The Indulgent Parent belief that most supports addiction is the ninth toxic belief, which is that avoiding problems is the best way to deal with them. Our Big Mac fan found out the fallacy of this belief. You don't get *pure* enjoyment out of things you overuse to avoid problems. This is a good illustration of how a belief can prevent you from learning the truth of your actual experience. The ninth toxic belief creates the denial that allows addiction to flourish. Unfortunately, the more you practice this denial, the harder it can be to see the lie within it. To combat this belief, your Adult must look clearly at how your Child really feels when you procrastinate. "Why do today what you can put off till tomorrow?" is funny when you're avoiding yard work. But it's destructive when you're avoiding feelings and issues that upset you or provoke you into harmful behavior, since these feelings won't go away until you face them.

Ingredients of Sobriety

In Alcoholics Anonymous[12] it's recognized that alcoholics need a sponsor along with group support to provide Adult and Wise-Parent guidance. Sobriety isn't simply stopping the addiction. Recovering alcoholics talk about how it's easier to stop drinking than to get sober and stay sober. Sobriety requires Adult self-mastery, which is what we're working on here. You must have sober friends both to prevent and overcome an addiction. Non-sober addict friends can't help you, and their Indulgent-Parent and Child parts will try to pull you back in.

Young people have weak Adults and need the strong Adults of their parents to guide them to a sober and fulfilling life. Don't expect your kids to avoid addictions if you're relying on one to handle your own stress. They won't respect what you have to say, and you won't be showing them the value, balance, and skills of a sober life. You need to know the rewards of staying on track before you can guide someone else to give up the field of flowers.

If you don't have addictive habits of numbing out your awareness, *don't assume you're immune.* The Child part of us humans is very powerful, connected as it is to our crocodile brain and our overly quick fight-or-flight reactions. To stay clear of addictions, you must monitor regularly to uncover and correct your Indulgent-Parent messages and the Critical-Parent beliefs that make your Child want to escape.

Recognize tendencies to want immediate gratification, which are expressed when your Child says, "I can't stand that I can't have what I want *now.*" Watch out for the third toxic belief (that people should be blamed when they don't measure up) and don't expect too much of yourself. If you cling to the third belief, your Critical Parent will punish you for your human tendencies and just make your Child more needy, resentful and desirous of a quick fix.

Sobriety when Life Gets Tough

Build your Adult and Wise-Parent strength to keep yourself from getting hooked on an addiction when life gets tough. Heighten your awareness of all the corrupting messages you're bombarded with and develop some tough phrases to shut them down. Be aware that when you have to endure a long, difficult experience—caring for a sick relative, coping with two or three young kids in diapers, recovering from an injury or being stuck in a negative work situation—your human nature will be at risk for an addiction.

Then you need to increase your self-care and your self-awareness to protect your functioning. Build your Wise Parent and Adult, limit your Critical Parent carefully and manage your Child kindly, but firmly.

Take some time to enjoy less-stressed, healthy friends. If you find yourself drawn into a mind-numbing activity, don't use it to hide from your problems. Limit your time with it and find a variety of activities instead of just one.

If you've struggled with an addiction before, remind yourself that positive new activities don't offer escape through the intense preoccupation your addiction provided. Gradually, however, they do fill the void and sustain you by enhancing your good feelings about yourself that the addiction would have destroyed. Include some activities that you can share with others who can nurture you when you need more support. Don't procrastinate and let your inner family get set into patterns that you can't break. The sooner you get support, the easier your readjustment will be.

Sources of Help

There are countless sources of help available to prevent or overcome addictions. Alcoholics Anonymous offers support along with its program for revamping beliefs that prevent sobriety. Groups for Adult Children of Alcoholics can be very powerful. Hazelden[13] and PubMed Health[14] offer many resources online for treatment and recovery. Stanton Peele emphasizes the capability of individuals to cope with addiction and describes a wide range of socially available tools you can use.[15] He endorses the concept that addiction is not a disease. And remember Lance Dodes' helpful book for refined self-monitoring.[16]

Because of human tendencies to get overwhelmed with stress, you always need to have the support of others to help you observe yourself. You can't count on your Adult to maintain its functioning when you cope with stress alone or your Wise Parent to be adequate for new situations. CBT works best when paired with the support of non-addicted, sober friends who can help you maintain your inner balance.

With support you can get back on the track of your journey and discover the self-esteem you can only earn when you stay on track, pulling your particular load all the way up the mountain. Then you can enjoy the real "high" of being capable and savor it for the rest of your life.

Here are some tough anti-addiction messages to get you started:

- When it seems too good to be true, it probably is.

- I can give myself a high anytime—one that builds me without tearing me down.

- If it's humanly possible, I'm sure I can do it too.

- I want to waste no time in learning how to use my own gifts.

- I want to be healthy to teach my children how to face life without addiction.

- I'm not entitled to more relief from responsibility than anyone else.

- Putting things off doesn't really reduce my stress.

- Disappointment is a normal part of life; I can bear it.

- Being smart doesn't mean cutting corners.

- What if everyone did what I'm doing?

- From Alcoholics Anonymous: let go and let God.

Notes

1. Watty Piper, *The Little Engine that Could* (New York: Philomel Books, 2005).
2. Stanton Peele with Archie Brodsky, *Love and Addiction* (New York: The Viking Press, 1980).
3. Daniel G. Amen, *Change Your Brain, Change Your Life* (New York: Three Rivers Press, 1998).

4. Sandra A. Brown, Matthew McGue, Jennifer Maggs, John Schulenberg, Ralph Hingson, Scott Swartzwelder, Christopher Martin, Tammy Chung, Susan F. Tapert, Kenneth Sher, Ken C. Winters, Cherry Lowman, and Stacia Murphy, "A Developmental Perspective on Alcohol and Youths 16 to 20 Years of Age," *Pediatrics*, Vol. 121 Suppl. 4 (April 2008).

5. Claudia Black, *It Will Never Happen to Me* (Bainbridge Island: MAC Publishing, 2001).

6. Jon E. Grant and Marc N. Potenza, *Pathological Gambling: A Clinical Guide to Treatment* (Arlington: American Psychiatric Publishing, 2004).

7. Lance Dodes, *Breaking Addiction: A 7-Step Handbook for Ending Any Addiction* (New York: Harper Collins, 2011).

8. Geneen Roth, *Feeding the Hungry Heart: The Experience of Compulsive Eating* (1982; repr., New York: Penguin Books, 1993).

9. Geneen Roth, Why Weight? A Guide to Ending Compulsive Eating (New York: Penguin Group, 1989).

10. Judith Beck, *The Beck Diet Solution: Train Your Brain to Think Like a Thin Person* (Birmingham: Oxmoor House, 2008).

11. Patrick J. Carnes, *Out of the Shadows: Understanding Sexual Addiction* (Center City: Hazelden, 2001); see also http://www.GentlePath.com, Accessed on June 7, 2012.

12. *Alcoholics Anonymous* (New York: Alcoholics Anonymous World Services, 1976).

13. Hazelden, accessed on May 25, 2012, http//www.hazelden.org.

14. PubMed, accessed on May 25, 2012, http//www.ncbi.nlm.gov/pubmed.

15. Stanton Peele, *7 Tools to Beat Addiction* (New York: Three Rivers Press, 2004); see also http://www.peele.net, accessed June 8, 2012.

16. Dodes, *Breaking Addiction*.

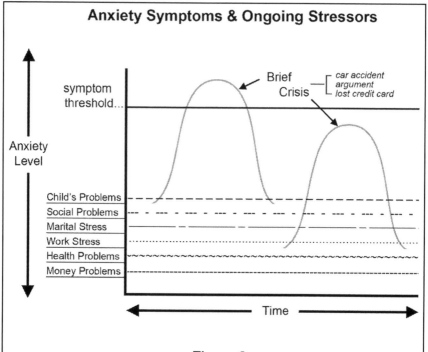

Figure 3.

Ongoing stressors like marital or financial problems add up, increasing brain chemicals that prepare you for fight-or-flight. The higher their levels, the closer you come to a full fight-or-flight reaction, which you may experience as a panic attack, headache, stomach ache, crying, or losing your temper. When ongoing stressors are at a lower level, brief crises don't push you over the threshold where you'll have symptoms.

II : 3

Anxiety Issues

When your Adult can't manage your inner family or cope with life stressors, panicky, anxious feelings can escalate into disabling symptoms. Victims of anxiety have an inadequate Wise Parent who can't guide or reassure their frightened Child. They may have a Critical Parent who presses them to take on more than they should in their life and then beats up on the Child when they fail to perform well. With this inner struggle, the Adult is overwhelmed and can't function.

Some people focus obsessive-compulsively on possible dangers, some exercise vigilance that allows them little rest and others are struck by alarming panic attacks that seem to come from nowhere. Heredity seems to determine which of these symptoms a person is likely to get when stressed. Parents afflicted with severe symptoms are poor role models too, unwittingly teaching unhealthy habits and beliefs. This chapter will describe why anxiety symptoms emerge as they do and how to overcome them through adjustments in your inner and outer worlds.

Reduce the Impact of Ongoing Stressors

Let's look at how getting overwhelmed in your life can create anxiety symptoms. Figure 3 describes how ongoing stressors can build up, gradually overloading your tolerance. Then a brief stressor comes along to push your brain chemistry over its threshold, and you have a symptom. Ongoing stressors are the worries about financial, health, community or relationship problems that can last a long time, and there are two ways to address these. One way is to summon your Adult to reduce your activities and commitments. Say no to more responsibilities, especially those your Critical Parent has driven you to accept. If you can't do this on your own, a therapist can provide insight and support until you strengthen your own Wise Parent and Adult.

The second way to reduce the impact of ongoing stressors is to identify what beliefs about each stressor could be changed, allowing you to handle them more easily. You may need to start by critiquing the belief that you *can't take* any more stress. That just scares your Child and gets your body all upset, as described in Part I, chapter 3. The truth is that you *can take* such stress but just don't want to anymore.

Focus your Adult to analyze your unwise beliefs about each stressor. For example, if you have nagging worries about your health but don't take care of yourself, you may subscribe to the ninth toxic belief (that avoiding problems is the easiest way to cope). Once you combat that belief, you can get a physical, eat healthy, scrub the toxins off your fruit, exercise and worry less. If you have financial problems but keep spending too much money, the same toxic belief is in effect and you may have other Indulgent-Parent beliefs that encourage your Child to have unlimited fun. Your Adult can combat the avoidance and guide your Wise Parent to manage your Child better. A Wise Parent message would be, "It's really more fun when we won't have to suffer later." Then you can find a good financial counselor or work with your spouse to develop a plan that's more affordable.

Reduce Your Symptoms and Your Fear of Them

At the same time you're working to take control of your life stressors, you'll need to reduce the symptoms that can disable you and prevent this effort. It's possible to do this without professional help in many cases but is often faster and less painful with help. First, reduce your fear of the symptoms themselves by realizing they're warning signals that you need to rebalance, like the buzz of a washing machine when all the clothes have gotten on one side. The washing machine isn't damaged, and neither are you. The Parent-Child struggle that has created the symptom can be interrupted by a distracting activity, like counting backwards by sevens from two hundred, working a crossword puzzle or focusing on your breathing. This may seem way too simple to address something as disruptive as a panic attack, but it's all several of my clients have needed to overcome their panic attacks. They had only experienced these attacks briefly in response to a specific stressor, and they weren't interested in learning all the reasons why they had them. They felt secure just by counting backwards at the onset of an attack.

How Panic Attacks Happen

For those of us who just want to understand better or have suffered panic attacks for a longer time, let's look at the mechanism for them. First there is a stressful event that overloads your normal coping ability (see again figure 3). This can be a life event like a car accident or something as simple as losing your keys when you're in a hurry. It can also be a mind-created stressor caused by a Parent-Child conflict your Adult can't hear. These inner-family-generated stressors account for panicky feelings that seem to come from nowhere when you're calm, like during your morning shower or while you sit in a boring meeting.

Your inner family inhabits what scientists have called your "default network," which operates outside your awareness when you aren't focusing on something in particular. Douglas Fox, reporting in the journal *New Scientist* (November 2008),[1] describes research going back over fifty years that reveals insight into the brain functions of your inner family. Dubbed the "default network" by Marcus Raichle and Gordon Schuman in 2001, it's continuously active when you're daydreaming and during the early part of sleep. Researchers explained that this default network processes the memories of your daily experience, editing and storing them according to their importance to your safety and functioning.

The default network of your inner family includes memory centers that hold beliefs from your childhood that, as we've noted, often lead you into fight-or-flight. The hippocampus, in the heart of the default network, funnels incoming information into these memory centers (see again figures 1 and 2). Processing occurs, and too often the decision is made to alert your body into action. Fox indicates that functional MRIs have demonstrated recently that this default network's activity level drops when volunteers focus their attention on a task like solving a puzzle or math problem. This is no doubt why counting backwards works so well to stop a panic attack; it shuts off your default network, which gives your inner family a rest. This discovery suggests that any extreme emotional reaction brewing in your inner family could be interrupted by focusing your attention on some demanding task. This technique was discussed earlier in Part I, chapter 3.

When your default network concludes you must go into fight-or-flight, it signals your body via your Vagus nerve. Then your body's reaction signals your brain to stay upset via the Vagus nerve. Your Adult is working to shut off this extreme reaction but is not feeling any change in your body. What's wrong? Eighty percent of the nerve fibers in your Vagus nerve run from your body to your brain to keep your brain engaged in fight-or-flight.[2] This means that even when you realize your body has been foolishly hooked in, your Adult must use the remaining 20 percent of the fibers in the Vagus nerve to quiet down *both* your brain and body. It's not surprising this may take longer than is comfortable, but knowing this can help keep your Adult from being overwhelmed by all the scary feedback. It must continue firm and confident with its reassuring message that there is no immediate danger that requires your body to run or fight.

It's much easier when your Adult can catch the message before it reaches your body and revise it. But you can still calm your body even when it does get hooked. A simple statement works best to override all this drama, such as, "This won't kill me" or "My life is not in danger." Why could this work? It's likely your brain is wired to react quickly to *clear* signals that fight-or-flight *won't* be necessary. The earlier you use these clarifying messages, the less your body gets involved. How could your Adult notice this sooner? Identify what *your* body does first when it receives the signal.

One of the first body changes in response to Vagus nerve signals is hyperventilating. This consists of quick, shallow breaths that people rarely notice. Why we hyperventilate when we feel threatened became clear to me during a walk with my dog. Dolly was a long-haired dachshund of eleven pounds who never realized she was a small dog. Even at seventeen years old, she still wanted to attack any dog she saw. We learned very early that we had to pick her up and restrain her at the sight of any animal. Her immediate first response was to puff intensely. It was clear that she was actively mobilizing her body to tear into action. Humans aren't often so obvious, but we hyperventilate to mobilize for action, just like Dolly.

How to shut off a panic attack

To prevent going into a full-blown panic, you must stop hyperventilating. A focused task like counting backwards stops you from hyperventilating indirectly by forcing your default network to take a break. But for some of you, that doesn't last, and your default network picks up where it left off, signaling for action again. When I had to overcome panic attacks in the early 1970s, someone told me to blow into a paper bag. It turns out Claire Weekes, a pioneer in treating panic in the 1960s and '70s, described how rapid, shallow breathing depletes carbon dioxide in the brain. Weekes recommended blowing into a paper bag to increase the carbon dioxide level.[3] I never had one handy, so I tried just breathing out, with only tiny inward breaths as much as I could for awhile. When I combined that with calming self-talk, I was able to stop my attacks.

This is what I've taught clients to do for over thirty years, and they've quickly recovered from panic attacks in most cases. Many clients report that doctors and emergency room staff tell them to use diaphragmatic, or deep breathing to stop their panic. This only increases the oxygen-carbon dioxide imbalance you've already created with your hyperventilating. **<u>Just breathe out deeply and take in only the smallest breaths you can until you're calm. You'll feel the calming effect immediately</u>**. It's a great relief to stop being afraid of the panic attack itself. A summary of the steps suggested to shut down a panic attack or other intense fight-or-flight reaction is offered in appendix C.

Shutting Off Your Intense Anxiety

When you're overwhelmed by intense anxiety, insomnia, obsessive thoughts or panic attacks, it takes a strong Adult-Wise-Parent team to firmly override your default network/inner family. At this point your inner family has already engaged your body to run or fight. My very anxious clients were more able to engage their Adult after I explained how the simple tasks I gave them worked in their brains.

For example, I recently I saw a doctor, "Paul," who dragged himself in after sleeping just two hours the night before. He hadn't been able to sleep more than a couple of hours a night for a year, he reported, and had slept only a little better the four previous years. He was in a constant state of anxiety and near-panic. He often felt hopeless, angry and depressed due to a combination of professional and financial stressors. He was afraid for his health and checked his blood pressure several times a day, finding it consistently too high at about 180/115. He refused any medication, and his life situation was not going to resolve itself quickly.

We listed his stressors, and I gave him an insomnia-tips handout drawn from Part I, chapter 2. Then I drew figure 1 and explained how to shut down the process that was keeping his body mobilized for action. I told him that every night as he listed each stressor, he should remind himself, "It won't kill me." He was also to note any plan he could make for each item in the coming days, as indicated in the handout. I urged him to remind his inner family throughout each day that *none* of the worries constantly on his mind were actually *life-threatening,* even though they threatened his quality of life.

As we discussed how to work with his brain, he commented that the ideas fit with his understanding of it. He said he felt much more relaxed by the end of our discussion and was yawning profusely. The next week he came in very excited about being able to sleep for four hours a night. Over the next couple of months, he gradually became calmer and his sleep increased. His blood pressure came into the normal range, and he stopped coming in for counseling.

A few months later, he sustained a concussion during a car accident and became very agitated again. His Adult helped his inner family stop overgeneralizing and identify that the car accident was over and he was no longer in danger. Then we added Benson's relaxation technique (Part I, chapter 5), and he quickly restabilized. Throughout this treatment his life situation continued to be very chaotic and out of his control, yet he was able to reduce his symptoms and function anyway by keeping his Adult in charge. The eighth toxic belief—that happiness depends on what happens to you in life—is not true.

Your Adult Prevents Fight-or-Flight Miscommunication

When you tell your inner family "it won't kill me," you offer Adult, factual information that has a powerful, stabilizing effect. To refine how you communicate, consider how you talk to your Parent or Child within. When your tension has become severe enough to express itself in symptoms like panic, obsessions and compulsions, or generalized anxiety, your Adult has to become stronger. Your Adult must quickly notice and combat Critical-Parent beliefs that blur the distinction between a disturbing situation and a life-threatening one. No, it's not true that you'd be better off dead than humiliated, financially ruined, rejected in love, etc. No, it doesn't mean your Child should feel ugly, stupid or worthless when things don't go well for you. No, it's not unbearable for you to fail, lose or get betrayed. And yes, you *can* stand it if you have another panic attack. Your body reactions reveal when your Child is hearing these things. Your alert Adult must intervene promptly with the facts.

You create more lasting stability only when you teach your Wise Parent to manage your Child all the time, keeping it feeling safe and comfortable with itself. Adult facts can blunt the Critical Parent and gradually reduce its power. Your stronger Wise Parent can carry your Child through life with a supportive, buffering bath of reassurance and encouragement. It says you're strong and capable; you've done tougher things before, like learn to swim, pass that math course or recover from a broken leg. Your Wise Parent says you can learn from your mistakes, which are like everyone else's. It says you can be happy with your gifts and enjoy a good life. Your Adult must peddle along, continually reminding your inner family that most of the time, you aren't likely to die. Your Wise Parent can help your Child feel more comfortable, even when you are going through the worst things.

Strengthen Your Wise Parent for Permanent Symptom Relief

Herbert Benson's *The Relaxation Response* (see Part I, chapter 5) can help your Wise Parent gain control of anxiety. In a later book, Benson describes how this response can be prompted by meditation, exercise and many creative activities along with the technique he describes.[4] He explains that the sympathetic nervous system releases adrenaline when the amygdala signals fight-or-flight. This system is the on-off switch you try to keep off when you remind yourself "I won't die from this." Adrenaline and other neurotransmitters cause the body reactions you experience when your anxiety is very high. These include increases in heart rate, blood pressure, breathing and metabolism.

Benson indicates that when you don't act to flee or fight, stress hormones remain to poison your body. Running or fighting would reduce the excess in your brain. The relaxation response he describes blocks the stress hormones' impact on the body and also soothes neural networks in the brain that persist in worry. Practice invoking deep relaxation to provide healing comfort for your Child, credibility for your Wise Parent and diffusion of any Critical-Parent fear-mongering. Benson notes that beta-blocker drugs also calm the body, but they don't provide the permanent changes possible with relaxation-response practice and healing self-talk. Other meditation techniques can provide similar long-term benefits.

For stable mental fitness, strengthen your Wise Parent all your life. Program yourself with new, realistic and comforting beliefs. Learn how to inspire your creative Child to embrace life. As with exercise programs for the body, mental exercise has to be fun to be maintained. As noted in Part I, chapter 5, I suggest you put up bulletin boards and fill them with cards to yourself, pictures of those who love you and brighten your life and quotes that touch your Child. Update them, removing messages you've absorbed and adding new ones for present challenges. Take odd moments to soak up their messages for you, the memory of when you got them and the thoughts they inspire. Keep looking for new input that builds your Wise Parent indefinitely.

During the five years I struggled without medication or knowledgeable guidance to overcome my panic attacks, I worked intensively on providing my Child with frequent encouraging messages and comforting activities every day. Since I also suffered waves of depression in the first year and insomnia throughout that time, I felt I could barely hang on many days. I found solid friends who were dependably kind and sensible, with strong Wise Parents to teach mine. I learned the crucial importance of having friends who have known you for a long time; they can remind you of who you really are when you get over-whelmed and distorted by severe stress.

It's important to get help if you get stuck, but don't let your self-doubt allow you to accept another person's input if it's not reassuring. I didn't talk much about my symptoms in the '70s, because there was little under-standing of them. I just applied what I was learning in graduate school, and my desperation fueled my diligence. There's lots of help available today, but there are still professionals who don't know how to teach you what you need to know. David Carbonell in his *Panic Attacks Workbook* (2004) calls the misunderstanding between brain parts that sets off a panic attack the "panic trick."[5] His workbook offers support for practic-ing new patterns to reduce the impact of any intense anxiety reaction.

Your Adult must identify helpers who don't further alarm your Child by ignorantly guessing about why you're having anxiety symp-toms. There's a name for this in the trade: "pathologizing the client." Your problems are hard enough; you don't need someone to make you think they're even worse. You need wise friends and professional helpers who aren't afraid for you. I remember the relief I felt when I told some new artist friends about my difficult move from Iowa City to Chicago. I expected them to sympathize with me, but one just beamed at me and said, "You're having quite an adventure!"

Super-Wise Care for Highly Sensitive People

In her work with the highly sensitive person (HSP) trait, Elaine Aron indicates that people with anxiety disorders are most often HSPs, but most HSPs don't have anxiety disorders. Panic disorder affects 1.5–3 percent of the population, obsessive-compulsive dis-order, 2.5 percent, and generalized anxiety disorder, 5 percent, with some overlap among these groups. HSPs make up 15–20 percent of the population. She indicates that HSPs are more susceptible to child-hood trauma and stress than non-HSPs, leading more often to adult symptoms for HSPs.

The sixth toxic belief (that a caring person must get very upset when those around them are hurting) is often hard for HSPs to com-bat. They may have trouble remembering that when they're sleep-deprived, irritable and suffering from chronic tension, they can't help those they care about as much or as wisely as they would wish. It's especially helpful for these people to learn how to allot realistic time frames for their activities, so they can allow time for rest. Improved self-organization with a calendar and prioritized lists can help give them the reassuring sense that they have some control in their lives. Such organization reduces the chance of errors that can lead to Critical-Parent abuse of their Child.

In her books and newsletter, *Comfort Zone*, Aron stresses the HSP's extra need for good self-care in all areas—diet, exercise, sleep, relationships, work environment and mental health practices.[6] HSPs are more likely to develop symptoms without consistent management of their own care. HSPs need to manage their ongoing stressors thoughtfully and not let their conscientious, perfectionistic nature pull them into doing too much. Cognitive-behavioral therapy work to reduce any negative influence of the Critical Parent and build the Wise Parent while strengthening the Adult's ability to self-observe is vital. This provides a foundation for many HSPs to prevent or reduce symptoms independently for a lifetime.

General Anxiety Disorder

When considering the case of General Anxiety Disorder, it's tempting to see affected people as exaggerated HSPs, whose intensified reactivity results from childhood and adult neglect of their emotional needs. I find that these HSPs work diligently in counseling to learn how to manage their lives and minds better. They often need a low dose of antidepressant medication and some help to get sleep for the first few months of therapy. HSPs are often (but not always) more sensitive to medication, too. If they can adequately modify their ongoing stressors, most can get off medication gradually in a few months. Even with really thorough work on their beliefs and self-care, they may need medication longer if their life stressors continue at an unhealthy level.

Obsessive-Compulsive Disorder

Similar basic care reduces the intensity of obsessive-compulsive disorder (OCD) symptoms, but rarely eliminates them altogether. All my OCD clients in the past ten years have scored in the upper half of

Elaine Aron's HSP self-test. The ninth toxic belief (that avoiding problems is the best strategy) is what sustains the OCD symptoms. The victim practices an obsession because it relieves an anxiety that is based on an irrationally inflated fear. For example, a client we'll call Jill fears she may be poisoned or infected with disease. She excessively washes her hands, uses surgical gloves to cook and clean and used to throw out lots of cans and cartons of food she thought might be tainted.

Jill has improved through the process described above and now forces herself to take the risk of exposure to germs in order to prove to herself that she's strong enough to weather them. When she backslides, Jill is avoiding the risk because the quick relief from anxiety feels better than the thought of future freedom from her obsession. The *OCD Workbook*, also a handbook for OCD,[7] gives detailed guidance for most types of OCD. It supports healthy beliefs about coping and teaches step-by-step how to change habits that reinforce OCD behaviors.

"Bob," obsessively checks for leaks or other damage to his house. He has needed medication (fluoxetine/Zoloft) for a few months at a time. Without it he loses his ability to follow instructions and understand the concepts taught in the *OCD Workbook*. He's found relief by telling himself "it won't kill me" when he doesn't check the house. Unlike Jill with her contamination fears, he's able to believe easily that an imperfection in his house won't kill him. Despite this understanding, Bob has times each year when he resumes taking Zoloft to help him overcome his compulsive checking. With his doctor's approval, he varies the dose or even takes it once in a while. This approach allows him to be off medication for much of the year, reducing its side effects. Both Bob and Jill are otherwise fully functioning people who manage demanding jobs and enjoy positive family lives.

Panic Attacks

Panic attacks often begin during a period of intense stress but have their roots in habits practiced since childhood. For the last ten years, I've given every client who has panic attacks Elaine Aron's HSP quiz. All but two of about 200 clients have scored in the upper half of the test. In my work I have found a pattern they share. In order to fit in as children and cope, they learned to stifle their awareness of when they were anxious or overwhelmed. Their Critical Parent listened when others told them they shouldn't be so sensitive. These conscientious HSPs habitually pushed themselves to handle more than they really could.

Eventually the habit of not attending to their feelings led to a buildup of anxiety. This resulted in panic attacks that seemed to appear without cause. To heal their symptoms, they had to reverse the tendency to stifle their feelings and pay extra attention to all their negative reactions through Adult monitoring. After they cleared out the built-up resentment and fear in their neglected Child and revised their Parent messages to be more supportive, their symptoms gradually subsided. They then had to work to maintain their self-awareness to prevent future buildups and resultant panic episodes.

Keeping Yourself Free of Panic Attacks

An example of how to remain symptom-free might be helpful. As an HSP therapist who works continually to monitor and maintain my mental fitness, I was proud that I had gone thirty years without a panic attack. I had gradually overcome them over a five-year period in the early 1970s and took many more years to feel confident that I could manage my anxiety adequately. A few years ago I even commented during a stressful time to my husband, "If I didn't know how to not have a panic attack, I'd be having one now."

A couple of summers ago, I was very busy working as a full-time therapist, doing large projects in my garden and caring often for my grandchildren. To keep up with all this, I planned and made lists continually. In April I began to have strange episodes that gradually increased in frequency over the summer. These consisted of having my shoulder muscles seize up and an electric pulse of pain go up through my neck muscles to my forehead and end suddenly, all in less than three seconds. I thought I had pinched something in my neck and went to a chiropractor.

By August these "shocks" were happening twice a week, and I became suspicious that they were sneaky panic attacks. I watched more closely until one day I had a clear stressor that was followed immediately by one of these episodes. I did remember that I didn't need to be afraid of these attacks. I laughed and realized that my inner family had developed this way of expressing anxiety because I would recognize the other kind of panic attack; sneaky indeed. I went shopping in a big, over-stimulating store (a known trigger in the past) and practiced breathing out while intensively monitoring for my stress level. That terminated the episode.

Then I did what I should have done sooner and scaled back my activity level. I went over my lists and extended the time allotted for activities out a year, allowing for less pressure and more downtime. I've had a few episodes since then while trying to complete this book. The recurrence of newly styled panic attacks has impressed upon me how dedicated our inner family is to protecting us from unhealthy self-management if it can, even if it means employing remarkably wily, creative and disturbing methods.

How to Use Medication to Manage Your Symptoms

Before you turn to medication to help manage your panic or anxiety, be sure to have your doctor evaluate any physical problems that may be contributing. Conditions that mimic the early feelings of a panic attack can trigger one, confusing your brain to believe fight-or-flight is required. Particularly the symptom of light-headedness or dizziness can be due to hypoglycemia, low blood pressure, an inner-ear balance problem or a brain injury. Several clients I've seen could only overcome their panic and fear of it when they discovered one of these problems was triggering them. Once they knew the cause was physical and not some unknown terror they couldn't identify, they could more easily reassure themselves. They stopped feeling they were hopelessly crazy and sought appropriate help for the physical root of their problem.

Daniel Amen offers a description of what would certainly be the ideal use of medication in treating anxiety and depression.[8] Unfortunately, what he describes is very rarely available to most people in most areas. Here's what he recommends: A specialist (psychiatrist), not a general practitioner, should be consulted. Medications should be applied with precision and with thorough understanding of the patient's particular type of brain dysfunction. Amen uses costly brain scans or special questionnaires to determine which areas of the brain to medicate. There should be careful and long-term follow-up when medication is being used. He describes his own brand of cognitive-behavioral therapy and how he integrates it with medication for his excellent treatment.

In reality clients are fortunate if their general practitioner has some competency in using medication for anxiety or depression. When one or two medications don't work, doctors often feel it necessary to refer to a local psychiatrist. I'm sure our area isn't unique in its lack of psychiatrists who are taking new clients and who also take the client's often-changing insurance. Child and adolescent psychiatrists are even harder to find. My clients can expect to wait a month in many cases and then they often get a cursory evaluation, which results in inappropriate and even harmful medication choices. Follow-ups are then fifteen minutes, and clients are often not heard when they make a complaint. Determined clients who can persist and get insurance support may try several psychiatrists before they find one who is thorough and offers thoughtful follow-up.

Once the medication is in place, many doctors don't follow up adequately. Prescribing doctors and psychiatrists very rarely contact the client's therapist before prescribing a medication, even though the therapist could offer valuable information to supplement the prescriber's brief observations from a first interview or even briefer follow-up sessions. Finally, very few psychiatrists offer skilled cognitive therapy like Amen does; most only offer medication.

In his 2011 article "Talk Doesn't Pay, So Psychiatry Turns Instead to Drug Therapy," Gardiner Harris describes how psychiatrists themselves expressed concern about this growing trend.[9] In my experience many don't provide therapy or refer clients for it. Daniel Amen emphasizes that counseling for habit changes that can last a lifetime should always be included.

Brendan L. Smith reviews recent research on medication for treating anxiety or depression in his article, "Inappropriate Prescribing."[10] He describes how pharmaceutical companies tripled their spending to promote use of psychotropic drugs between 1996 and 2005, with five times as much direct advertising to consumers. Psychiatrists, general practitioners and patients themselves find it less expensive to use medication than psychotherapy, resulting in a drop in patients receiving it during that time, from one-third to one-fifth.

However evidence consistently indicates that cognitive-behavioral psychotherapy (CBT) frequently provides as much help with fewer side-effects as medication and results in long-lasting improvement. Smith notes that in 2011 the British government spent 400 million pounds to make CBT the first treatment to be offered to patients with anxiety or mild depression, after reviewing studies demonstrating the ineffectiveness of medication and the long-term positive impact of CBT for these disorders.

I suggest you use a cautious, Adult-in-charge approach in seeking medication. First find a skilled therapist who can help you evaluate your reactions to any medication and support you in demanding thoughtful consideration from your medication provider. When you're fighting anxiety symptoms, you need to be self-protective in discussing medication with prescribing doctors. Much of the medication that relieves anxiety symptoms quickly is very addictive, like the benzodiazepines Xanax (alprazolam), Klonopin (clonazepam) and Ativan (lorazepam). Bliss Jones offers her story and research for how to get off these drugs in her book *Benzo-Wise: A Recovery Companion.* [11]

When carefully administered, these medications can be very helpful. Long-term regular use can result in dependency that can leave clients intensely anxious when increasingly larger doses fail to work anymore. These medications can also encourage clients to put off getting therapy, fostering the avoidance that fuels anxiety symptoms. The ninth toxic belief (that procrastination and avoidance are the best solutions) can lead to a dangerous circle in which anxiety provokes drug use, which encourages avoidance, which leads to chaos in your life and more anxiety.

Antidepressants like Zoloft (fluoxetine) or Lexapro (escitalopram) can be very helpful in the short term (six months to two years) to help your Adult resolve your inner-family-created symptoms. They should not be used in lieu of working on the mental and lifestyle habits that will ultimately resolve your anxiety symptoms. But in the correct dose, they don't promote avoidance; they help you focus and problem-solve. You need to do that as efficiently as possible and then, with your prescribing doctor's guidance, *gradually* go off the medication. James Harper and Jayson Austin offer a strong warning about the dangers of continual use of antidepressants and guidance for how to get off them in their book *How to Get Off Psychoactive Drugs Safely: There Is Hope. There Is a Solution.*[12] Peter R. Breggin and David Cohen describe the negative effects medication can have in their book *Your Drug May Be Your Problem: How and Why to Stop Taking Psychiatric Medications.*[13]

Remember that if life gangs up on you in the future, you may be able to go back on the meds again, tune up your self-care and then get off gradually again once things settle down. Your doctor must advise you about whether this would be safe for you. If, for example you have bipolar disorder, you must stay on your medication or it won't be effective. Antidepressants do have significant side effects that are still being discovered. They can cause alarming and disabling symptoms if you go off them too fast. These problems will be discussed further in Part II, chapter 6. Many people with anxiety disorders can build up the confidence and skills to cope without medication or with minimal medication occasionally. But it's not a contest; be kind to yourself and let your Adult, Wise Parent and treatment providers work together to make the best choice for you.

Help for Those with Persistent Anxiety Symptoms

I've seen a few clients who have come in after several years on various medications for panic and generalized anxiety but have had little or no psychotherapy. Their physical symptoms of anxiety, diarrhea, irritable bowel syndrome (IBS), heart palpitations, and hours-long episodes of panic are so severe, they sometimes end up in a hospital emergency room. Once there they're often tested thoroughly over a period of hours for heart problems, since an intense panic attack can mimic a heart attack. This is all devastating to the victim's confidence in himself and in his medical providers. Fear of having a panic attack or an IBS episode can keep people from traveling or even from leaving their homes.

There's a comprehensive program that has worked beautifully to help these people overcome their habits of panic and become fully functioning. Lucinda Bassett, who cured herself after twenty years of panic attacks, wrote *From Panic to Power*.[14] This slender paperback has inspired hope in many clients, especially those who focus on fears of illness and death. Her program involves an audio-disc program that systematically leads people through the steps needed to heal. She includes a fifteen-minute daily relaxation exercise that my clients have found extremely helpful. Clients can replay these discs to reprogram themselves with reassuring self-talk. These can be found at Bassett's website, which is quite commercial; don't let that put you off. Pharmaceutical companies spend literally billions on advertising annually to convince you and your doctors that drugs are the only thing that will work for you.

Steps to Remember

To put your Adult in charge of your inner family fight-or-flight anxiety reactions and keep it in charge, remember these steps:

1. Take Elaine Aron's HSP self-test and begin following her suggestions along with those in Part I, chapter 5 of this book to improve your self-care.

2. Identify your ongoing stressors and work to eliminate or reduce them as described in Part I, chapter 5.

3. Practice your Adult monitoring to manage your inner family self-talk and reduce your fight-or-flight tendencies as described in Part I, chapter 4.

4. Decide with the help of your primary care provider whether you should consider medication and see a therapist. This should be step one if your symptoms interfere with your functioning.

5. Develop self-talk and lifestyle habits that keep your Child confident and comfortable.

Here are some messages that can help you reprogram yourself:

- I deserve to enjoy my sensitivity, not suffer from it.

- I am the best judge of what works for me.

- I'm conscientious; I don't have to be perfect too.

- I'm strong and capable; I can stand the stress of being human.

- Fight-or-flight is almost never necessary.

- I can find the courage to face—rather than avoid—my fears.

- I can stand it that I have to work harder than others to manage my reactivity.

- There is no such thing as courage in the absence of fear.

- I can learn to take excellent care of myself.

- Looking back in five years, what will seem important?

- I can give myself enough time to enjoy my activities.

Notes

1. Douglas Fox, "The Private Life of the Brain," *New Scientist*, November 2008).
2. Bessell A. van der Kolk, "New Frontiers in Trauma Treatment," workshop by the Institute for the Advancement of Human Behavior, 2007.
3. Claire Weekes, *Hope and Help for Your Nerves* (1969: repr., New York: Signet, 1990).

4. Herbert Benson, *Beyond the Relaxation Response* (New York: Berkeley Books, 1985).

5. David Carbonell, *Panic Attacks Workbook* (Berkeley: Ulysses Press, 2004).

6. Elaine Aron, http://www.hsperson.com, accessed June 8, 2012.

7. Bruce M. Hyman and Cherry Pedrick, *The OCD Workbook (Oakland: New Harbinger, 2005).*

8. Daniel G. Amen and Lisa C. Routh, *Healing Anxiety and Depression (New York: Penguin Books, 2003).*

9. Gardiner Harris, *"Talk Therapy Doesn't Pay, So Psychiatry Turns Instead to Drugs," (The New York Times 5, 2011). See also http://nytimes.com/2011/03/06/ health policy/06doctors.html.* Accessed 6/25/2012.

10. Brendan L. Smith, *"Inappropriate Prescribing," Monitor on Psychology (June 2011).*

11. Bliss Jones, *Benzo-Wise: A Recovery Companion* (2009, rev. ed., Nichols: Campanile Publishing, 2010).

12. James Harper and Jayson Austin, *How to Get Off Psychoactive Drugs Safely: There Is Hope. There Is a Solution (* 2005, rev. ed., Charleston: CreateSpace, 2011).

13. Peter R. Breggin and David Cohen, *Your Drug May Be Your Problem: How and Why to Stop Taking Psychiatric Medications* (2000, rev. ed., Philadelphia: DaCapo Press, 2007).

14. Lucinda Bassett, *From Panic to Power* (New York: HarperCollins, 1997).

II : 4

The Grief Process and the Resolution of Anger

Grief and anger can disrupt your efforts to keep your Adult mind in charge. How can you keep from being sucked into painful Child feelings when you have losses? Your Adult mind has to keep your Parent and Child parts from jumping to the conclusion that a loss or disappointment is life-threatening. Anger and fear diminish when you prevent the common inner-family misunderstanding that provokes your body into fight-or-flight reactions. A calm Adult mind can handle situations more effectively and prevent you from other losses caused by your Child's acting out. Grief and anger are normal and necessary feelings in response to life. Your increasingly capable Adult and Wise Parent can recognize when your Child reacts and offer comfort.

A Process for Healing

When you feel cheated in life, hurt by the loss of a loved one or discouraged with your own accomplishments, how can you take a fresh look at your future? Humans have a natural process for healing after a loss. It's probably a necessary adaptation in our wiring that ensures our survival. It's called the grief process and is usually discussed when a loved one dies. The primary stages of the grief process are denial, bargaining, anger, sadness and acceptance.[1]

When you feel terribly hurt, disappointed or hopeless, your Adult can focus on working through this process and open a door to the future. You can apply it to any dream you've had to give up. Perhaps you need to grieve the childhood you wish you'd had, the schooling, the parents, the siblings or the acting out you did. Then you can reduce your anger and sadness about it to levels that don't prevent your growth. You must navigate all the way through the grief process and not get stuck in a state of dysfunction.

Denial

Denial distorts how you look at your life, creating dishonest relationships and empty goals. To recognize beliefs that sustain denial, monitor your feelings for a few days. The most prevalent belief for this stage is that it's better to avoid pain than face it (the ninth toxic belief). This stems from your inner family's belief that your Child couldn't stand to endure the pain of your loss. But it isn't really easier to put off suppressed grief. It simmers within your Child, sapping its joy and energy. Pretending that you've had no pain also prevents you from empathizing with others who admit their hurt. You've surely been annoyed by the phony bravado of people who are "too strong" to admit to any problems in their lives.

Bargaining

As a transition from the denial to the angry stage of the grief process, bargaining happens when you glimpse your loss but use irrational schemes to pretend you don't really have it. A client described how she tried to believe that her aunt, visiting from across the country, was enough like her mother to fill the terrible void she felt when her mother died. For more confusing losses than the death of a loved one, the bargaining can go on a long time. You might say to yourself: Maybe my childhood was pretty normal if I can believe one of my parents was healthy. Maybe I don't have to face that Dad was terribly negligent and self-absorbed and I don't have to feel my anger toward him, too. Maybe my mother didn't know I was being abused and would have defended me if she knew. Maybe my sister doesn't really have invasive cancer. If I pray hard, maybe she'll get well.

Not to deny that miracles can happen, but we wouldn't say they're in the realm of what we'd rationally expect if we weren't *bargaining*.

Anger

After bargaining comes the anger stage in the grief process. The guy with the chronic chip on his shoulder is stuck in the anger stage of grief and can stay stuck the rest of his life. That's why I think anger is so prevalent; it's sustainable. You can vent it in sarcasm, put-downs, complaints and all kinds of acting out. Blaming others or even yourself for what happened at least gives you an answer. That unreasonably inflated answer distracts you from really feeling your loss. Your Child is distracted from its loss by angry ruminations or rants and doesn't want to stop. It believes it "can't stand" to feel *sad*. You can live your life stuck in your anger, and many people do. Where does all this anger begin?

Since it's likely no one taught you to have *entirely* realistic expectations while you were growing up, you may still struggle with the issues you had upon entering adulthood. Of course as you get older, there are more disappointments and unfair experiences. These all need to be grieved all the way through. You must embrace reality, though it feels like an icy shower at first. A student of Albert Ellis once quoted him as saying, "It's better to walk around being pleasantly surprised than bitterly disappointed." Bitter disappointment is the root of anger. I wondered why therapists were called "shrinks" for some years. Then I realized our job is to "shrink" people's unrealistic expectations.

Combat the toxic beliefs that set you up to be angry. Almost all of the twelve toxic beliefs can lead to intense anger unless your Adult takes charge. We're angry when someone rejects us and we believe we must have their approval (the first belief). We're angry when someone else wins the contest we worked so hard for (the second and seventh beliefs). We're angry when we don't get the job, the support, the raise, the life circumstances we feel we must have to be happy (the eighth belief). We're angry when we give a lot of care to others and they don't respond as we expected (the eighth and tenth beliefs). We're angry when we lose someone we love if we believe we can't get along without them (the sixth and tenth beliefs). We're also hurt when these losses occur but often resist knowing about our hurt, because that takes us into sadness, which makes us feel weak and vulnerable.

How to Manage Your Anger

The first thing you must do to manage anger is shut down your body's intense fight-or-flight reactions. You can do this more easily if you catch them early in their process. To do this your Adult must monitor regularly for reactions in your particular body that indicate your Child is getting angry. David Kucklick, working with angry boys at the Jesse Dyslin Boys Ranch in the 1980s, used a drawing of a person and had them practice circling where they noticed a reaction. They'd circle their fist or jaw, eyebrows or stomach. What would you circle?

One day while counseling a couple who were being verbally abusive to each other despite my efforts, I noticed a prickling sensation on the back of my neck. My adult recognized that this was a sign I was getting angry before I had the awareness of anger. This helped me laugh at how I was now reduced to the level of my male dachshund, Henry, and I was able to remain professional in my work with them. Henry was quite reactive and easily had the fur on his neck puff up when he felt threatened.

The first thing to do when your Adult notes a fight-or-flight reaction that comes from anger is to calm your body by reassuring your Child quickly that you're actually safe, using a thematic prompt like "no need for fight-or-flight." This quick intervention creates the sense of a boundary around you, shielding your Child from the negative vibes coming at you. You may not always catch yourself early in this process. You may already be yelling or heading out the door with a slam. Your Adult may have only the shakiest hold on your Child.

It's never too late to stop fight-or-flight by reminding yourself this level of reaction is unnecessary. But as noted in Part I, chapter 3, once your Vagus nerve has gotten your body upset, you only have 20 percent of the fibers in it taking your calming messages back to your body. Eighty percent are still going from your upset body to your brain, flooding it with neurochemicals to keep you fighting or running away. So take a break until your Adult can get back in charge. If this is a regular pattern between you and someone else, like your spouse or a friend, discuss this with them and agree to separate to cool down if either of you notices fight-or-flight has begun trashing the communication.

Anger You're Wired to Have

Some beliefs seem to be hardwired into our minds. For example, let's tackle the seventh toxic belief that it's unbearable if you don't get rewarded when you work hard and persistently for something. First note that "it's unbearable" is one of those phrases that trigger your Child feelings and bodily reactions into fight-or-flight. Rarely would this be necessary, even if you were unfairly fired and had to be homeless. Fight-or-flight only helps with immediate, life-threatening dangers; it won't help you get a new job or a new home. So it's bearable, but you may still feel really angry.

One very bright, hard-working and intelligent woman came in after having been fired from her job. At forty-three, Fiona had experienced continued success in her education and career. She was devastated by this treatment and took months to heal from the real trauma of it, both the anger and the hurt. Her whole sense of herself, held in her wounded Child, was damaged. We worked hard to teach her Wise Parent how to cope with the seventh toxic belief. The first two beliefs—that she should expect approval and could always compete well with others—weren't too hard for her to revise.

Fiona just couldn't accept that hard, capable and diligent work for a company wouldn't automatically be rewarded. She felt like the foundation stone of her belief system had been torn out. We discussed how in her daily newspaper she read about people all over the world experiencing similar disappointment and devastation that was often worse than hers. We discussed that perhaps her superiors couldn't communicate their expectations to her adequately, which wasted her efforts through no fault of her own. We discussed that the all-male firm may have discriminated against her.

Her Child was quieter, but not much comforted yet. She decided to investigate to find an answer for why she might have been fired as she was, with little warning or explanation. Her Adult recognized it needed more information to settle her Child down. She discovered there were two women before her who had received similar treatment and concluded she had indeed been discriminated against. Having this knowledge relieved her of some of her tension, but she needed to do more due to her anger over the injustice done to her and feelings of helplessness that resulted. She joined with the other two women for support and to explore suing the company.

You can imagine that other people with different styles of anger might react differently in this situation. They might drink themselves into becoming an alcoholic. They might get an illness or have an illness worsen. They might go back to the company and yell a lot or shoot someone. They might write a book exposing the company's behavior. Anger takes many forms, but it all amounts to the same thing: your angry and hurt Child believes it just "can't stand" that it wasn't treated fairly.

Where does the seventh toxic belief come from? We've discussed how people grow up being taught these beliefs by their parents or society in general. But when we look at how intense and long-lasting anger can be, we see that the problem may go deeper. Fiona's situation reflects some of B. F. Skinner's findings about pigeons. He describes how a pigeon taught to peck a disc on the side of the cage reacted when no kernels of corn were given after a long period of being regularly rewarded. The pigeon flapped its wings, squawked and turned its back on the reward chute and disc.[2] Fiona expressed the human version of these reactions, and you can probably think of times like this for you.

A key element in the degree of frustration felt in this situation is that Fiona had nearly always been rewarded for her hard work. Skinner found that varying the reward frequency led to more tolerance of frustration, a situation I'll discuss in later in the chapter on parenting. For now focus on the fact that when you work long and hard for something, your Adult should be prepared for your Child's disappointment if you don't get it. Your natural reaction is to be very disappointed to the point you might give up.

Your Adult must redirect your efforts and not allow you to quit trying, which would lead to simmering anger and depression. Your Wise Parent must encourage your Child not to blame itself and feel like there's something wrong with you. Your Indulgent Parent can't be allowed to give your Child this example as an excuse for not trying your best in the future. This example of how your Adult can combat and revise the seventh belief can be used for any toxic belief that causes you to be angry. Your goal is not to eliminate all your hurt and anger, but to reduce them down to less toxic levels.

Refer to the eight steps of cognitive-behavioral therapy available for reference in appendix A for the complete description of the process. Here are the steps for focusing on your anger:

1. Monitor to find where anger might be occurring in your body.

2. Identify how intensely you're feeling the anger.

3. Choose what you must do to reduce immediate fight-or-flight tendencies and do it. Refer to appendix C to blunt your reaction quickly.

4. Once calm, explore to identify which belief or beliefs are triggering the reaction.

5. Work to revise these beliefs or use a thematic prompt to access your already revised self-talk to calm and reassure yourself.

6. Reengage with the person or situation to address problems that might cause similar hurt in the future.

You can stay in anger indefinitely, denying your hurt, but you'll live with less energy for love, less insight for compassion and less freedom for creativity. You need a strong Wise Parent to reassure your Child it can withstand feeling the reality of your hurt after your shrewd Adult sees the denial. Revising your toxic beliefs will ultimately bring relief and peace. But at first you often feel betrayed, cheated and angry. For example, revising the eighth belief is especially hard, as it involves having to accept that you must supply your own happiness and that others really can't be expected to do that. It feels cold and lonely before you know how to do it. These feelings in your Child can prevent your Adult from seeing how to change your beliefs to make losses bearable. A therapist can offer Adult insight along with Wise-Parent support as you work to help your Child feel secure and comfortable with these new realizations. It must learn to depend on your own Wise Parent instead.

Social Influences and Anger

I've mentioned how humans are probably wired to be angry in some types of situations. We're also influenced by our life situation as we grow up, which can make it harder to combat our natural tendencies. Our society raises children to enter adulthood with unnecessary losses to grieve. We're set up to have many expectations of others and life that are unrealistic. Our Child is filled with dreams about achievement and fairy-tale relationships, and this leaves some people feeling entitled to impossible fulfillment. Surreal images of beauty are held up in airbrushed pictures as ideals everyone should look like. Consider the whole Barbie-doll phenomenon for our little girls. How about the monsters and superheroes for our little boys?

As teens many girls focus too much on finding the romantic ideal with a boyfriend and neglect their school work. Look at what kind of clothes are popular for them. Too many teenage boys immerse themselves in video games, where they can have virtual superpower capabilities and neglect development of their social skills and school work. These activities provide more regular kernels of corn than real life. When these kids must join others in real relationships and jobs, they're often upset or angry to discover that they aren't rewarded as faithfully for their efforts. This problem is compounded if they've failed to develop the skills they need to navigate real life. How would Skinner's pigeon do in the barnyard? Laura Kastner and Jennifer Wyatt offer tips for how parents can guide their children through these new threats to their development.[3]

No doubt there have always been social influences that make Adult management of our natural reactions to disappointment more difficult. As scientists have studied these influences more systematically during the last century, more of them have been examined. Skinner describes at length his research and conclusions about how the use of punishment creates emotion, including anger. He describes many forms of punishment, including taking a reward away. His work in this area is very concise and informative.[4]

People have worked for years to identify ways Skinner's findings could be used to teach children more effectively in our schools.[5] Many of his findings have been incorporated with good results. My seven- year-old grandson has his card turned over if he doesn't follow classroom rules. He doesn't have his knuckles rapped or get placed with his nose in a circle on the blackboard in front of everyone to invoke the effects of social punishment.

To handle anger your Adult must be aware that your Child has tendencies to get angry that are not your Child's fault. Skinner describes how demoralizing guilt and disabling trauma can gradually form due to punishment your Child experiences as you grow up.[6] Remember that your Child can only learn and thrive with kernels of corn and Wise-Parent guidance. As you revise your toxic beliefs situation by situation, you'll create the conditions for a Child that is not often losing its energy to anger.

Sadness

Sadness is the fourth stage of grief, the stage you're taught to fear. Movies about angry heroes are box office hits; not many are made (or watched) with heroes who are simply sad. As a culture we have a deeply rooted belief that we "can't stand" to be sad. We're terrified that we'll get lost somehow if we let ourselves embrace our sadness and cry. Look at the expressions we use when we do that: "I lost it," "I went crazy" or "I was completely out of it." If a client goes to a doctor saying she's been crying a lot and cries in his office, she will almost certainly leave with a prescription or two. If a man does that, he may get even stronger drugs.

Therapists are trained to watch for suicidal tendencies when someone is very sad and stay in closer touch with them. That's appropriate, because sadness embraced and supported is sadness eased. I've observed that it's when you hang onto anger that you can become harmful to yourself or others. People don't tend to cry and suffer in pure sadness for long. It's an exhausting, miserable, yet cleansing state that gives some relief from tension. The exception to this is when people are traumatized by some aspect of their loss, like the circumstances of someone's death, abusive treatment during a divorce or severe problems in childhood. In these cases desensitization to the trauma as described in the next chapter can allow people to resolve their sadness.

An example of how anger intertwined with trauma and sadness can get you stuck can be found in the case of a couple I saw whose son had been killed three years before. The husband had come to accept what had happened, but his wife was still in constant torment. She blamed herself for having been so angry at her son for his drug use and violent lifestyle that when he lingered dying, she didn't pray for him well enough. During therapy she uncovered this detail and realized she was assuming her prayers could have been more powerful than God's own decisions. This was not what her faith taught her. After this she immediately began reassessing her feelings of guilt and anger on the way to processing her sadness. She'll feel sad about losing her son indefinitely, but not with the painful intensity she'd suffered for years.

Acceptance or Adjustment

With revised beliefs and enough support, you can move through sadness and into what has most often been called acceptance. A woman I saw who was coming to terms with being unable to have children said she could *adjust* to, but not accept, her fate. Adjustment is probably a more possible goal. Acceptance seems to require that you agree that the loss was OK. You must somehow adjust to the fact that very painful losses are unavoidable as you go through life. Your Wise Parent must grow strong enough to comfort your Child through them. Some people, like the mother who founded Mothers Against Drunk Drivers (MADD) after her child was killed by a drunk driver, need to transform their grief in order to adjust. Fiona had to try to change the company that discriminated against her. Transforming grief gives meaning to a loss that felt unbearably wasteful; now it counts for some future benefit, even though you still feel your pain.

The sadness that remains after a completed grief process is not disabling, but it does linger and color your life in many ways, some enriching. You can savor memories of your loved ones, perhaps learning to enjoy something they used to enjoy—a recipe, a craft, a volunteer activity. You can focus on what they gave you and resolve to develop that more in their memory. Many who've successfully grieved the childhood they didn't get become therapists and social workers committed to helping others avoid what they suffered. If you've lost a job, maybe you can think of ways to use or retool your skills for another job that gives you even more meaning. Resolution of grief requires a comforted Child who can bring its creativity to the process.

Resources and Support

Resources for discovering beliefs that could keep you stuck in denial and anger are plentiful. Therese Rando describes different kinds of grief, emphasizes that resolving grief is hard work and defines how to do it.[7] John James and Russell Friedman offer a way to structure working through your grief using simple but powerful self-study tools.[8] Matthew McKay and Peter Rogers offer a comprehensive program for recognizing, managing and overcoming damaging anger in their *Anger Control Workbook*.[9] Ronald and Patricia Potter-Efron describe various ways people express anger to help you detect your own.[10] Carl Semmelroth and Donald Smith address anger as a habit and describe how you can redirect yourself.[11] Les Carter and Frank Minirth discuss how you can get stuck in the "trap" of anger.[12] Finally, Martha Whitmore Hickman offers wonderful healing and inspiring quotes to comfort you and build your Wise Parent as you work through the grief process.[13]

When you have a lot of hurt to process, you owe it to yourself to seek a therapist and other human support to help you sustain your courage for the work. It's easy to look back and see that you were foolishly embracing a toxic belief, but while you're still under its influence and unaware, you may suffer terrible anxiety and despair. Even when a therapist works hard to help you see the errors in your thinking, it can be very tricky and difficult. You'll know it's time to get extra help if you become anxious and upset as you read one of these resource books. Stop reading until you have wise support; then a book may be a great source of homework between sessions.

Your therapist or local hospital referral system may be able to recommend groups for support, like Compassionate Friends for parents who've lost a child, divorce support, alcohol- and drug-related support groups or veterans groups. Sharing with others who've suffered similar losses is often a necessary part of healing. It supports Wise-Parent growth while comforting your Child and provides new information to your Adult. Support can help reduce Critical-Parent pressure to feel guilt or toxic anger toward others involved in your loss. Blaming others is like taking a poisonous pill and hoping someone else will die, a wise friend once said to me. Sharing with others can keep you from getting stuck in your grief process.

Once you process your grief all the way through, you can accept (or adjust to) your losses as part of the shared human experience. This allows your Child to give up the infuriating notion that you've been singled out for unfairness. Read the local newspaper, and you'll see how random unfairness is. It's good to say, "I've been lucky for a while, and now it's my turn for some unfairness," rather than "Why me?" This helps you stay current, so your past can't drag down your future. It also helps you remember to keep your expectations adjusted to reality. Then you'll be able to walk around being pleasantly surprised instead of bitterly disappointed.

Here are some phrases to help you navigate your grief process:

- Why do I think I should be spared unfairness?

- What was I expecting in this situation?

- What does my experience teach me I should expect in this situation?

- Am I setting myself up to be angry or hurt?

- If I take this action, I need to be prepared for the possible negative outcome.

- How can I make this pain count for something good?

- I would rather be pleasantly surprised than bitterly disappointed every day.

- Resentment is like taking a poisonous pill and hoping someone else will die.

- Human existence is full of pain, but we are designed to handle it.

- I cherish the many memories I have from knowing her.

- His influence has inspired my life.

- My grief teaches me compassion for others and their losses.

Notes

1. Elizabeth Kübler-Ross and David Kessler, *On Grief and Grieving* (New York: Simon & Schuster, 2005).
2. B. F. Skinner, *The Science of Human Behavior* (1953; repr., New York: The Free Press, 1965).
3. Laura S. Kastner and Jennifer Wyatt, *Getting to Calm: Cool-Headed Strategies for Parenting Tweens and Teens* (Seattle: ParentMap, 2009).
4. Skinner, *The Science of Human Behavior,* 182–193.
5. B. F. Skinner, *The Technology of Teaching* (New York: Appleton-Century-Crofts, 1968).
6. Skinner, *The Science of Human Behavior,* 182–193.
7. Therese A. Rando, *How to Go on Living When Someone You Love Dies* (New York: Bantam, 1991).
8. John W. James and Russell Friedman, *The Grief Recovery Handbook* (New York: HarperCollins, 2009).
9. Matthew McKay and Peter Rogers, *The Anger Control Workbook* (Oakland: New Harbinger, 2000).
10. Ronald T. and Patricia S. Potter-Efron, *Letting Go of Anger: The Eleven Most Common Anger Styles* (Oakland: New Harbinger, 2006).
11. Carl Semmelroth and Donald E. P. Smith, *The Anger Habit in Relationships: A Communication Workbook for Relationship, Marriages and Partnerships* (New York: Writers' Showcase, 2000).
12. Les Carter and Frank Minirth, *The Anger Trap* (San Francisco: John Wiley, 2003).
13. Martha Whitmore Hickman, *Healing after Loss* (New York: HarperCollins, 1994).

II : 5

Dissociation, Self-Preservation and Post-Traumatic Stress Disorder

The preceding chapter described how you must complete the grief process when you suffer losses in order to keep your Adult mind in charge. When you experience trauma along with losses, you can get stuck in the turmoil of anger, sadness and fear. This turmoil overwhelms Adult functioning when you need it most. In this chapter we'll explore the dissociation underlying traumatic stress reactions and its adaptive function. I'll describe how trauma can lead to a long-term disabling mental condition called post-traumatic stress disorder (PTSD).

I'll analyze the components of PTSD and discuss how new discoveries about the brain have led to techniques for simple and effective restructuring of trauma-induced confusion. I'll lay out the steps I've found necessary for safe and thorough resolution of trauma and will address some individual differences known to affect people's reaction to trauma. This chapter is directed to readers who have experienced a trauma that needs healing. If you haven't had one, you'll be more able to understand those who have and better prepared for a future trauma of your own after reading this section.

In this chapter I've taken a different approach by describing what you should expect in therapy for trauma in more detail. I've done this for two reasons. First, if you're going to claim your own mental fitness, you need to know that your trauma can be safely healed. Second, you may have difficulty finding a therapist who is trained adequately to help you. You may enter into therapy with symptoms of anxiety, depression, insomnia and mood swings that are very extreme, but that doesn't necessarily mean that you have an anxiety disorder, bipolar disorder or classical depression. One or more of these disorders are commonly diagnosed (and medicated) when PTSD hasn't been recognized.

If your therapist doesn't know treatment must be different for you, you won't get well. You may even get worse as your therapist recommends increasing doses of sedating medications to try to shut down those terrible nightmares and intense feelings. Your therapist may get frustrated with you because you don't respond to her guidance, which will leave you feeling worse about yourself. Years of this kind of treatment can result in clients who no longer believe they could ever lead normal lives. You need to know how to recognize competent treatment at every stage of trauma work; then you can confidently leave a therapist who is incapable of helping you and search for one who can. Even a competent therapist may not give you all the guidance you need. Learn what you can, then try a new therapist if you remain distressed until you reach the peace you deserve.

Dissociation and Post-Traumatic Stress Disorder

I noted that when people have a loss that is compounded by a trauma, they can get stuck in a knot of anger, sadness and fear. Just how does this happen? When you have to handle a traumatic event, your inner family creates a separate compartment for it to insulate your Adult mind from the trauma. This separation—called dissociation—frees your Adult to cope with life events at the time. As I've noted, your inner family focuses first upon ensuring your survival. Dissociation prevents a fight-or-flight response to a traumatic event when your inner family believes it would be too dangerous. You may even be able to cope as though nothing has happened.

Eventually this dissociation breaks down, and you begin to get flashes of the trauma in nightmares or as moods that don't make sense. These reactions are symptoms of post-traumatic stress disorder. Let's examine each aspect of this process to understand how it happens and therefore how it can be cured. Your trauma may have been terrifying, but your recovery from it need not be filled with terror. You adapted and you survived. Now it's time to reach for better quality in your life. You can do that with your Adult leading your inner family out of its confusion.

The term dissociation may carry an aura of sinister mystery. But it's easily understood as a continuum of separation in your mind that allows you to function in a wide range of situations. At one end of this continuum, your Child takes over and has some fun. Sometimes you decide you can eat extra dessert, buy some indulgence or take some time off, but then later you ask, "What was I thinking?" Or you may get focused on a work project and ignore your Child completely while you burn through the hours to get it done. You're a little out of balance but can easily readjust. At this end of the continuum, your Adult can just refocus to access the whole memory of your experience.

Your inner family increasingly blocks Adult awareness of memories as they appear more threatening. When a loved one dies, people often say, "I did okay until the funeral was over, and then I fell apart." You may remember only parts of an angry exchange with your spouse and block any disturbing words you might have said but are ashamed of. You may have fragmented memories of a car accident, even if your head wasn't injured. At the less traumatic end of the dissociation continuum, you can connect to the whole memory in minutes or days.

Dissociation and Self-Preservation

As you move into more traumatic events at the other end of the dissociation continuum, your inner family blocks your Adult awareness of the event to ensure what it interprets to be your survival. For example, the morning after a child is sexually assaulted by her father, she's still expected to dress herself and function at school. If there's a battle in which soldiers see their friends killed, they still have to take appropriate action immediately. People vary in their sensitivity to trauma and how quickly their inner family moves to block a memory.

Long-term dissociation of traumatic memories occurs because of beliefs held in your Child and Parent parts. Once these parts believe a memory threatens your survival, there will be no easy release of that memory; the memory of the traumatic event is stuck in time. When you connect to it, you feel like you did at the time it happened. The abused little girl couldn't call the police, drive away or take care of herself on her own. When she revisits the traumatic memory years later, her Child feels that same helplessness, which overwhelms her sense of herself as a capable Adult. Her Parent parts automatically protect her as they always have, believing she "couldn't stand" to know, and that she'd become dangerous to herself if she knew. They believe that she'd lose the relationships that she needed for survival as a little girl. Thus entrenched in a system that worked in the past, your inner family may resist allowing you access to a dissociated memory.

Symptoms of Post-Traumatic Stress Disorder

As long as traumatic memories are blocked, you're at risk of suffering the symptoms of post-traumatic stress disorder. Dissociation can work very well, allowing you to keep going through your daily life. You might have no recognizable symptoms for years. Two women I worked with who had multiple personalities due to long-term childhood sexual abuse functioned well and raised very capable children. When they were in their forties, intense symptoms made them aware of their dissociation and they struggled to heal their childhood trauma. In cases where the trauma is less severe or shorter-term, it's usually more accessible and produces symptoms sooner.

Symptoms are often triggered by situations that remind the person's inner family of her trauma. Terrible nightmares, intense anxiety or sadness may seem to come from nowhere. A pervasive, unshakable depression and feelings of dread may last for years. Medication won't really overcome these feelings, even in doses that make the person zombielike. Fight-or-flight reactions can be frequent and in some cases violent. When you feel like this or know someone going through this, you may be very frightened. Despair and even suicide are possible for those who can't get help to break through their confusion.

Treating Post-Traumatic Stress Disorder

How can you reconnect your Adult to the traumatized, dissociated parts of the Child and Parent? This reconnection or integration is necessary to heal the trauma and complete your grief process. Your Child and Parent parts need Adult guidance to reinterpret the original traumas and recognize that present stressors don't pose a similar threat. In their traumatized state, they will overwhelm your Adult and keep you stuck. Remember that the Vagus nerve has 80 percent of its fibers communicating from the body to the brain. When the body is in frequent fight-or-flight mode, the Adult brain can't calm it down with its meager 20 percent, even when it's clear about what needs to be done. How can you shut this maddening process down?

Scientific breakthroughs in the past fifteen years have revolutionized the treatment of people trying to recover from trauma. Functional MRIs and intensive experimentation have revealed ways to help the brain heal itself. Having worked with trauma and abuse victims for fifteen years prior to these discoveries, I've been very excited to apply the new techniques. The old strategies most often left people significantly impaired, but with more insight into their situation. I often told myself that there has to be a way to break through this; there is.

Safety First: Four Steps to Prepare for Desensitization of Trauma

Despite having PTSD, you may be holding yourself together fairly well much of the time as you go to your therapist's office. Your inner family is working hard to protect your functioning. It's alert for any threat to the precarious balance that exists in your confused mind. It doesn't have confidence that the therapist won't make you worse by unleashing your blocked memories. Therefore, it's the therapist's duty to reassure your inner family. In doing so she creates a safe space for your Adult to communicate with your traumatized parts.

1. First, you need to feel safe and comfortable in the therapist's office. You may need to talk with a few therapists before you find one who inspires your trust and confidence. Ask about

their training and experience for treating PTSD and what professional consultation they have available if you run into a block in resolving your trauma. Ask them what plan they have for treating you and whether there are any websites or books you could study to support your understanding and growth through the process. You must have a clear understanding about what, if any, limits there are to confidentiality. For example, what does the therapist have to report to authorities regarding past child abuse? When would they feel they had to contact your doctor or a family member, and how would they work with you on that? You should know how long you can continue in treatment, what it will cost and how you can reach the therapist between sessions if needed. Much of this may be covered in the therapist's disclosure statement but needs to be specifically clarified to treat PTSD, especially if you're an anxious, sleep-deprived client. Availability of medication and the support of a primary care doctor and/or psychiatrist should also be ensured.

2. Second, your therapist should assess your feelings of safety and support at home and work. If you're in a very abusive relationship at home or in a hostile work environment, you should receive guidance on how to protect your security and sometimes the security of children and pets. This ensures your safety and also lets your Child know you'll get help in the ways that count most. Without this trust, the inner family won't loosen its lock on memories that might threaten your functioning. During the first session or two, it's also important to determine how well you're supported for the work. Can you find comfort among family or friends? It's good just to be with people who love you without having to talk about your trauma.

3. If you can't get into therapy yet, just work on building your Wise Parent and making connections with friendly people. For resolving lesser traumas, this may be all you need to create the security that will allow you to access and rework your trauma

using the monitoring and analysis described previously. Don't try to uncover more serious traumas without therapeutic support; your Child may withdraw even further from help, and you may get disabling symptoms like severe insomnia, panic attacks, irritable bowel syndrome or fibromyalgia.

4. The third step is to determine what self-care skills you have to nurture yourself while working through your trauma. Your therapist should describe what work needs to be done, if any, prior to addressing your trauma directly. You may need time and guidance to stabilize things at home or work before you can be calm enough. You may need new coping skills, like knowing how to combat some problem beliefs or how to confront someone assertively, for example. Your use of alcohol, drugs or prescription medication must be evaluated and adjusted. Appropriate prescription medication can help a lot; alcohol, marijuana or other drug usage can prevent your brain from processing your trauma all the way through. You don't need to be left with all the feelings and more detailed knowledge, but no resolution of your trauma.

5. The fourth step is for your therapist to get an overview of your experience with trauma. If your traumatic experiences are well contained, allowing you to list them in a history without being triggered, it can be very helpful for your therapist's planning. This also gives her insight that will help her offer valuable support as you review your memories. If you're triggered when relating your history, the therapist can often proceed with just a brief outline of your traumas and about when they occurred. I've often found it unnecessary to require a client to go through a detailed history before we desensitize and then again as we go through the reprocessing. It's useful to review some positive memories of times when you have overcome something difficult or received help when you needed it. Your therapist can remind you of these when your Child feels helpless as you recall a traumatic experience and help you recognize your important strengths by the end of it.

If you come into therapy very soon after a trauma and are sleepless, constantly replaying the experience and extremely upset, your therapist will have to develop rapport and make her assessments more quickly. If you've had prior traumas that aren't resolved, your therapist should focus on helping you calm down with simple breathing techniques and stabilizing self-talk. If this is an isolated trauma or if prior traumas have been worked through, I find proceeding quickly with desensitization can be very helpful to the client.

Processing Your Trauma

You're finally ready to have your trauma or traumas addressed. There are two techniques I use to help provide relief from the symptoms of dissociated pain. I learned to perform traumatic incident reduction (TIR),[1] which involves having clients review their trauma over and over in one session, describing it aloud with increasing detail until they feel it's resolved. It was very exciting to see people emerge from this process with their symptoms greatly alleviated. There were two problems, however. Sometimes clients had too little recall of the experience and became blocked very easily by their protective inner family. The second problem with TIR is that it can be traumatizing for a client to describe a humiliating experience in detail several times to resolve it. But when a client has good rapport with the therapist and wants to share every detail, it can be very effective to resolve the trauma.

EMDR and BioLateral

The next technique I learned is Francine Shapiro's eye movement desensitization and resolution. Her 1995 book with that title offers information on how it was developed and why it works.[2] The very active EMDR website offers updated information about the international organization, EMDRIA, and lots of new discoveries around the world. More is being learned about this and other techniques for treating trauma every day through experimentation and study of the brain. I've trained in using this and related techniques for over ten years and have found an approach that doesn't retraumatize clients, but most often helps them reduce their symptoms. This resolution allows them to complete the grief process around their trauma.

Shapiro first explored eye movements because of the observation that during sleep, rapid eye movements accompany dreaming. She questioned whether these movements actually functioned in some way to help people process experiences in their dreams. Much research has revealed that this is true and gone on to try to identify how this happens in the brain. Daniel Amen and Lisa Routh describe how three brain areas made overactive by trauma can be quieted with EMDR in their book *Healing Anxiety and Depression*[3]

It was discovered that bilateral stimulation of specific brain areas through hearing, touch or your kinesthetic sense also functions to push through resolution of trauma. Deliberate bilateral stimulation while you mentally replay a trauma can help you resolve traumas that are too disturbing for your dreams to process. The early research focused on using eye movements. For this, you sit opposite the therapist while your therapist moves a wand back and forth to help your eyes track back and forth as you review a traumatic experience. Some therapists use a light bar to guide their clients' eyes.

Your therapist can also alternately tap the backs of your hands or use a device that taps to help you process. When a client has trauma that may be overpowering and trigger too much feeling or too many memories, tapping works best. Ulrich Lanius asserts that this works better for some clients because the sense of touch is not as widely articulated in the brain as sight and hearing and therefore arouses it less.[4] He notes that when using eye movements, covering one eye and working for short periods helps reduce triggering. One of my clients with multiple personalities could only tolerate briefly tracking back and forth with one eye to stop the physical pain of an abuse flashback.

BioLateral Music: Comfort through the Process

A third bilateral technique uses the avenue of hearing. David Grand has developed tapes and CDs with a vibrating, subtle "boom boom" sound that alternates from one earphone to the other. It's often embedded in soothing instrumental music. He calls these "BioLateral."[5] This is the technique I've come to use most for several reasons. Clients can sit comfortably and interact with the therapist easily while the music-embedded sound plays at a low level. Clients report that they find the music very comforting. They can change the volume or turn off the sound as they wish. Sensitive, supportive communication is enhanced when the client and therapist can make eye contact and read each other's expressions. Long sessions are more comfortable in this natural sitting arrangement. Sometimes I will shift into hand-tapping to help ground and support the client. Other times I'll use a pencil and eye movements to focus more intensely on a situation. Most of the time, the BioLateral music works very well on its own.

Following the guidelines of Shapiro, I first have the client enjoy the BioLateral music while he identifies and mentally connects with a place where he has felt safe and happy. We discuss how he can choose to take a break any time and revisit that place. Then the client begins to remember a trauma we've identified, and I check on his level of distress, using a number between one and ten, before he begins. We also define a phrase describing how he hopes to feel when he has resolved the memory. I check on the distress level as needed throughout the processing and at the end.

When there's just one trauma to process or a cluster of closely related traumas in the past, the time for processing is brief. In fact, clients find it reassuring to hear that the memory won't be re-experienced in the same amount of time it took to happen. It's processed in dream time, where an hour can speed by in seconds and long episodes are compressed into minutes. As the client reviews his memory, he's free to talk about what he remembers or just review it privately; either way works for the brain. I encourage clients to talk enough so that I can work with them to revise any beliefs or assumptions that would keep them upset. Any of the cognitive-behavioral therapy techniques described previously can be used to help the client while he listens and reprocesses and after he has completed review of the memory. This process directly connects the client's Adult with his traumatized inner family, allowing the healing that precedes resolution of his grief process.

For clients who have more than one trauma to heal, the BioLateral technique is very comfortable. When there's one primary trauma and a couple past traumas that come up in association, we just continue through until all the associated traumas are processed in one session. When clients have a long history of traumas, as with an abusive childhood, we work in sections, sometimes chronologically, sometimes taking the most traumatic first and then working through associated traumas in declining levels of distress. Generalization from reprocessing each trauma makes the work shorter; similar traumas are desensitized at the same time. We only have to reprocess representative traumas, not every single one.

I've found it appropriate to respond flexibly to the client's needs as she goes through these longer reprocessing experiences. Since insurance companies aren't so flexible, I work with partial pay (or, rarely, with private pay) to provide necessary care that would not be covered. This is some of the most rewarding and exciting work I do. Sometimes I'll schedule two-hour sessions or two sessions in a week for as long as necessary, depending on the pressure of the memories and the symptoms of the client. Many other therapists also offer extended sessions and reduced fees for service when clients need them. Find one with this commitment if you have a lot of trauma to process.

It's best to allow time for processing between sessions, so that the client's inner family can work on the new understanding in its own way. In some cases there's too much pressure for this; then it's compassionate to allow the client to get through her pain. In doing this work, I've come to admire what I see as a drive to heal coming from the inner family. Once it realizes it's safe to unload the traumatic memories, it can be impatient to do so. I often find myself working to hold it back and slow things down to support the client's functioning.

After Reprocessing the Trauma

What you can expect following a reprocessing session varies with the nature and timing of the trauma. With one major past trauma, the result is often immediate, dramatic and profound. Clients will often weep and express disbelief that they could feel so much relief in such a short time. More often, with recent traumas or a series of traumas, clients will report some feelings of relief, rating it a four on a scale of one to ten, rather than a one or two. They also may experience some mild confusion about what's going on inside. For a day or two, they may find their senses are more reactive and even a little raw. This soon passes, and they gradually report feeling better over the next few weeks. After a few months of intense reprocessing, many clients who've been on a lot of medication to try to suppress their PTSD symptoms are able to eliminate most of their drugs.

Trauma Resolution, Support and the Grief Process

When the trauma happens to a young child or is a violent assault on the person's body or sense of security, as in a rape, house fire, car accident or in war, it must be reinterpreted for complete resolution. This work is part of the last stage of the grieving process, adjustment and transformation. With PTSD the intense wounds to a person's sense of himself, trust in others and hope for his future may require more support than therapy can offer. After or near the end of therapy, if you can find a group of people who have survived traumas like yours, you'll discover ideas for how to complete your healing and transform your grief into helping others.

Without this step you may indefinitely be at risk for depression, even when you're free from the flashbacks and intense anxiety you suffered before therapy. The next chapter includes more information about how to deal with any depressive tendencies due to PTSD. Further resources and concepts to help you cope with your own or a loved one's PTSD are offered in Glenn Schiraldi's *Post-Traumatic Stress Disorder Sourcebook.*[6]

Below are some phrases to remind you of your new sense of reality; you can add more to this list as you grow.

- I am safe now.

- I know how to protect myself and get help now.

- The past need not determine my future.

- My suffering can be turned into understanding that will help others.

- Now I can face things that would have scared me too much before.

- Now I can explore my possibilities more freely.

- If I have survived this far, I can surely function even better from now on.

- Now I can join the world of the lucky people who haven't been traumatized.

Notes

1. Gerald D. French and Frank A. Gerbode, *The Traumatic Incident Reduction Workshop* (Menlo Park: IRM Press, 1992).
2. Francine Shapiro, *Eye Movement Desensitization and Reprocessing: Basic Principles, Protocols and Procedures* (New York: The Guilford Press, 1995).
3. Daniel Amen and Lisa C. Routh, *Healing Anxiety and Depression* (New York: Penguin Group, 2003), 106-108.
4. Ulrich Lanius, "Dissociative Processes and EMDR: Staying Connected" (workshop, Seattle, WA, October 5, 2001).
5. David Grand, http://www.BioLateral.com, accessed June 8, 2012.
6. Glenn A. Schiraldi, *The Post-Traumatic Stress Disorder Sourcebook* (New York: McGraw Hill, 2009).

II : 6

Release the Grip of Depression

Remember Joe from the first chapter of this book? He actually inspired me to begin writing this when, after I'd explained in detail why he needed more sleep, he said, "Doc, I'm so tired I can't remember what you're saying; could you write it down for me?" I'd just told him his lack of sleep interfered with his Adult functioning. But I was still trying to give him complex explanations. So if you're depressed and you're reading this chapter without having read part one of this book, especially chapter two ("Prepare Your Brain"), do go back and read that. You'll feel better and will be more able to understand and apply what I am about to discuss here.

Joe easily identified with the pigeon that had its feet shocked in a Skinner box. He sat on his couch immobilized night after night, feeling overwhelmed, anxious, frustrated and depressed. Wisely, he did not expect others to solve his problems and sought counseling to help him help himself. People who are more depressed than Joe often can no longer recognize that they're depressed. They suffer feelings of sadness, anger and hopelessness that overwhelm their Adult and make them believe there is no help available.

You're seeking lifelong mental fitness. To grow and maintain your new skills, you must learn how to avoid falling into depression. Once you are severely depressed, you may need others to pull you out. As I discussed in Part I, chapter 5, others aren't always there to help you. You can't have secure confidence in your ability to manage what life throws at you until you know how to prevent depression.

Without this confidence you may depend too much on the support of others and will suffer intensely each time they let you down. Even the most well-meaning and devoted friend or mate will have times when they can't pull you up because of their own life struggles. Less devoted friends will get tired of trying to cheer you up and keep you from being depressed. You need to develop a strong Adult and secure inner family to have enduring, positive relationships.

Basic Self-Care to Prevent Depression

If you've been practicing the habits described in Part I, you've taken important steps to prevent depression. If you're still struggling, make sure you get adequate sleep and a thorough medical checkup. Your doctor should evaluate you for physical problems that can cause depression; a nonfunctional thyroid, certain medications, major surgery and hormonal imbalances caused by menopause, a hysterectomy or the birth of a child are some of the more common problems.

Rubin Naiman observes that insomnia is both a cause and a result of severe depression. One year of inadequate sleep has been shown to lead to severe depression.[1] This lack of sleep can have both physical and emotional causes. Sleep apnea and chronic pain are common disruptors, and insomnia makes chronic pain worse. Naiman urges using the least medication possible to allow for normal and restorative sleep. Be sure your doctor and counselor are working together to find the best medication for both your insomnia and your depression if medication is needed.

CBT, the Inner Family and Depression

Once you're getting some rest and your Adult is available again, you can begin to sort out the basis of your depression. What are the beliefs that deplete your energy and leave you hopeless? First try asking the question, "What do I need to grieve?" or "What disappointed me?" As noted in the chapter on grief (Part II, chapter 4), if you've been feeling sad for a long time, you need to look deeper to discern what's made you angry, disappointed, frustrated or traumatized. Life events really can gang up on you unfairly. The eight steps of cognitive-behavioral therapy and the twelve toxic beliefs are repeated in appendix A.

It's natural for your Child to feel picked on or guilty at times, but it shouldn't be stuck with those feelings by itself. Wise-Parent and Adult functions should guide it into a calmer state. When your Child isn't managed well, you can remain depressed for a long time. This is why the more depressed people get, the more they focus in on themselves; their distressed Child takes charge. In this state they can barely take care of themselves, much less anyone else. If you're a depressed parent, realizing this should help motivate you to get help.

Let's look at the inner-family beliefs and self-talk that occur most often with severe depression. I've grouped the first six beliefs with the Critical Parent (CP) and the second group of beliefs with the Indulgent Parent (IP). Some of these beliefs can belong to both Parent parts.

Your Critical Parent torments your Child into angry despair.

1. If someone is disapproving, the CP blames your Child for being unworthy, rude, not listening well enough, being ugly, stupid, etc.

2. If you lose at a game or do worse than someone else in a job, the CP calls your Child a failure.

3. If you fail to meet one of your own standards of honesty, neatness, punctuality, preparedness, etc., the CP is all over your Child, placing blame for what the CP perceives to be lack of character. Your CP will also encourage resentment toward others for their shortcomings.

4. If something bad happens, the CP will accuse your Child of not worrying about it enough.

5. The CP insists your Child will never amount to anything because of prior experiences, like a history of abuse, acting out or failing in something.

6. The CP will accuse your Child of being a bad friend, parent, spouse, etc., for not sacrificing your peace of mind every time a loved one is upset.

It's easy to see that without a strong enough Adult and Wise Parent, a CP that buys into several toxic beliefs could keep your Child angry, sad and hopeless. While the CP dominates the inner family when you're depressed, it's wise to be alert for an undercurrent of IP messages that set you up for CP trouble.

Engage your Adult to observe whether you're taking shortcuts because you've bought into IP messages.

7. Your IP tells you it's terribly unfair that you didn't get the promotion or win the contest you worked hard for, because you deserved it. After a few more disappointments, you don't try so hard and you blame others when you lose. Then your CP will call you lazy or even incompetent.

8. Your IP tells you that your problems aren't your fault and that other people or circumstances are responsible when you run into trouble. Our caged pigeon, little children, extremely disabled adults and prisoners of war have reason to believe this. But if you continually fail to look for what you have the power to do in your life, you'll end up angry, hurt and feeling helpless. Your CP may even attack others for causing you distress. Then your CP will call you worthless, stupid and lazy.

9. Your IP may say you deserve to play instead of tackling chores on time. Your CP may say you aren't capable of facing and handling your problems. This causes you to avoid or procrastinate when you could have faced a responsibility. Then your CP will blame your Child for not getting things done on time or losing the job or relationship your avoidance cost you.

10. Your IP says you deserve to have others you can depend on for many things. Then when they let you down, your CP tells

you you're not strong enough to handle life's problems on your own and blames your Child for being too needy or foolish about whom you've chosen as friends.

11., 12. Your IP says you're too smart or too deserving to have to follow the rules that most people accept. Should you really spend your bill-paying dollars to gamble your way into big money because you can outsmart the casinos? Are you really such a gifted driver that you'll never hurt someone when you speed? Are you really such a deserving person that you don't have to work diligently at your job? Your CP will torment you when you've blown your money, wiped out a family driving too fast or gotten fired because you were too important to show up on time for work.

As noted in the chapter on addiction (Part II, chapter 2), it's human to seek breaks from focusing your Adult on what you should be doing all the time. To avoid depression you must develop a balance between intense Adult monitoring and your Child's need for rest and enjoyment. This requires that you rewrite your Parent messages to be more accurate and reasonable. I've begun here to identify what you're likely to discover as you monitor to manage your inner family. A resource to expand your understanding is William Knaus's *Cognitive Behavioral Workbook for Depression.*[2] It can help develop further your cognitive-behavioral therapy skills.

Working with your Adult, your Wise Parent (WP) can bring fairness, reason and comfort to your Child. Your Adult must recognize when the CP is operating out of a toxic belief, correct it and prompt the WP to give the Child a fair and supportive message. You'll probably find just a handful of beliefs your Adult needs to correct. Follow your CBT system to identify, challenge and revise beliefs that cause your feelings of anger, hopelessness and despair. Be creative and find brief phrases (thematic prompts) you can pull out any time to combat your CP's attacks on your Child. It's helpful simply to shut off the CP at times with phrases like, "I'm not going to do that to myself right now," "I *never* deserve to feel *that* bad" or "I won't be useful to anyone if I get down over that."

Just Say No to Addictive Negative Self-Talk

There's a kind of self-talk particular to depression that functions as an addiction and short-circuits your healing as addictions do, and that's the recurring thought of "ending it all." People in this state of mind believe it would be easier that way, and they have a point; why struggle to eat healthy, exercise, build mental fitness, etc., if we could just leave for good? It's important to recognize this addiction for what it is and shut it down quickly. The immature coping that accompanies addictions makes this "answer" tempting. This kind of self-talk should alert your Adult to the fact that you need professional help. Your Child has become too hopeless, and its feelings of fight-or-flight will overwhelm your Adult capacity to search for better answers.

When people dwell on suicide as an answer, they don't give methods like the ones described here a chance. If you find yourself thinking this way, you must find other people with Wise Parents much stronger than yours, like a therapist and mentally fit friends. They can help you discover that you have what it takes to build a life of joy and worth. Addicts need not apply; they will offer drugs, alcohol or other mind-blockers to "ease" you through your pain. Religious faith can be a strong deterrent for actual suicide but may not prevent habitual thoughts of suicide. The thoughts themselves short-circuit growth. Get help to combat these thoughts and give your life a chance.

Sample Comfort to Prevent Depression

Your Child won't believe your new, encouraging self-talk unless it can experience what it's like to feel better. Even a weak Wise Parent can find some ways to soothe your Child, perhaps by drawing from your own youth. What music made you happy? What special places made you feel safe? What movies or TV shows made you laugh? Old *I Love Lucy* episodes were a great comfort and release for me when I fought serious depression. Children's shows and books can be surprisingly supportive. I used to choke up often, in a good way, watching *Sesame Street* with my son. I can still sing the alphabet like Big Bird and most of Kermit the Frog's "It's Not Easy Being Green." What a great message for remembering to value myself that song gave!

For severe depression you need to plug in many daily breaks for comfort. Plan for fifteen minutes at a time when you can monitor very closely for how you're feeling as you try very brief things to calm and comfort you. If you're trying to read and you can't, listen to a soothing CD. If that makes you cry, try watching a light TV show. When the commercials irritate you, take a hot bath. Pot a plant, organize a drawer, weed in the yard or talk about the weather with a neighbor. Do all these and other things you discover to distract your Child from its mood and remind it that things aren't so bad.

Gradually you will find a group of brief activities you can count on to pull you out of a downward spiral. Engage in them quickly when you notice the tug, so that you can keep your Vagus nerve from taking your body and Child into scary discomfort. Outdoor activities help a lot because they lift you directly through light and exercise into healthier brain chemistry. If it's a nice day, you may be cheered by its loveliness. It's important to put your Child to bed early and provide a reassuring close to the day's thoughts as described in Part I, chapter 2 ("Prepare Your Brain").

Once you've pulled out of the worst stages of depression, you must begin to build habits that can protect you from getting depressed again. It's good to develop your own formula to keep you on track in the future. Keep a notebook or make a file listing the beliefs you've combated and your revisions of them. One client developed a brief "urgent care" file of quotes, phrases and pictures that could very quickly calm her Child. Begin habits that are fun, like making time to enjoy special pictures, music, movies, mementoes and quotes. Find a hobby or craft to comfort you when you're alone or to share with friends. Mental fitness, much like physical fitness, is easier to maintain with activities you enjoy.

You must keep updating your positive activities all your life as your interests, health and circumstances change. It's likely that people sometimes get depressed in old age because they don't expect they should have to update and change what they enjoy. If your shoulder goes out and golf is the only activity you love, you should *expect* to cultivate one or more new beloved activities. What you like will change over the years, but you won't always know which activities you will enjoy. Expect you'll have to try different things until you find some that nurture your Child. This isn't just fun; it's medically necessary to prevent another siege of depression.

Connect with Others to Prevent Depression

To prevent or overcome depression, evaluate your satisfaction with your work and community connections. In her book *Passages: Predictable Crises in Adult Development,*[3] Gail Sheehy describes how men in this country tend to get depressed if they don't feel valued in their jobs, can't earn enough to support their families or can't find work that allows them to express their talents. They will then be prone to a midlife crisis in their early forties. She suggests that women are less vulnerable in the work area, because they also value themselves for their functions as homemakers and mothers. However, women whose main focus is a career may have a similar problem with their midlife passage. It's especially important for men or women who are disappointed about their careers to feel valued by their families.

The most difficult thing for people to do when they're depressed, I've observed, is to go out and make new friends. Even those who were outgoing before their depression will resist this. It's like pulling teeth to get socially anxious and depressed people to make a consistent effort to go out and build social support. This is often true of Elaine Aron's highly sensitive people. To begin it's helpful to find some activity you can enjoy by yourself: a craft, a new author to read, gardening or something to research on your computer. Then you can begin joining with others who have the same interest. Take a class, join a book club, volunteer at a community garden or look at Meetup.com and see what others are doing with your activity. The shared interest gives you something to talk about with your new acquaintances.

You may find a few people who share other interests of yours that you can do together comfortably. The activities distract you from your feelings of depression, develop your talents and improve your feelings of competence. The new friends make you feel more confident socially and boost your hope that life could feel better. They help strengthen your Wise Parent. You need to meet with people regularly to get to know them well enough for friendships to develop. Friendship at first sight is as rare and instable as love at first sight. Trust and respect develop as you work or play with others, and then friendship can grow. I'll discuss this in more detail in Part III.

I saw one very shy young man who overcame much of his social anxiety but had no hobbies and no friends. He was still somewhat depressed. He came back in after a few months and declared, "I have one!" I knew he'd found a hobby. He had bought himself a metal detector and was having fun finding treasures all by himself. Of course, I was excited about how he possibly could meet people in groups who got together to do this, but he wasn't going there. A few months later, he came in again and said, "I've got another one, and you'll like this one better." He had discovered he could enjoy antique toys and was talking with the dealers at shows comfortably. He had even dated briefly and began to feel more confident in that area.

Once you've committed not to withdraw from relating to others for the rest of your life, you've taken a big step away from clinical depression. Extraverts who thrive on being with others have an easier time maintaining their social functioning. Many HSPs and introverts who just like to spend lots of time on their own activities have to work hard at this. The point here is that you do have to maintain adequate social connection to avoid depression. Friends naturally help grow your Adult and Wise Parent as you go through life. They help you appreciate your strengths and help you eliminate weaknesses that could undermine your well-being. They share your interests and encourage your Child to try new things along with them. They make lots of the tasks for keeping mentally fit easy and fun.

Genetics, Bipolar Disorder and Depression

There have long been discussions and studies to analyze whether there are inherited tendencies to become depressed. I think there are inherited tendencies for the most common forms of depression, but we don't know how they're sorted out yet. There's a significant exception to this when we deal with bipolar disorder, which used to be called manic-depressive disorder. This is clearly inherited and usually requires medication. Medication prevents the severe swings from profound depression to intense activity. This activity, called mania, can be expressed in either extreme positive or extreme negative emotion.

I refer the reader to James Phelps's website, Psycheducation.org, for information and resources.[4] He emphasizes the need for bipolar people and their families to become informed about bipolar disorder in order to be sure appropriate treatment is found. He is especially concerned that people with bipolar II are thought to have a lighter form of the disorder because they have less mania. He stresses that they in fact have more frequent depression than bipolar I clients and kill themselves twice as often. They're especially at risk for this when given selective serotonin reuptake inhibitor (SSRI) antidepressant medications, like Paxil or Lexapro, which can trigger a negatively charged manic episode.

Jay Carter describes the bipolar trait as a spectrum on which only people with a higher genetic loading are diagnosed.[5] At the lower end of the spectrum, people have a temperament where they get overly talkative and have sleep problems when stressed but don't escalate to the extremes. Like Rubin Naiman,[6] he indicates that people significantly deprived of sleep can exhibit psychosis similar to that which occurs in an extreme manic episode. Like Phelps, he indicates that bipolar people are more sensitive to sleep deprivation and have more problems sleeping. Carter notes that solving the sleep problems, usually with medication, can resolve or reduce many bipolar symptoms.

Carter describes the risks of mania for the destruction of people's lives and possible suicide. He notes that most of the time, mania is not a positive "up" as is generally thought. Instead, 80 percent of the time, people in their manic state are intensely angry, negative, agitated and sometimes abusive. He contends that bipolar depression and mania can occur in people who otherwise have good mental fitness but who have brain abnormalities that create chaos for them. This happens due to brain chemistry that disables Adult functions to regulate them.

Diagnosis by a capable professional before people with bipolar disorder damage their own lives and those of their loved ones is critical. A psychiatrist or psychiatric nurse practitioner is best able to work with clients to find the medications that will work for them. If a therapist is involved, he needs to coordinate with the prescribing doctor, making sure she's aware of problems the client is having due to incorrect medication, dosage or failure to take the medication as prescribed.

In therapy it's especially important to help the client remain hopeful about eventual improvement if he keeps working with the prescribing doctor. The client must be informed that the medication doesn't work if taken in response to a manic or depressive episode; it must be taken continually to work. Young clients with immature Adults and bipolar intensity can take very black-and-white views of their situation. They get excited when the medication helps and very dejected when it doesn't. Cognitive therapy can help their Adults maintain a perspective on their situation that helps keep them consistent with their meds and stable in their outlook for themselves.

Medication for Depression

Medication for depression that cycles in and out (major depression) or the lower grade depression that can drag on for years (dysthymia) has been studied and prescribed extensively. As it becomes possible to differentiate between what are likely to be several types of depression in these categories, medication issues may become clearer. It's known through decades of studies that severe depression requires medication along with psychotherapy for the best outcome. Primary-care providers can often find appropriate antidepressants and refer to a psychiatrist for cases that require more expertise in finding what will help. What I've observed is that with major depression, people's ability to comprehend and follow through with the work of psychotherapy is impaired until they get medication to improve their Adult functioning.

For dysthymia, I've observed that antidepressants don't work on a long-term basis. People with dysthymia are usually still capable of learning in therapy without medication. Antidepressant medication should be used only when it's really needed and for only as long as it's needed, because it is not harmless. In Part I, chapter 2, I discussed Naiman's comments about medication's negative impact on sleep and dreaming. Other recent studies also suggest that SSRIs may cause harm, especially with longer-term use. Oril van Mourik reported on Helen Fischer's neurological studies, which revealed that SSRIs cause both sexual dysfunction and a loss of emotional bonding in relationships.[7] Research on people over fifty found that SSRIs may cause increased bone fractures.[8]

I encourage people with dysthymia to use medication in as low a dose and for as short a time as possible if any medication is needed.

Patients can usually resume medication in the future if their symptoms recur. Your prescribing doctor can advise you about this in your case. The beliefs that cause dysthymia can lead to recurrent episodes for life. The belief that happiness is controlled by life circumstances (the eighth toxic belief) is a major contributor. You ask, "How can I possibly feel good when all this is going on?" You owe it to yourself to focus your Adult, look honestly at your life situation and resolve to change what you can. You are not a prisoner of war or a little child.

You shouldn't medicate yourself to stay indefinitely in a bad job, a hurtful marriage or an unhealthy organization or community. You should try what you can to change these or change your reactions to them. If these efforts fail to relieve your depressed feelings in the situation, you should leave it. The clients I've seen with long-term dysthymia feel trapped in their situations and struggle to identify ways to leave. They can sometimes find new ways to cope, reducing their discomfort. Is it ethical to medicate them for years, when increased awareness of their pain could motivate them to improve their life circumstances? In Part II, chapter 3 on anxiety, I noted the increased tendency for psychiatrists to offer medication—and not psychotherapy—to their clients. Depressed clients should at least be referred for counseling when they're given medication.

Depression over World Problems

Besides the problems in your immediate situation, you may fear an uncertain future in a troubled world. Daily news about the suffering that people all over the world endure can leave a caring person sad and hopeless. How do you enjoy that hot bath or that gourmet meal without a troubled conscience? How do you enjoy all the trappings of holidays with your family when there are millions starving to death? In light of these feelings, you must provide yourself with "happy spots" every day to stay healthy.

Some people try to block it all out by not reading the paper or watching the news on television. They're setting themselves up for a bout of overwhelming stress when (not if) their lives are touched by problems others face. When you increase your Adult awareness, you inevitably connect more to the world around you. You must find a way of understanding it all that doesn't leave you sick and immobilized with depression.

A major source of wisdom in our Western world, the New Testament of the Bible, offers a parable about how to do this. Jesus's disciples ask him how they'll be able to know what prophets to follow after he is gone. He answers, "You will know them by their fruits" (Matt. 7:15–20). A wise prophet has wise and positive followers; a healthy tree yields nourishing fruit. We don't call our major influences "prophets" today, but they imprint on us the beliefs that guide our lives. These "belief trees" should be pruned or chopped down if their fruits are anxiety and depression. You must water and fertilize belief trees that lead you into a life where the fruits are a capacity for concerned action and for great love and joy.

When you find yourself mildly depressed, that's a good time to journal and reflect, allowing your Adult and Wise Parent to coordinate. This reflection provides deep roots for your mental fitness. Dale Carnegie wrote a wonderful, comforting book, *How to Stop Worrying and Start Living*, which tells the stories of people during the Great Depression of the 1930s. He offers ideas from them for how to feel better each day, like counting your blessings instead of your problems.[9]

Most depression is at least in part the fruit of poor habits of mental fitness. In order to overcome a present bout of depression, you must practice the skills described in the previous chapters. Even with inherited depression like bipolar disorder, people can choose to work on keeping their Adult mind in charge. You have to *believe* you're capable of managing your life and deserve to be fulfilled in order to work at getting there in earnest. As with diabetes or heart disease, there are inherited components. Some of you have to work harder than others to manage yourselves wisely and reduce your chances of getting sick. As you work to revise the belief that happiness is controlled by outside events (the eighth toxic belief), you must remind yourself: "I can't control or fix all the world's problems, but I can manage my own. Only then will I have the enduring capacity to help just a little in this troubled world."

Here are some questions to help your Adult peddle past your depression:

- What am I dreading?

- What might I need to grieve?

- Am I creating space for my Child to rest and play?

- What could I find to comfort and renew me?

- Are my connections with others in need of a tune-up?

- What beliefs may be preventing me from doing these things?

- What new beliefs would lead me in a better direction?

- What blessings can I count tonight?

Here are some phrases to keep you hanging in there:

- I'm free to choose how to look at things.

- I have all the gifts I need to make my life good.

- There must be something helpful I can learn from this.

- My being depressed doesn't benefit even one person in this troubled world.

- Staying positive gives me the energy to contribute.

- Unfairness happens to everyone, including me.

- I'll do my best, and that's got to be good enough.

- There's help if I get stuck on my journey.

Notes

1. Rubin Naiman, *Healing Night* (Minneapolis: Syren Book Co., 2006).

2. William J. Knaus, *The Cognitive Behavioral Workbook for Depression* (Oakland: New Harbinger, 2006).

3. Gail Sheehy, *Passages: Predictable Crises in Adult Life* (1976; repr., New York: Ballantine Books, 2006).

4. James Phelps, http://www.PsychEducation.com, accessed June 8, 2012.

5. Jay Carter, *Bipolar: The Elements of Bipolar Disorder, A Practical Guide* (Wyomissing: Unicorn Press, 2008).

6. Naiman, *Healing Night*.

7. Oril Van Mourik, "SSRIs and Love," *PsychToday*, April 2007.

8. J. Brent Richards, Alexandra Papaioannou, Jonathon D. Adachi, Lawrence Joseph, Heather E. Whitson, Jerilynn C. Prior and David Goltzman, "Effect of Selective Serotonin Reuptake Inhibitors on the Risk of Fracture," *Archives of Internal Medicine*, Vol. 167 No. 2 (2007), 188–194.

9. Dale Carnegie, *How to Stop Worrying and Start Living,* (1944; rev. ed., New York: Simon & Schuster, 1984).

Behold thou desirest truth in the inward being.
Therefore teach me wisdom in my secret heart.
(Psalm 51:6)

II : 7

Keep Your Adult in Charge for Life

The Wise Parent you began to develop in Part I in order to manage your mind has now grown in Part II to include understanding of your inward being. With this knowledge your Adult can guide you to correct false beliefs as you go through your days. Your Adult must recognize when an inherited tendency is likely to affect its functioning. It must keep reprogramming your Parent parts to keep Critical- and Indulgent-Parent influences from sinking you into an addiction or setting off an extreme reaction. The emotional pressures from your Child of anxiety, anger, grief or despair must be caught early to keep you on track. Your increasingly strong Wise Parent can provide the stability to reduce their impact.

How can you keep your Wise Parent growing to maintain wisdom in your secret heart, where your Child lives? You've begun to embrace new beliefs that can keep your Child feeling capable, hopeful, energetic, curious, compassionate toward yourself and others and excited about your future. Your cognitive-behavioral therapy skills help you eliminate false beliefs. The "prophets" or wise thinkers you study can help you discover even more fair, valid and inspiring beliefs. As noted in the previous chapter, you must look carefully at each thinker, testing especially whether his fruits are sound.

It's confusing to try to sort out wisdom from all the possible prophets offering a way to live. But your Adult can gradually sort through what you encounter and help your Wise Parent grasp only the best fruit for you. Where do people start? Some find answers in their religion, which they were brought up to follow. Your Adult must evaluate what you've been taught and challenge religious teachings if they don't make sense to you. Don't blindly follow a leader without considering where he would take you. Don't let others pressure you to join them out of fear. Fight-or-flight is rarely helpful in making life choices, as you've discovered.

Don't Throw the Baby out with the Bath Water

For each prophet or belief set, be sure to look at the whole tree, not just the branch filled with tent caterpillars. Try to recognize and accept what good fruits are being offered. Most Roman Catholics use birth control, even though that's against their church's teachings. Most Muslims define jihad as "good energy," not violence or war. The first step in the AA Twelve-Step program puts off many intellectual or non-religious people. It involves acknowledging that one has lost all control over his addiction and must turn his life over to a higher power. What if we revise this to say, "I've lived my life under the belief that I can handle things on my own but now see that some kind of help might be needed." Then the next eleven steps can be very useful and even lifesaving.

Use your own judgment and be creative in finding what parts of these belief systems you can make your own. Your Child will always push you to seek quick fixes. You can't let it choose your beliefs, though you must consider its input as you try on a habit. This is where your Adult must be very alert along your journey, so it can look for the long-term effects of what you choose at each step of the way. Your Wise Parent must help your Child be patient and stay comfortable when you have to wait for feedback that you're on the right track. When your job feels like a dead end, a relationship disappoints you, a flood washes out your home or a loved one dies, your Child can become demanding of immediate comforts that would sabotage your long-term well-being. You must somehow remain clear about what your goals and values are to avoid an addiction. This is how you hold truth in your inward being.

Prophets to Guide the Beliefs of Your Inner World

A Wise Parent garbed in a strong belief system can keep your Child comfortable and well-managed. Religious training can offer a short-cut to forming a system that maintains your inner family in harmony. Some who reject many religious concepts are nonetheless committed to living a well-thought-out, self-aware life. In either case your Adult must organize your beliefs to avoid stumbling into an addiction, anxiety attack or bout of depression. There are rules shared by most thinking people to help you keep on track. Jesus's golden rule to "do unto others as we would have others do unto us"(Matt. 7:12) is basic for human empathy and promoting fairness and justice between people, whether they believe God is watching or not.

Years ago I heard a Jewish rabbi discuss the concept of forgiveness as a visiting minister to my church. It was the time of the Jewish New Year, and he noted that Jews try to enter each new year with a special kind of forgiveness. The rabbi explained that this forgiveness does not mean that Jews accept that previous hurtful things were right; they just acknowledge them and pray for God's help to leave them fully behind. This is similar to the last stage of the grief process; after you face a loss, you travel through your anger and sadness until you're ready to let go and move on.

Michael Newton offers insight from a different perspective. Newton has spent decades studying the reported experience of clients under hypnosis who described places and times in the past, prior to their present lives. He recorded many of these reports and shared his structured techniques with other hypnotherapists. In *Journey of Souls: Case Studies of Life Between Lives* [1] and *Destiny of Souls: New Case Studies of Life Between Lives* [2] he describes his sessions with clients he had questioned about what it was like between one life and the next. Newton edits a book named *Memories of the Afterlife: Life Between Lives: Studies of Personal Transformation*, where hypnotherapists from around the world report similar findings.[3]

Some of you may find his work a challenge to your Adult's effort to keep an open mind. You could try to look at this as yet another reason to keep developing your mental fitness. If it is true that you have more opportunities to explore living than just your present life, it might be easier to let go of hurt and disappointment. If souls vary in their wisdom due to their experience incarnating, there's another reason to stop wanting to blame or punish anyone. Newton's work challenges Western thought particularly, yet actually supports belief in a higher power who is always working in unfathomable ways for our good.

Some of those who don't believe in a higher power can still see the benefits of committing to courageous action to change things and exercising patience when they can't. Jean-Paul Sartre, speaking from an atheistic and existentialist point of view, emphasized the need to continually ask yourself what kind of community you would have if everyone were to do what you're about to do.[4] A well-functioning Adult considers what the inner family is pressing it to do in light of the probable impact on others in the outside world. A strong Wise Parent helps support inner-family courage instead of fight-or-flight and acceptance when it's necessary to tolerate disappointment. Together your Adult and Wise Parent can guide you to do what is best for yourself and your community, whether you believe in anything beyond this life or not.

It's helpful to maintain and update a journal or file of beliefs that keep you feeling balanced and positive. Watch for new quotes that grab you and make a note of them. Then go through them and consider how they relate, how you'd sort them and which are most important to you. Try reading what some of the authors of these quotes have to say or join a book club. Discuss new ideas with respected friends. This activity by your Adult helps strengthen your Wise Parent to manage your Child for the most positive expression of who you are.

Find Balance and Direction

Once you're stabilized with a working tree of beliefs, consider how to join with others in positive ways. You can't grow your tree in isolation. Remember that the twelve toxic beliefs all involve how you relate to others. How can your Adult keep from being overwhelmed by the outside world as you try to make well-considered choices? There are too many possible areas for investing your energy. Should you go after a college degree, a beautiful home, a wonderful marriage, lots of money, being a politician, being a minister, being a policeman, being a teacher or being a corporate CEO? For each of these, you would prioritize your goals differently, depending on your beliefs about what matters most.

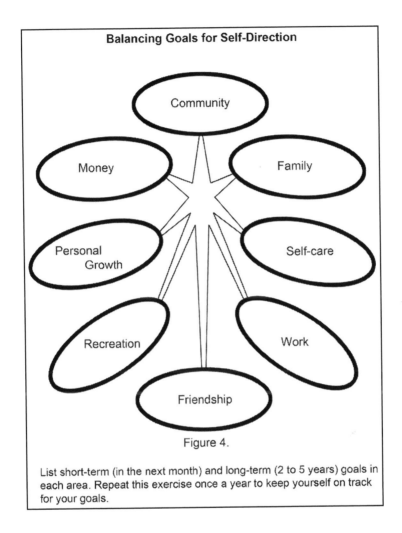

Figure 4.

List short-term (in the next month) and long-term (2 to 5 years) goals in each area. Repeat this exercise once a year to keep yourself on track for your goals.

It's a tough job to balance these priorities but it is possible to manage if you can keep your Adult in charge for each choice. This isn't how we usually function; we usually focus on one or two of these areas and just slide into the others with little thought. You need a handle on how to plan in order to find your direction. You can begin to create a big-picture view of your life ahead with a simple exercise. Divide your activities into eight areas and think of short- and long-term goals for each one. You'll find that these categories include activities that help you build your Wise Parent. Figure 4 suggests eight categories. Here's an example with one short-term and one long-term goal in each category. You'll want to define more in the categories you're focused on at this point in your life:

	Short-term goal	**Long-term goal**
Work	Apply for a job	Get promoted at work
Recreation	Learn how to knit	Make scarves for birthday gifts
Money	Save money on a DIY project	Build savings for retirement
Family	Call a relative	Move closer in retirement
Self-care	Walk five miles a week	Hike up a mountain
Friendship	Have lunch with a friend	Go for a weekend with friends
Community	Help plant a local garden	Organize a garden-tour fund-raiser
Personal growth	Find a mentor	Teach an inspiring class

When you consider these eight areas, you'll find that attention to all of them over several years is required to prevent conditions leading to depression, trauma or anxiety. Many of these areas allow you to find people who will become your friends and supporters. Fortunately most activities address goals in several categories. For example, planting a local garden gives you a chance to improve your community and connect with new friends for you and your family. Through them you could learn a healthy new recipe and find a buddy to walk with. You might learn about a friendly church or a good therapist for yourself or your ADHD third-grade son. You could even get a lead on a new job. You'll feel happier and have more energy to keep growing with all this friendly input right in your neighborhood.

Define your short- and long-term goals in each area once or twice a year to keep on track with growing your competence in all eight areas. You'll notice that you have lots of short-term goals in some areas and few or none in others. This is appropriate, since each stage of your adult life offers a different set of challenges. Gail Sheehy describes these stages with examples of people going through them in many walks of life.[5] Although you can only focus on a few goal areas at a time, it's best for your long-term fulfillment to try to set even a small goal for each area. Experiment to find what short steps are realistic for you. Gradually you'll find activities that allow you to develop all eight areas with less confusion.

As you work at this, you'll discover new ways of thinking about your future and surprise yourself with ideas for more meaningful goals. You're beginning the relationship work that will be further explored in Part III. As you master the principles for your own mental fitness, you become stronger within yourself and ready for healthy relationships. You can learn to stop punishing others and expecting them to change as you learn to stop punishing yourself. Learn to do unto yourself as you would do unto others as you monitor with your Adult. You can learn to guide others effectively as you learn to guide yourself. You can refine your understanding of your beliefs as you apply them with others, honing them in the human cauldron.

Get Support to Keep Your Adult in Charge

Forty years ago when I hit my bottom (as the AA people would say), I had to discover, mostly on my own, the lessons in this book to climb out of it. It's good to know that now there are guidelines from science to help us get started when wisdom seems unavailable. As the references included here indicate, there are many studies that show how new techniques can help resolve anxiety and depression. The safest belief tree you can climb when you're at your bottom is that of a well-grounded therapist. Get a referral from someone reliable.

Therapists are taught to help you find your own guiding beliefs, not confuse you with their own. Most will tell you when your questions need to be directed to a spiritual leader.

You may feel uncomfortable at first with a therapist who's helping you confront things you've avoided. She should work from the understanding that you need kernels of corn to grow and help you see your strong points and what you need to work on. But one therapist is not likely to give you all you need; you must direct your own search, keeping your Adult attuned to your inner family while you explore to find the beliefs that work for you. If your first therapist doesn't help you enough, try another one. You'd do that for a car you liked if your first mechanic couldn't fix it. You could also try some other support for a while before trying again with a therapist.

When (not if) life gets overwhelming, don't cop out to your Child and succumb to an addiction of any kind. Quick fixes just delude you into thinking you're doing well and dull your Adult's awareness. The sooner you address your confusion, the less chance there is for your Critical Parent to get ammunition to crush your Child's spirit. AA or Al-Anon (if it's a family member who's dragging you down) can help. Find another support group, your pastor, a wise friend or neighbor who inspires and nurtures you until you feel strong enough to try again. Most importantly, believe you can grow much stronger.

Six Steps to Keep Your Adult in Charge

Here's a summary of what your Adult must make sure you're doing all the time:

1. Monitor consistently to manage your beliefs and expectations.

2. Strengthen your Wise Parent by defining and practicing beliefs that comfort and inspire you. Practice activities alone and with others that nurture your fragile new beliefs.

3. Keep a bridle on your Critical Parent, allowing messages needed to protect you but shutting down beliefs that upset and immobilize you.

4. Learn to manage your Child with wisdom and kindness. Give it space to rest, create, play and explore. Limit it when it feels entitled to more indulgence than is good for you. Correct Indulgent-Parent beliefs that corrupt your Child.

5. Connect with others to grow in all these skills, noting both positive and negative examples. You'll grow the tree of your understanding and discover your unique talents for participating among others.

6. Make regular time to reflect on what you're learning and adjust your direction as your new insights guide you.

Stay open to wisdom from any direction. A child, a puppy, the busybody next door, a TV show, a clerk in the grocery store or an old book can all offer new Wise-Parent messages to enrich your life. Put these messages up where you can see them often until they become a part of your mind. Your Adult is strengthened as you remain aware of what you can learn from each moment. Become friends with your body and listen when it signals that you need to adjust a belief to prevent fight-or-flight reactions. Remind yourself that you almost never need to be on guard for threats to your life as you go through your days. You can peddle your bicycle as you monitor along in peace.

Notes

1. Michael Newton, *Journey of Souls: Case Studies of Life Between Lives* (St. Paul: Llewellyn Worldwide, 1994).
2. Michael Newton, *Destiny of Souls: New Case Studies of Life Between Lives* (Woodbury: Llewellyn Worldwide, 2000).
3. Michael Newton, ed., *Memories of the Afterlife: Life Between Lives: Stories of Personal Transformation* (Woodbury: Llewellyn Worldwide, 2009).

4. Jean-Paul Sartre, *Existentialism is a Humanism* (New Haven: Yale University Press, 2007).

5. Gail Sheehy, *Passages: Predictable Crises in Adult Life* (1976; repr., New York: Ballantine Books, 2006).

Introduction to
Part III:
Applications in
Relationships

Once you have studied parts 1 and 2 and have begun to claim your own mental fitness, you'll be ready to apply your understanding and skills in relationships. This is where you can practice your new beliefs and make them your new natural way of being. This is where you'll be tested continually as you try to keep your Adult mind in charge while others lead with their insecure Child. This is where you discover you must be the leader in your relationships, inspiring others to try to keep their own Adult in charge. When you encounter others who share your understanding about how to manage their minds, it's a delightful relief and huge support for your continued efforts. Relationships with such people can be much more relaxed and free of drama.

Part III includes examples of how the twelve toxic beliefs play out in the many kinds of relationships you have. We'll explore how each type of relationship reveals these beliefs from different angles. Your Adult and Wise Parent will grow more astute as you uncover these beliefs in your own relationships. Take for example the third toxic belief, where you blame and punish others when they don't meet your expectations. Since you bring different expectations to each type of relationship, you could blame others for different failings in each. As you sort these out, your Adult can learn to recognize the toxic beliefs for each relationship type and correct them.

Even the names for your relationships carry an emotional flavor rooted in your Child. You could feel hurt because you thought someone was your friend, until a confidence wasn't kept. Remember when your fifth-grade teacher taught you what a friend was? If you do, you went to an exceptional school. How often do you and a prospective friend discuss the ground rules for your friendship? It's a good idea but rarely happens.

What about your mother, brother, cousin or aunt? You'll have unexamined and unspoken expectations of these people too. With family relationships your expectations must evolve as you go through your life. Are you keeping up with the necessary adjustments? How about your ideas of being a parent? If you plan to be a parent, you'll probably expect to be a good one and feel terrible if anyone suggests you're failing. Do you even know what's required?

For each type of relationship, your Adult must identify what beliefs and expectations you bring, evaluate them and modify them if they're expressions of the twelve toxic beliefs. Part III will describe some of these expectations and suggest more reasonable beliefs for you to store in your Wise Parent. As you work on these, you'll find new ways to combat your Critical- and Indulgent-Parent influences while you exercise your Adult. Only through relating to others can you develop mental fitness, because such interaction teaches you about your beliefs. You'll catch yourself operating out of a crazy expectation and you will observe others doing that too. It's more fun to see someone else losing their temper than to find yourself doing it, but both can grow your Adult. The challenge is to view your interactions with others as a training ground, rather than a final exam.

God grant me the serenity
To accept the things I cannot change,
The courage to change the things I can,
And the wisdom to know the difference.
—Reinhold Niebuhr*

III:1

Friendship Holds the Keys

The Serenity Prayer, cherished by those trying to recover from addictions in twelve-step programs, offers all of us a mantra for coping with other people. It summarizes elegantly what you need to remember to keep your cool and hang in there. You need the wisdom to know the difference between friendship and other relationships to guide you in what you try to change and what you decide to accept. You can begin to identify how your expectations should change for other relationships in order to make them function well. Your Adult needs this information to keep your Child from being upset in other relationships when people don't behave like friends. Your Wise Parent must have this understanding to maintain nontoxic beliefs as you relate to others in your family, neighborhood, workplace, or community.

Friendship is a concept that you can idealize to the point where it's no fun anymore. You can be hurt, elated, enraged or comforted in your friendships without engaging your Adult to define your concept of what a friend is. One thing we all seem to agree on is that friendship involves hanging in there with another person, but how long, how

---

*AA History and Trivia (http://www.aahistory.com), an Alcoholics Anonymous website, gives the history of how AA came to use the Serenity Prayer. It describes their communication with Reinhold Niebuhr, who wasn't sure if he'd written it but gave permission for AA to use and share it. The site describes other versions of the prayer and also offers the complete prayer as Niebuhr presented it.

how intensely and how comfortably we hang in there varies with each relationship. Your Adult and Wise Parent can form friendships that have the best combination of these factors.

When you engage with others, you're pressed to manage your reactions quickly and to consider complex issues. What's good for both you and them? Will they understand your intentions? How much trouble can you get in? Anxiety can reduce your ability to function, as it causes you to focus too much on keeping yourself safe and comfortable. In such cases your Adult gets overrun and you move into subtle fight-or-flight behavior. Remember that you can recognize that your brain has misunderstood when your body shows signs of discomfort, like a knot in your stomach, a flash of heat or tension in your muscles. This confusion stops you from offering the best you have to others and can prevent both courage and serenity.

Friendship cushions you from interpersonal stress. Friends can provide stability for your life like no one else. They can be family members, neighbors, coworkers or grade-school buddies. They can be older or younger, wealthier or poorer, more or less gifted. They value you and try to be available when you need support or just companionship. Their expectations of you reflect how they see you. From this continual feedback, you're helped to know who you are from the outside in. With several friends you get several ways of seeing yourself. When friends know you well and you can trust them, you gain a solid sense of how well you're carrying out the expression of what you value. You become free to share your talents and the fruits of your efforts with others, beginning with your friends.

A Supportive Reality Check

You need feedback from friends as a reality check in order to balance your work to be mentally fit. But you must rely on your own judgment and self-observations to keep your Adult in charge; you can't depend on another person's evaluation of you to know how you're doing with that. You must monitor and work on building your own set of valid beliefs to keep your inner family from taking you into fight-or-flight over the smallest incidents. You can't see yourself as others see you, because you'll always have blind spots and tendencies to see things solely from your own point of view. Your friends trust that you mean well no matter what and they help you to be a good friend when you can't do it on your own. You do the same for them.

During time with trusted friends, you can relax your vigilance over your fight-or-flight tendencies. You have a space to be lighthearted, express your Child without fear and feel safe. You grow your Wise Parent just by basking in the Wise Parents of your friends. You can take risks and be creative in your humor, your projects and your fun together. You can draw on the memory of time with friends to sustain you when you're feeling down. Troublesome people lose much of their power when you can remind yourself of how your respected friends see you. Gradually, your view of yourself becomes more like your friends' view of you and your self-esteem is strengthened.

When your Critical Parent tries to interfere too much, a friend's gentle observation may help you correct the Critical Parent's false interpretation. When I was a young single parent, I barely had enough money to pay for our needs. I didn't get a credit card until I was thirty-five, because I couldn't see how I could ever pay it off. So once in a while, I'd make an error and bounce a check. This would put my inner family into major fight-or-flight—mostly flight. One day I mentioned how anxious this all made me to my wise friend Peggy, a math professor who certainly didn't have this kind of problem. She smiled at me warmly and said simply, "It happens." To this day when I make some error like this, her kind assurance helps me manage my Critical Parent. That moment with Peggy is now part of my Wise Parent.

Who Can Really Be Your Friend?

Friends can differ from you in many ways, but in some ways they need to be like you. What are these ways? Does a friend need to share your interests and like to have fun the same way you do? These traits allow for companionship but don't ensure friendship. People who share your interests but not your values may make better acquaintances than friends; you can occasionally have a good time with them. The friends you count on for safe havens and solid feedback need to share your key values. You can't really relax when your Child might be lured into activities your Critical Parent will bust you for later. You can't rely on some friends' feedback about you, because they may not actually understand you and what you're trying to do in your life. They may have trouble seeing why your values are important to you.

What values should you hope to share with friends? First they must share similar values about what friendship is. They must value fairness, kindness and honesty to allow your Child to relax. They need to have insight into their own false beliefs and Critical-Parent messages, as you try to do. They must also work to manage their fight-or-flight reactions in order to be measured and thoughtful in how they give you feedback. They must understand the value of positive feedback for building people and the limitations of punishment. Why would you want to hang out with someone who continually complains about your minor flaws? If what you consider minor they consider major, your values are different.

Other values relate to your prospective friend's capacity to maintain her Adult in charge. If she indulges in addictions, she will not grow. If she's done this for some time, she won't have learned the self-management skills that you've struggled for without relying on an addiction. She probably won't appreciate what you're trying to do and may resent your refusal to join her Child in its out-of-control behavior. If your friend has untreated anxiety, depression, grief or trauma, she won't be able to step out of herself reliably to be with you. You can offer support, but not so often your insights, which could be easily misunderstood as simplistic and unsympathetic. No one wants her friend to act like her therapist. You should encourage such friends to seek the guidance of a counselor who is trained to help them move out of their pain.

There are practical considerations, even with people who share your values as friends and like you a lot. How many close friends can each of us manage? Friendship requires opportunities to share time together. With comfortable friends you can feel connected at once after not speaking for several months or even years. But you need a few friends who are available often to enrich your life and help you maintain yourself. You can enjoy people of varying ages, but it's helpful to recognize what stage of life your friend occupies. Fifty-year-olds whose kids are grown-up may have more time and need different support than twenty-five-year-olds with two kids in diapers. Your focus and the values you emphasize will change over time, as Gail Sheehy so well documents in her book *Passages: Predictable Crises in Adult Life*.[1]

How Can You Be a Good Friend?

What are the obstacles that you bring to a relationship? You've been working to overcome these in parts 1 and 2. Let's examine how the principles you've learned could help you to be a better friend. Continue to monitor your reactions to be sure your Adult steps in when your body signals that your Child needs reassurance or your Critical Parent needs correction. Even before your Adult knows just what's bothering you, it can nearly always assure your inner family that there's no life-threatening danger present and therefore no need to mobilize for fight-or-flight.

Scan for whether you're getting hooked by one of the twelve toxic beliefs by following the process described in Part I, chapter 4. These beliefs result from a lack of wisdom, lead to failures of courage and crush your serenity. They're listed in their basic form in appendix A along with cognitive-behavioral therapy guidelines for your quick reference. Since these beliefs trigger your Critical Parent to upset your Child (and mobilize your body), you must try to combat them every time they appear until you've replaced them with more reasonable beliefs. To be there for your friend, you must maintain your Adult and Wise-Parent functions.

Here are a few examples. When your friend fails to keep a promise, the third toxic belief (that you should blame others when they let you down) would have you fire off an e-mail or text conveying your anger and disappointment. A modified belief would allow you time to talk with your friend to try to understand what happened from his point of view. When you counted on your friend to come over to comfort you after a loss and he couldn't, the tenth toxic belief would have you feel betrayed and desperate. Try to remember that you don't *need* someone there for you; you *want* him there, and you can wait to understand what was happening for him before you conclude that he just doesn't care about you.

When you're sad because of a loss, the sixth toxic belief would have you feel hurt that your friend went out and had fun. It's not true that a caring person must get very upset when someone else is hurt. Your friend can choose other ways of supporting you besides sitting with you for hours while you cry, at least after the first day or so. The first toxic belief can leave you resentful of a friend every time she disagrees with you, because you think you must have her approval to feel secure. Neither of you can be your own person in a friendship if you can't agree to disagree. The eighth toxic belief would have you feel your day is ruined if your friend couldn't join you for an activity. But happiness doesn't depend on outside realities; you must create it from within. When you can manage your beliefs and expectations, you can be a more fair and comfortable friend.

Keeping your Adult alert, you'll offer better friendship as you deliberately work to overcome these relationship-busting beliefs. You and your friend must both be willing to work at this for a strong friendship to flourish. Later in this chapter, I'll discuss how to cope when friendships become less rewarding or end. This discussion will assume that you've done your best to talk with your friend to understand and resolve problems like those described above, which occur due to toxic beliefs. I'll give your Adult more information about how to do this below.

Where do I stop and you begin?

The tenth toxic belief (that caring means being very dependent on another person and vice versa) fuels problems with *boundaries* between friends. Your primary boundary is like an invisible bubble around you which occurs out of the reality that only *you* can manage yourself. Your Wise Parent must help you remember that you can only change what's in your power to change. You can't change another person's feelings, behavior, attitudes or choices. If you believe caring means intense mutual dependence, you'll try to erase your boundaries and force yourself and the other person to feel, think and behave the same. Friendship is suffocated by this effort. It's impossible for two people to be that much alike and in tune for any length of time; our bubbles can only overlap a little.

The sixth toxic belief (that a caring person must get very upset over his loved one's problems) compounds the boundary confusion. When a friend confides about a loss at length and many times over a period of months, how can you remain supportive? Remember that you each have a boundary around your own experience and must keep your Child comfortable. You don't need to get upset for your friend each time you listen. If you do, you'll stop being supportive and begin giving unrealistic advice in your desire to relieve not just her pain, but also your own. Your friend must go through her own grief process. You don't have to grieve unless you've both had the loss, and even then your grief process won't be just like hers for many reasons. You can endure a friend's struggles and maintain your serenity by staying in your own bubble.

When both people in a friendship subscribe to these toxic beliefs, there will be intense ups and downs when their Adults are overwhelmed by Parent-Child confusion over how serious a problem is. These beliefs can quickly trigger you into fight-or-flight out of the belief that your life is threatened not only when you get upset, but also when your friend gets upset. As the drama escalates, the relationship can become very painful and dysfunctional. When alcohol or drug use further compromises both friends' Adult, serious risky behavior can actually develop, hooking their inner family into intense fight-or-flight activity. This is how violence or stalking behaviors can develop. Good boundary management can prevent all of this. Charles Whitfield offers profound and comprehensive guidance in his book *Boundaries and Relationships: Knowing, Protecting and Enjoying the Self.*[2]

If jealousy plagues you, repair your Wise Parent.

Two beliefs can lead you into feelings of jealousy. The most important one is the notion that you can only be happy if external events go as you wish (the eighth toxic belief). This belief makes you jealous over your friend. You can torture yourself every time a friend enjoys or values another person if you believe you can't be happy without her friendship. Your inner family may interpret the situation as life-threatening, and there you are in fight-or-flight mode again, stewing in your own misery. You may try desperate things to extract reassurance from your friend, when it is your own Adult that should be calming your inner family. There's really no danger to your survival if you lose someone. Have the courage to be yourself and give up trying to change yourself to keep a friend.

The next belief that can cause jealousy is the second toxic belief, which is that to feel worthwhile, you have to compete with someone else and win in one or several areas. This belief makes you envious of your friend. Should you doubt a friend's affection or respect because you feel less attractive, less intelligent, less talented or less socially graceful than she is? How can you then relax and enjoy her company? How can you genuinely support her when she gets recognition for an accomplishment? How can your friend assure you of her respect when you're lacking it for yourself? You will have trouble trusting her. Your Critical Parent, caught up in the second toxic belief, is riding you for not being as good as someone else and needs to be shut down. Have the serenity to accept the differences between you and your friends gracefully.

Jealousy undermines your relationship with your friend and with yourself. When you find yourself feeling jealous of anyone, it's time to look at what you value and what you've been working on in your own life. If your Wise Parent is strong, it will remind you that you're on your own journey, not someone else's. It will help you remember the thoughtful effort you've made to live according to your own values as you discover them in your life. It will help you remember your successes and appreciate your own strengths.

There's no reason to measure yourself against anyone else. It's comparing apples to oranges, because there's no one else like you. If you find your Wise Parent chronically lacking in its ability to support your self-esteem, it's time to reevaluate your belief system. Search for beliefs that allow you to be satisfied with the equipment you have for your life—your body, brain, talents and temperament. Otherwise, friendship will be very hard for you to receive or to give. You must judge your belief tree by its fruits. The ability to enjoy friendship is a precious fruit you need for mental fitness.

Avoid gossip to build trust and loyalty in your friendships.

Boundary confusion and jealousy combine to create problems with trust and loyalty. In addition to the boundary bubble around yourself, you need a second boundary around each of your relationships. This bubble is created out of the trust that forms as you connect in a special way with another person. You share things with each friend differently, and this is based on your reading of their capacity to understand you. You're a little different with each friend because of the unique intersection of interests, experience and personality traits between you.

When you talk about one friend with another, be careful to maintain the boundary for each friendship. Avoid trying to gain the approval of one friend who is present behind the back of another, as this is a manifestation of the first toxic belief. Gossip for entertainment is damaging. It doesn't have to involve any secrets and can simply be a disloyalty expressed in how you talk about a friend.

You can't sound off with just anyone who happens to be there when you're frustrated with a friend without damaging your friendship. Gossip destroys trust. The people you're talking to will trust you less, even if they're laughing with you. What will you say about them when they're not present? It will hurt the person whose confidence you've violated, and he *will* be told some of what you say to others. To prevent an eruption of anger about a friend, remain aware of your feelings in the friendship and process them in a timely manner with her.

However, there can be times among trusted friends that talking over a concern about another friend will help process a problem. This only works if the third party will keep your concerns to herself because she respects the boundaries of the friendship you're discussing. She can't go talk to your friend; you need to do that. She also can't discuss it with someone else. Women often find help in coping with their husbands with friends they trust in this way. In my experience I've noticed that men rarely seem to attempt this and have less support in dealing thoughtfully with their wives. When they understand boundaries, friends can help each other have more honest and sensitive relationships with others.

It would be amazing if we all could follow these rules diligently. However, we're not capable of keeping our Adult in charge all the time, for all the reasons discussed in parts 1 and 2. Therefore, you must keep reminding yourself that the third toxic belief (that we or others should be blamed and punished for failing to live up to our standards) is the most damaging of all for relationships. When you forget to keep your Adult in charge and make a mistake like betraying a friend's confidence in a weak moment, rest assured that a strong friendship will recover from it. It's a sign that you and your friend are mentally fit when you accept that there will be mistakes between you and you can trust each other to forgive them. Have the courage to keep trying and the serenity to accept that both of you will occasionally fail.

Assertive Skills Sustain Friendships

To keep a friendship free of simmering resentments, your Adult must be aware of when you need to express your annoyance, hurt or frustration to your friend. When your Critical Parent is under control, you can offer constructive feedback. You have several choices. You can choose to simply let an incident go because you aren't that disturbed, for example, that your friend kept you waiting a half hour for lunch. Perhaps you understand what happened or you were late the last time yourself. If this is a repeated offense, you should ask your friend to be more thoughtful of your time.

Many people won't try to talk things through; they fear the friend won't respond as they would like and they avoid confronting him, even gently. They don't realize they're subscribing to the third toxic belief when they say to themselves, "He should know this is disrespectful to me without my having to tell him. If he doesn't, he's not much of a friend and I just won't plan to meet with him any time soon." If the often-late friend asks what's wrong, most often this avoidant friend will say he's just been too busy to get together.

What does this avoidant behavior do to a friendship if it's repeated a few times? The level of trust plummets between the parties, the frequency of time shared is drastically reduced and the relationship cools, sometimes permanently. To maintain strong friendships, both parties need to accept that annoying or thoughtless behavior is bound to appear over the course of years on both sides of the friendship. You need to realize that your friends can't see their behavior the way you do unless you share how it looks and feels to you.

If you're reluctant to try to resolve a problem with someone who has been a solid friend, engage your Adult to examine why you won't put out this effort. If you're simply avoiding something that could be unpleasant, remember the negative consequences of the ninth toxic belief. Avoiding an opportunity to resolve a problem with your friend may result in the end of this valuable support in your life and all the happy times you could have together in the future. Consider seeing a counselor to help you understand where this exaggerated fight-or-flight reaction is coming from and learn how to communicate assertively in these situations. This avoidance is a damaging habit that will short-circuit your growth and may take you into Adult-blunting addictions.

Assertive confrontation—where each of you simply express how you see it and how it feels to you—is a necessary skill for solid friendships. Manuel Smith offers many entertaining illustrations of how to speak assertively in his book *When I Say No, I Feel Guilty*.[3] It's courageous to require yourself to try at least once to discuss your feelings of hurt or annoyance with your friend before you get irritable with him or distance from him. You'll often be surprised to learn what he was experiencing from his end. This effort won't hurt a solid relationship and will likely bring you closer through building more trust between you.

Incomplete Empathy Twists Communication

Two caring friends may have a very hurtful encounter when they fail to offer Adult-managed empathy. Consider the following example. Lisa tells Bobbi about how she felt at work when a coworker talked behind her back, saying damaging things.

Bobbi says, "I know how you feel! I was so humiliated by George when he put me down recently."

Lisa says, "I was angry; it wasn't my fault. Why do you think I should have felt embarrassed? You know I'm a perfectionist and work really hard at my job."

Bobbi responds, "You can be honest with me. You know that really made you feel like crawling into a hole."

Lisa, angry now, answers, "I *am* being honest with you; why do you think I'd lie? I was just *angry!*"

If Bobbi won't accept Lisa's self-description at this point and keeps trying to get Lisa to "own up," a real rift could occur in the relationship. When your friend tries to demand that you admit to feelings you don't have, you feel violated, not understood.

So what happened? Bobbi tried to empathize by walking in Lisa's shoes. She asked herself, "How would I feel in her place?" What she failed to do was make an adjustment between herself and Lisa based on her long-term knowledge of Lisa. That's what prompted Lisa to remind her about her perfectionism. Bobbi's error left Lisa feeling alone and invisible. Bobbi also refused to accept Lisa's correction of her interpretation, effectively calling her friend a liar. She tried to insist that Lisa had to have the same response Bobbi thought she'd have in a similar situation. This is where Lisa could feel violated and, if unconfident, confused and anxious. If Lisa gets mad and calls Bobbi self-absorbed, Bobbi may feel unfairly attacked, as she believes she tried to be a thoughtful friend and walk in Lisa's shoes. This dynamic happens frequently with couples.

What can you do to ensure that you give support that's actually supportive? Your Adult must realize that empathy is difficult if you only listen to your friend. You have to listen actively to be sure you're following what's really going on in your friend's mind. You must assume you *won't* easily understand, instead of jumping in, sure you've got it on the first try. You should clarify ambiguous comments by asking what was meant. Try to repeat what you thought you heard and ask if you've heard correctly. Give your friend time to sort out her thoughts without interruption.

Then she may feel your empathy and work to help you understand her.

This kind of communication is very powerful to help you connect when a friend is upset or excited and wants to share but lacks the Adult presence to do it well at that moment. Stay comfortable in your bubble with your feelings and let your Adult help her express all she needs to say. Paul Donoghue and Mary Siegel offer more suggestions for communication that builds friendship in *Are You Really Listening? Keys to Successful Communication.*[4] John Gottman and Joan DeClare provide wonderful insight and exercises for how to connect better in all your relationships in *The Relationship Cure: 5 Step Guide to Strengthening Your Marriage, Family and Friendships.*[5]

Individual Differences in Friendship

Your Adult needs to recognize when individual differences may be affecting a relationship. I discussed how these can interfere with Adult functioning in Part II, chapter 1. When you find that a friend has consistent problems with offering you the empathy or consideration you would like, consider whether she's actually able to do any better before you get angry or hurt. You would want your friends to do that for you if you had attention deficit disorder and couldn't stay organized or if you were a highly sensitive person who wanted more reassurance than most. Is your friend capable of remembering things as well as you are? How can *you* compensate if you're having trouble, say, remembering a meeting with a friend? Especially when significant individual differences occur, you and your friends will get along more easily if your Wise Parent dominates. Part III, chapter 4 deals with dating and describes how individual differences can interfere with close relationships, offering references that describe several examples in detail.

When Friendships Wane

It can be very painful to realize that you're losing a friend. To protect your Child, your Wise Parent needs to cope well when this happens. Remind yourself that losing a friend is not life-threatening. A racing heart or an upset stomach won't help when you have to face hurtful behavior by someone you counted as a friend. There are four key concepts to plant into your Wise Parent for this occasionally inevitable situation.

First, the ability to be honest and assertive is necessary for a healthy relationship. Was your friend willing to talk with you about behaviors that upset him? How did he respond when you asked him what was wrong? Try not to blame or punish people who won't level with you. And you can't force them to be open and honest with you, either. When a friend won't level with you, what might it mean? You have to guess, because he isn't telling you. You might wonder if you've done something so unforgivable that he won't try to discuss it; if you can guess what that might be, you could try to apologize.

If this pattern continues, however, you should consider whether this friend has changed his view of your friendship and chosen to distance himself from you. Hard as that may be at times, it's best for you to accept his choice. It's bad for your self-esteem and mental fitness to try to be close with someone who requires you to read his mind. His behavior also suggests that he assumes he can read yours and finds you in some way lacking. Any couples' therapist will tell you this pattern is both common and often very hard to break. Many people believe they can only feel loved if the other person can guess what they need. This is no doubt related to their subscribing to all the beliefs described above (the first, second, third, sixth, eighth, ninth and tenth toxic beliefs).

Second, you must be thoughtful about who deserves credibility as a judge of your behavior. Your Wise Parent must be very cautious about whose feedback you will take seriously. Someone who won't try to understand you or who can't see that you're doing the best you can doesn't qualify. This applies to acquaintances as well as friends. Of course, it's wise to *consider* all feedback, since you can't see yourself from the outside. But choose only the feedback that your own Adult and Wise Parent find helpful.

If you want to change some of your habits, like interrupting, being ten minutes late or forgetting things, regard the change as an experiment, rather than throwing yourself into it out of guilt. You may find that what you're trying to change is so difficult that you can no longer relax or be spontaneous. Increased anxiety won't help you be more sensitive to others. In this case it's best to seek friends who are more tolerant of your foibles because they value your strengths. Jan Yager offers excellent guidance for how to work with yourself and your friend when problems arise in her book *When Friendship Hurts: How to Deal with Friends Who Betray, Abandon and Wound You*.[6]

Third, what about when you find *yourself* wanting to reduce time with a friend? Search your feelings and evaluate whether you have built up a grudge because you didn't check out your assumptions. If that isn't the problem, check whether you're drawn to new friends because of a change in your interests or focus. You can choose to spend less time with a friend and allow your friend space when she needs it too. You can still maintain this friendship at a good level with less frequent one-on-one time, if both of you trust that you still value each other. When neither one of you jumps easily into fight-or-flight reactions due to feelings of deep rejection as circumstances change in a friendship, you can often remain friends for life.

Fourth, to risk opening up to a new person, you need to know how to limit or end a friendship when you no longer have time or energy for more friends. You also must accept that others may choose to do this with you. You can't keep up with everyone you like and value. As your life unfolds, you'll develop different interests or take on new responsibilities. The more you recognize this, the less hurt and anxiety you'll have when a friendship must end. Sometimes people take refuge in anger to avoid grief and will pick a fight to end a friendship. As noted in Part II, chapter 4, our society is phobic about sadness. You can accept the change in a friendship with serenity when your Wise Parent helps your Child feel okay, even if the other person expresses anger or hurt.

You can tell that a friend is distancing in a number of ways. You may find that the quality of communication between the two of you is uncomfortable, despite your efforts to clear up misunderstandings. Your friend may no longer initiate getting together or may cancel when it's time to meet. You also may feel less like being with your friend. If you've tried to resolve any issues between you, it's often best to let the friendship pass without confrontations or hand-wringing. This will make it easier to reconnect in the future. You should avoid lapsing into the third toxic belief and saying hurtful things to each other. People shouldn't be blamed or punished for not being able to maintain every friendship they begin. When your Wise Parent understands this, you can initiate a new friendship without concerns about how unpleasant it may be if one of you loses interest.

Flexible Friendship Requires a Secure Inner Child

As you navigate friendships from your earliest encounters through the ups and downs, draw on your own capacity to comfort and nurture yourself. When a close friend moves away or you lose a friend, how do you maintain yourself in the void? You can stay in contact at a distance and spend more time with other friends. Strengthen your Wise Parent to keep your Child feeling hopeful and open to new people. You'll still grieve the loss of the regular support and company of your friend.

Allow yourself to feel your sadness and don't try to minimize your pain by denying how much the friendship meant to you or finding fault with your friend. As described in Part II, chapter 4, you can only heal by completing your grief process. Getting stuck in anger or denial sets you up to be less open to making new friends. Anger or denial will also make you less likely to stay in touch with a distant friend. You may both need the special support your unique friendship provides you, even if you can't get together in person. It's a shrinking world after all.

Exercise your best self-care to bridge the gap caused by a change or loss in a friendship. Your Wise Parent can find lots of ways to distract and comfort your Child as you gradually come to accept your loss. Don't find ways to blame yourself or unleash your Critical Parent with all its bogus beliefs. When you find yourself pretty much alone in your life, don't assume that you're unlovable; this can happen to anyone along the way. Jan Yager offers her ideas for how to cope with the natural changes in friendships in her book *Friendshifts: The Power of Friendship and How It Shapes Our Lives*.[7]

Comfort yourself and remember the good times in your friendships. Learn anything you can from them to improve your future ones. You're on a journey to grow and learn. You don't know now what you'll know in a year or two as you keep exploring life and relationships. You didn't know before what you know now and you can't fairly chastise yourself for that. Your old friends have the same handicap and so will your new ones. If you bring to them an increased compassion, tolerance and openness, your friendships will unfold with greater ease. Begin to look for new friends among your acquaintances. Roger and Sally Horchow offer a lively discussion with lots of tips for how to further develop your friendship-making skills in *The Art of Friendship: 70 Simple Rules for Making Meaningful Connections*.[8]

Your understanding of friendship offers wisdom for all your relationships. Your Wise Parent will gradually internalize realistic beliefs about what to expect from people in various situations. Its wisdom will inspire you with the courage to confront another person when that's needed or the serenity to accept a situation when that's more suitable. For each choice your Adult must consider how much you and the other person value the relationship and how close you both want it to be. You'll gain confidence that you have the courage to hear feedback from others—even when it's painful—and use it to grow. You'll find the self-acceptance that allows you a basic serenity, even when you make mistakes or lose a friend despite your best efforts. This comfort in your Child will allow you to explore getting to know many people with enthusiasm instead of fear.

Here are some Wise-Parent beliefs to help you enjoy friendship:

- Gradually, I can learn when to express courage and when to find serene acceptance in my friendships.

- I don't need any particular person; I just need *some* friends.

- I don't need to fear either giving or receiving rejection; it's just part of life.

- Fight-or-flight bodily reactions signal that I've bought into some toxic beliefs.

- When another person is very angry with me, I don't have to join in or hide out. I can offer my skills to help us problem-solve with our Adults if she's open to this.

- It never hurts to clarify what's being communicated.

- I can find friends who want to have healthy, honest relationships if I hold out for this.

- I'm not responsible for keeping others comfortable, though I can offer caring support.

- If I don't have the power to change something or someone, I can't have the responsibility.

Notes

1. Gail Sheehy, *Passages: Predictable Crises in Adult Life* (1976; repr., New York: Ballantine Books, 2006).
2. Charles L. Whitfield, *Boundaries and Relationships: Knowing, Protecting and Enjoying the Self* (Deerfield Beach: Health Communications, Inc., 1993).
3. Manuel Smith, *When I Say No, I Feel Guilty* (New York: Bantam Books, 1975).
4. Paul J. Donoghue and Mary E. Siegel, *Are You Really Listening? Keys to Successful Communication* (Notre Dame: Sorin Books, 2005).
5. John M. Gottman and Joan DeClare, *The Relationship Cure: A 5 Step Guide to Strengthening Your Marriage, Family and Friendships* (New York: Three Rivers Press, 2001).
6. Jan Yager, *When Friendship Hurts: How to Deal with Friends Who Betray, Abandon or Wound You* (New York: Simon & Schuster, 2002).
7. Jan Yager, *Friendshifts: The Power of Friendship and How It Shapes Our Lives* (Stamford: Hannacroix Creek Books, 1999).
8. Roger & Sally Horchow, *The Art of Friendship: 70 Simple Rules for Making Meaningful Connections* (New York: Quirk Packaging, 2005).

III:2

Acquaintance Skills: Civility and Smooth Cooperation

Acquaintances are the people you encounter regularly but don't usually engage as friends. They include most coworkers, neighbors, and community organization members. These people make up most of your social environment. From them you'll eventually glean a few close friends and mentors. In relating to them, many concepts for friendship apply but with some key modifications. People bring different goals to these relationships. Your focus with them can't be to meet your deep needs for support, love and validation.

Your first concern must be to find ways to maintain *civility and smooth cooperation* at work and in your family, neighborhood and community. This means you must consistently lead with your Adult. You can't expect acquaintances to put your needs first half the time like your friends do. You're best prepared if you expect your needs to be very low on everyone's priority list. You must try to handle your own needs first and then join the world of acquaintances.

Dale Carnegie's *How to Win Friends and Influence People* hits the mark for how to manage these relationships.[1] He offers suggestions based on the cheerful acceptance that people admire others who show a sincere interest in *them*. For example, he states that people's own names are "the sweetest sound" they can hear. Learn your acquaintances' names and be sure you know how to pronounce and spell them correctly. While you should bring gentle acceptance and tolerance for others' self-absorption, you must overcome your own to thrive with acquaintances. Remember that you can't assume that any given person has your understanding of how to manage fight-or-flight reactions. You can be a leader in bringing mental fitness to your world if you practice what you've learned.

Social Anxiety and the Cloak of Invisibility

If you're anxious when you meet new people or have to participate with people you don't know well, try to recognize the reality of acquaintances. Our brain makes it so that it's "human" to be self-absorbed—not selfish, but focused primarily on ourselves and our own worries and goals. When you're anxious, you're self-absorbed and worried about how others will react to you. I like to recommend an experiment to my socially anxious clients. Walk over to an acquaintance and draw him out about what brings him here, his hobbies, family, work, etc. Let him talk for awhile and then venture a few relevant words about yourself. See how long it takes for him to look at his watch. You're really beginning to understand why the third toxic belief, where we blame people for their human frailty, is unreasonable if you can laugh about this. Guess what? You like it when people want to listen to you, too.

If you're socially anxious, it's a great relief to realize that others not only aren't thinking negative thoughts about you, they aren't really thinking much about you at all. As people mature beyond junior-high social Darwinism, in most cases they cease to focus on what they can ridicule about others to make themselves popular. Many socially anxious and highly sensitive people withdrew from others in junior high and assume people will always be like they were at age twelve. You can grieve that trauma and wake up to the world of more reasonable and fair-minded people. Of course there is the occasional perpetual adolescent who can be nasty, but most others won't look up to that person any more.

As an adult you can feel comfortably invisible among others much of the time unless you choose to engage someone in talking. There will be some outgoing people who will initiate talking with you. They'll also talk longer if you make the conversation about them. Just a few are aware of this concept—people who work in sales, for example—and they'll work to keep the conversation about you. When you realize someone else is trying to keep the conversation about you, you can laugh about it together and make more of a connection sometimes.

When you encounter the rare person who doesn't look at his watch but wants to have a shared conversation with you, enjoy him. He either just likes you for some reason, has more wisdom about human relating than most people, or both. He may not have time for another friend but he likely has the potential to be a friend. Remember that your goal is just to get along and be comfortable.

You can't be anxious about trying to land a friendship when you're relating to acquaintances. This requires repeated opportunities to meet, in most cases. You'll both know if you have so much to talk about that you'd like to meet again for coffee. You don't need to try to make it happen or avoid it, either. Civility and smooth cooperation give you a positive environment for friendship to grow naturally. Chapter 4 will describe how dating complicates this.

Boundaries Keep the Social Wheels Humming

As you lead with your Adult when relating to acquaintances, you're practicing how to maintain the boundary bubble around yourself while allowing others to maintain their own. Our bubbles most often touch lightly with those of acquaintances. With repeated contact they touch more and may even merge a little, but we don't get a second bubble around both of us until the relationship deepens into friendship. This isn't a rule, it's a description of how things work in reality.

Until that second bubble forms, stay mostly within your own bubble by limiting your Child and Parent communications. Once you've become friends, strengthen your mutual bubble by sharing your friendship away from the acquaintance group. This allows space for you to develop your special connection away from the interruptions, jealousies or insensitivities of others who may not appreciate your new friendship.

Among acquaintances don't share your grief, your joy, your judgments or your sympathy without your Adult considering the circumstances. Be more cautious about the possible misunderstandings of people who don't know you or trust you yet. Will they feel patronized if you offer comfort? Will they find you irritating if you giggle? Will they resent you for gloating when you express joy? Will they complain to the boss if you cry on the job?

You can share some of these feelings, but in limited ways. In fact you're expected to share some of yourself to make others comfortable with you. For good acquaintance-relating, always remember that others prefer conversations where they talk the most. Even then, limit the conversation if you think their Child has taken over and they may be uncomfortable with you later for having shared so much. Nurture them by noting the strengths you see in them that will help them cope.

Coworkers, supervisors and supervisees impact your comfort at work.

Let's focus first on work situations. As with all acquaintance relationships, civility and smooth cooperation are the primary goal. At work the cooperation is focused on producing the goods or services of the company. As with most acquaintance situations, you and the others involved aren't together just for fun. You need a paycheck, and the company needs your work. Out of consideration for this, your Adult must help you look beyond yourself at the impact of your behavior on everyone else and the goals you're trying to accomplish in the work situation.

In a business workers must be led to cooperate. Many problems occur when companies ignore management capability as they promote someone to supervise. Verbal abuse, negligence due to avoiding employee problems, sexual harassment and demoralizing communication all may occur when supervisors lack the training to lead. Proper training, like learning employee review guidelines or rules for a productive meeting, can give them techniques for their Adult to use. It may also include guidance for how they can maintain their Adult functioning under pressure. However, some supervisors seem to think positive feedback is for sissies. They don't respect the evidence that punishment won't build their people.

For decades many companies have paid to enroll employees in the Dale Carnegie Personal Relations Course to help them develop more confidence and compassion in relating to others. Employers must promote people with technical expertise into management positions, and the course helps employees gain the interpersonal skill they'll need. Carnegie's books *How to Win Friends and Influence People* and *How to Stop worrying and Start Living: Time-Tested Methods for Conquering Worry* [2] provide the basis for the course. Having marketed the course for two years in the mid-1970s, and seen the personal growth of the forty-some people in each class many times, I highly recommend it to everyone. It brought me to tears when I saw how beautifully this program creates the conditions for people to grow. The program's focus is based entirely on wise positive feedback and positive role models.

To function best at work, survey the realities you encounter there with your most objective Adult. You'll be more relaxed and focused on your job if you develop realistic expectations about what you can accomplish. There are avenues for you to offer input at work. However, there may be limited reception to what you offer, no matter how hard you try to communicate. Courageously experiment, but make sure your Wise Parent helps your Child not to be hurt or feel inadequate when you can't be heard. Your boss has the power to ignore employees who don't pull their weight and give an unfair load to you. Your boss may even believe she's complimenting you with the extra work, but over the long-term such compliments lead to burnout.

You need the serenity to accept what you cannot change until you decide to change jobs. It continually amazes me to see how inefficient our workplaces can be, despite all the management training that has been available now for decades. If you're frustrated daily by how others reduce your effectiveness, you'll damage your mental fitness and annoy your coworkers. Complaining repeatedly about the same issues doesn't help the day go by. No one likes a whiny Child. You're more likely to be promoted to a position where you can have a little more impact if you just offer smooth cooperation.

Getting along with coworkers is another challenge where your Adult and Wise Parent can guide you. As with other acquaintance relationships, you can't give your Child freedom to interact. If you become friendly with a sympathetic coworker and begin to pour out your heart about your boyfriend, your job frustration or your financial worries, she'll find this burdensome. She and your boss will lose respect for you, and this will make you insecure at work. You must get many of your needs for friendship met outside of work, though you'll see others who don't. Roland Barth offers clever and funny descriptions of workplace people and situations in his book *Lessons Learned: Shaping Relationships and the Culture of the Workplace.*[3] His humor will help you regain your Adult perspective, and his suggestions could help you navigate better at work.

If a coworker decides to harass you, there's a limit to how much help you may get from management. Assess the situation and plan how you can avoid feeding this worker's out-of-control Parent-Child parts. Don't respond with the hurt, fear or anger he's trying to elicit. Stay businesslike and cordial. Sometimes it's best to be breezy in your manner with difficult coworkers, giving them no idea you're at all affected by the unfriendly treatment. Steve Lurie offers a comprehensive program to build your relationships at work in his book *Connect for Success: The Ultimate Guide to Workplace Relationships.*[4] He describes boundary issues, differences in personal styles and communication skills for you on the job.

While all twelve toxic beliefs feed inappropriate reactions in a job situation, two may occur most often at work. The second toxic belief, which leads you to get upset if you can't perform better than someone else, can reduce cooperation. If you see that a coworker is more capable than you, it may hurt your self-esteem. But if you feel you performed better than a coworker who got the promotion you wanted, the seventh toxic belief comes into play, which leaves you feeling betrayed for not getting something you worked hard for. Clinging to this belief will only bring you misery in situations where many capable people are competing for a very few opportunities.

The seventh toxic belief develops another dimension when you're laid off or needed that promotion just to cover your bills. It's hard not to get hooked into fight-or-flight when you really do fear for the survival of your family's standard of living. You have every right to grieve work losses but you need to grieve them all the way through to preserve your mental fitness. Your Adult must help you to see that employers have no legally enforceable responsibility to offer you fairness or adequate pay, unless there's a very clear case of discrimination.

Even with discrimination there's often little recourse. Coworkers won't put their own jobs on the line very often to support a friend who's being denied opportunities because the boss shows prejudice over race, gender, age or sexual orientation. One local company had two class action lawsuits successfully brought against its managers for discrimination against women. Some clients I saw were paid three thousand dollars each time, which doesn't even come close to what their lack of promotions had cost them over the course of their careers. It was cold comfort for the hurt and anger they felt along the way as they were mistreated. Unions try to raise the bar in this area but have little power in many cases. It's self-protective not to get your expectations too high and keep serene in the recognition that you can gradually position yourself to leave. Of course, if the discrimination is blatant enough, you can sue your company, like Fiona in our chapter on grief (Part II, chapter 4).

With acquaintance relationships, including those with coworkers, your Adult must help your Child maintain its sense of your own worth. The focused goals of the situation allow less time for you to be known for who you really are, even when others may be interested. When your work is criticized, your Critical Parent may try to convince you there's something wrong with you; don't buy it. You may learn from this painful feedback how to do things differently the next time, or you may not have anything you could improve. Your Adult must make your final evaluation, not your boss.

Don't immobilize yourself with punishing self-criticism. Use the resources available to improve your position at your workplace, obtain a different one or find a new way to make a living. Think creatively about what kind of work would allow a greater expression of your strengths, unless you're already in your favorite kind of work. Remember that the seventh toxic belief is false; hard work only *improves your chances* of being rewarded, it doesn't *guarantee* a reward. But no one can take away the personal reward of knowing you did your best. Unfairness happens everywhere; personal satisfaction is all you can really count on. You'll keep yourself energized to improve your situation if you stay positive with self-talk kernels of corn. Find support outside work with liberal doses of friendship, family and private time to recharge yourself.

Neighbors can create a safe haven.

Unless you and another family planned to move next door to each other, you have with your neighbors another situation where civility and smooth cooperation are more important than becoming close friends. You're stuck with each other, just as you are with your coworkers. Boundary issues become concrete, and people's feelings of ownership can trump good acquaintance behavior. Keep your Adult in charge as you work for pleasant relationships with all your neighbors.

Neighbors most often want to get along and have a happy neighborhood. Neighborhood-watch parties or potlucks help busy families get to know each other. Exchanges of cups of sugar, plants or animal caretaking can make life run more smoothly. Neighbors can often be called upon to help out in an emergency. They can hold a key to let the police in if your burglar alarm goes off. They can drive you to an appointment, and you can drive them. This pleasant situation is created when neighbors bring realistic expectations and a commitment to be neighborly. It's great when you can easily become good friends with a neighbor, but proceed with this thoughtfully. It's better to have a good acquaintance with clear boundaries than a friendship turned sour right next door.

Of course, there are neighbors who have no concerns about civility or making the neighborhood a happy place. They are most often overwhelmed with their own concerns and coping badly. What can you do in this case? I remember taking down an ugly twelve-foot-tall fence between the first house we ever owned and a neighbor's home twenty feet away. We learned after we'd committed to buy the house that those neighbors were most uncivil. They had ugly fights laced with shouted profanities and two dogs that they shooed over to our yard to do their duty. One was a Doberman with a reputation for biting when you crossed him. The other was a dachshund named Heidi who needed to go potty at 3:00 a.m. every night but wouldn't come back until the wife hollered "Heidi! Heidi! Heidi!" for fifteen minutes. This woman once whacked our annoying but very sweet cat over the head with her dustpan, giving him a bad concussion. There was a pretty row of cottonwoods on the property line that they cut off at eight feet once when we were on vacation.

We never confronted them because we'd learned that our predecessors had feuded over their horrid behavior for the entire time they lived there. They finally put up the spite fence we removed because they couldn't stand to look at them anymore. We had as much peace as possible and never got bitten. We did call to see if we had any recourse about the trees—we didn't. We had no proof that the wife had hit our cat. We realized that it was best not to get into a screaming match with them over these things. I did enjoy a fantasy about hooking up loud speakers to shout "Heidi! Heidi! Heidi!" about an hour after her nightly calling every night but didn't follow through. Fantasies help discharge anger and give you a chance to laugh privately at the villains in your life. We were happy to move away, but the ugly behavior had diminished by then because we never fed it.

When faced with neighbors who are incapable of functioning with their Adults, you're best served by using your Adult for both of you. Think carefully about your strategy and don't get drawn in to their pain and abusiveness, unless you have to protect someone in their family or yours. Interfering won't get you any thanks, but there are some things you can't ignore just to keep the peace. Report any abuse of a child, elder or pet, drug activities or a terrorist plot being perpetrated next door; otherwise, keep your distance. Bill Adler offers hilarious and instructive stories about people who can't be civil and how their neighbors often shrewdly handled them in his book *Outwitting the Neighbors: A Practical and Entertaining Guide to Achieving Peaceful Coexistence with the People Next Door.*[5]

Churches, charities and clubs offer the potential for great satisfaction.

The same guidelines for acquaintance relationships apply in these situations, where there's often less clarity about who's in charge than at work but more need for active smooth cooperation than with neighbors. As you consider joining a group, evaluate whether you can accept its goals and structure or lack of structure. You may in time be able to lead a group in a different direction or improve its structure, but don't join it with that in mind. In most groups there are already people who have invested a lot of themselves to make it just the way it is now.

There will be cliques, favoritism, turf issues and all the behaviors people engage in when they aren't clear about what they seek when they join a group. Your Adult functioning can help you be more comfortable. It may win you the respect and trust of some group members, who may want you to take some leadership role because you're level-headed. Refrain from doing this until you've earned the right in the minds of most of the people in the group by pitching in with the more humble chores the group must do.

Many people who join groups don't have enough support outside to maintain their Adults while they participate. A minister once said to me that a church is a "hospital for souls." If you know this going in, it will help keep your Critical Parent from popping out when others appear self-centered in what they do. They may behave like adolescents in trying to form friendships, getting jealous or hurt easily. They may take on more than they can handle in order to get recognition. They may become hurt, passive-aggressive or bitter when even the smallest task they manage is shifted to someone else. They may seek to be the group leader's favorite, because their own Wise Parent is inadequate to nurture their Child.

You'll note that in all these cases, the less people can contain their fight-or-flight tendencies, the more intense their reactions will be. Observe the dynamics of the group before you commit to it. Whether you want to help kids in a charity, play cards with a bunch of neighbors or worship in a friendly church, keep in mind that leadership by people who lack Adult self-management can ruin the experience. Participation by some of these people is inevitable. Any of us can find ourselves without adequate support at times in our life, and we'll bring our needy selves into groups to get more support. If your Adult can predict how your Child might get upset in the situation, you'll have a better chance of maintaining yourself in a well-led group.

Despite all the potential difficulties you may encounter in community groups, there's potential for great satisfaction. Charles A. Bennett describes how volunteers thrive from helping others in his book *Volunteering: The Selfish Benefits.*[6] When you connect to your wider community, you meet people who can enrich your life in untold ways. Increasing the number of people you meet is the only way to expand your circle of friends and discover people who may help you grow in new ways. Take with you reasonable expectations, keep your Adult and Wise Parent active and have new adventures.

How to Express Civility and Smooth Cooperation

Below is a summary of the things to remember when you participate with people who are present for other reasons than to get to know each other. See appendix A if you want to refer to the basic form of the twelve toxic beliefs.

A. Remember the limits of the group's purpose and stay focused on it.

B. Maintain civility through good acquaintance manners.

　　1. Express sincere interest in the others involved.

　　2. Be wise with what you share about yourself.

　　3. Remember your boundaries and develop friendships outside the group.

C. Keep your Adult alert for toxic beliefs that would prevent smooth cooperation, such as:

　　1. Intensely feeling you must have someone's approval.

　　2. A strong need to compete with someone else, despite your intent to cooperate.

　　3. Tendencies to blame or criticize others or feel shame yourself when there are problems.

　　4. Excessive worry about relationships or projects in the group.

5. Holding another person's past behavior against him, despite evidence of change. Refusing to try something new because you failed to do it well in the past.

6. Expecting people to become very upset if someone in the group has a problem.

7. Extreme disappointment if you work hard for something that others don't appreciate.

8. Blaming depressed or anxious feelings on your experience in the group.

9. Procrastinating about following through with commitments in the group.

10. Expecting others to be dependent on you and you on them beyond group needs.

11. Demanding more recognition than others in the group.

12. Cutting corners when you promise to carry out a group task.

Acquaintance activities give you a chance to practice your Adult skills for managing your inner family in a wide range of situations. This practice can build your confidence, self-esteem and awareness of what your unique talents can offer others. This growth prepares you to have mentally fit, closer relationships and satisfaction in your community connections.

Notes

1. Dale Carnegie, *How to Win Friends and Influence People* (1936; rev. ed., New York: Simon & Schuster, 1981).

2. Dale Carnegie, *How to Stop worrying and Start Living: Time-Tested Methods for Conquering Worry* (1944; rev. ed., New York: Simon & Schuster, 1984).

3. Roland S. Barth, *Lessons Learned: Shaping Relationships and the Culture of the Workplace* (Thousand Oaks: Sage Publications, 2003).

4. Steve Lurie, *Connect for Success: The Ultimate Guide to Workplace Relationships* (Lawrence: Empowered Work Publishing, 2009).

5. Bill Adler, Jr., *Outwitting the Neighbors: A Practical and Entertaining Guide to Achieving Peaceful Coexistence with the People Next Door* (New York: The Lion's Press, 1994).

6. Charles A. Bennett, *Volunteering: The Selfish Benefits* (Oak View: Committee Publications, 2001).

III:3

Relatives and Expectations

Your relatives can also be considered either friends or acquaintances, but with a twist. Especially with close relatives, people usually *expect* to enjoy the benefits of friendship without considering what real friendship requires. Just by virtue of being in the same family, people expect their relatives to be there for each other, giving time, energy and sometimes financial help when a family member needs it. Boundaries and bubbles are often trampled because you somehow owe a family member your support. Your Adult can observe all this and say it's unreasonable, even impossible. But how can you satisfy your Child's need to feel connected to your family and your Parent's commitment to loyal and responsible participation? There's the twist.

Fortunately, acquaintance skills for civility and smooth cooperation can ease the family ties that bind. As your connections with relatives evolve over the years, some may become real friends. Family gatherings can provide you with the regular contact that allows a relationship to grow. Meanwhile, you can offer your family civility and smooth cooperation, no matter how they behave. You can choose to confront an unruly or mean-spirited relative using your best assertive skills, just as you would with a neighbor or coworker. Your Adult should weigh the possible consequences and decide whether it's really worth it.

Adult Coping with Parental Expectations

"Kids always want to be accepted for who they are but never want to accept their parents for who *they* are." That was how my complaints to a therapist about my father (when I was in my thirties) were greeted. After catching my breath, I considered what he was saying. This insight saved my relationship with my dad for the next thirty years. So who are these parents we're supposed to accept for who they are? What do parents want from their kids? They want more respect from their kids than from their friends. They expect to be honored for the sacrifices they made when their children needed care.

Rarely, negligent or abusive parents will acknowledge that they don't deserve their kids' respect. But most parents remember what their kids don't even know about: those years when it took more than they felt they had to cope, the times when they were scared, broke or alone and still tried their best to provide care or the times when they were not so functional due to emotional problems or financial stress. They often can't walk in their kids' shoes at all. Most parents just want respect, loyalty and love, no matter what they did or what they do.

If you keep hoping your parents will change and feel you must confront them, don't expect them to thank you for the feedback. Remember, parents don't really want their kids to teach them how to be. Since you don't have the power to change your parents, you don't have the responsibility, even if your parents are making themselves miserable. If your parents really want friendship, they'll listen to feedback about how they can help you feel more comfortable in the relationship. Don't ask them to change their political or religious beliefs or their personal style any more than you would a friend. As an adult living separately, you do get to choose how much time and energy you'll extend to your parents. Realizing that you have the right to limit your time with them can relieve a lot of your tension.

Abusive parents reveal in therapy their intense beliefs that their children should anticipate their needs and read their minds. They lack the ability and understanding necessary to meet their own needs. They feel like abandoned children as they manage their kids and lash out through desperation. Some are cruel due to deep feelings of anger and worthlessness that grew out of their own parents' cruel abuse of them. Even when these parents recognize something is wrong, they have great difficulty developing a functional Adult and adequate Wise Parent in therapy. It's hard for them to trust a therapist, when their own parents had been so destructive. Therapy takes years, and relief for their kids is neither consistent nor certain along the way. Of course, most abusive parents never recognize their own problems enough to seek therapy; alcohol or drugs often handle their pain instead.

If your parents were very abusive to you, you must unburden yourself of feeling the guilt they tried to lay upon you from your youngest age. It was unreasonable for them to demand that you take care of them by not making mistakes or acting up when you were upset. You couldn't even take care of yourself. If even skilled therapists would have had trouble helping them, how could a three-, six-, twelve- or fifteen-year-old kid? Why should a young adult struggling to find his way in the world or an older adult trying to create a healthy family feel bad because an abusive parent still thinks he should? Your Adult must revise your beliefs about what you should have done to help your family as a child. Then your Adult must re-evaluate what you actually can do for them as an adult. Susan Forward describes abusive parents and how to overcome their influence in her book *Toxic Parents: Overcoming Their Hurtful Legacy and Reclaiming Your Life.*[1] Karyl McBride's book *Will I Ever Be Good Enough? Healing the Daughters of Narcissistic Mothers,*[2] offers insight that can help you understand where some of your lingering self-doubt came from and how to cope with a narcissistic parent as an adult.

I once heard of a support group for parents of children with severe developmental deficiencies. They supported each other to grieve the children they should have had in order to accept fully the kids they did have. This application of the grief process can help you find serenity in your relationship with your parents. That same disconcerting therapist I saw in the 1970s commented that "with family, anger doesn't bring you peace; only acceptance does." It takes courage to let yourself feel the sadness that comes when you realize your parents somehow couldn't be the parents you should have had. This sadness helps dissipate your anger and carry you into the serenity of acceptance. You may accept your parents' efforts a little more if some day you struggle to be the kind of parent you wish you could have had.

What Kids Expect from Their Parents

What do you want from your parents? As we grow up, most of us wish our parents could become our friends. Review the description of friendship in Part III, chapter 1 and see if you don't want those feelings of trust and appreciation between you and your parents. Then review the twelve toxic beliefs listed in appendix A. It may have been easy to see that your parents' expectations can be unreasonable. How crazy are your own? The first toxic belief, that they must have their parents' approval, is the one that most damages kids' ability to be friends with their parents. Kids don't just want acceptance from their parents; they seek validation, respect and pride in their accomplishments.

You needed to depend on your parents when you were a vulnerable child, and you haven't lost those brain connections. Only with the most diligent Adult work can you rewire your inner family to believe that you don't actually need your parents' approval to be content and confident anymore. You don't even *need* their respect. But you'd prefer to have it, especially if you want to maintain some connection with your family throughout your life. Your own Wise Parent is now in charge of your self-respect, and your parents are only consultants who may or may not have good suggestions.

What do you automatically expect of your parents because they're your mom and dad? Have the courage to look carefully at this. You want respect for who you are, but what are you showing your parents that tempts them to correct you? Are you keeping your Adult in charge to prevent your Indulgent Parent from leading you into chaos when your parents aren't there to guide you? How are you handling your finances? Will you ask your parents to bail you out? Are you limiting your alcohol, gambling and computer use to protect your Adult functioning? An addiction will draw in caring parents to challenge your choices. Your Child wants to enjoy freedom, but your Wise Parent needs to create safe limits for it.

If you're being responsible and managing your life pretty well, you may still expect things from your parents that you wouldn't from a friend. Engage your Adult to recognize when this happens to keep friendship possible with your parents. Don't call them only when you want some help and expect them not to feel used. Don't ask them to put your schedule or activity ahead of their own, as they would have when you were their dependent child. Keep it fair between you and consider their need for a life of their own. Don't expect your parents to babysit; plan with them for what they feel comfortable doing and be flexible. Find other sitters to rely on as well. Don't borrow things and return them damaged. Don't expect them to pay the bill when you go out to dinner with them; go dutch. If you treat them with the same respect you'd offer a valued friend, you may experience more respect from them.

After chiding me about my expectations of my father, my old therapist told me that I needed to take control of the relationship. He advised that I consider what I should offer as a good daughter; then I should practice that no matter what my father did. This would prevent the action-retaliation pattern that had been putting us both into fight-or-flight. He told me to send the Father's Day card I'd announced that I wouldn't send, call my dad (who lived across the country) regularly and visit as I felt I should. That way I could feel good about myself, even if he wasn't satisfied with me. I learned to prepare myself for our calls by saying to myself, "If there's anything you feel like saying that's in the slightest way critical, bite your tongue." My developing civility and acceptance very gradually helped us to have a warm, mutually respectful relationship, if not the friendship I would have liked.

Parent-Child Relating over the Years

As your kids evolve through their adult life, changes occur in both of you that can improve your relationship if you stay somewhat connected. Your arrogant, ungrateful teenager discovers a world where he also doesn't receive the respect and special treatment he thought he should get. When your kids become parents, they may realize how hard it was at times when you raised them. They'll want their kids to have a loving relationship with you and may even request some babysitting so they can have an evening out together. They may become more deeply confident and require less cautious communication from you. Friendship may grow if you offer consistent and respectful care, setting limits as with any friend. I'll discuss more on parenting adult children in the last chapter, "Mental Fitness and Parenting."

Your parents may lose some of their arrogance as they bump up against work problems and losses of friends and family. They may come to value your opinion and expertise as you become more capable of navigating your new world than they are. When a civil and cooperative kid helps his parent with a computer problem, many walls can begin to crumble. When a civil and cooperative parent asks for help and expresses appreciation, many wounds can heal. Your Adult can stay alert to signs your parents are changing over the years, and you can experiment with new ways of connecting.

When parents need their kids to care for them, both may come to see each other in new ways. Several clients who were abused or neglected as children have remarked that they finally got to be friends with their parents while they cared for them in their final years. Eleanor Cade offers guidance for how to cope in this situation in her book *Taking Care of Parents Who Didn't Take Care of You: Making Peace with Aging Parents*.[3] Even if your parents did take good care of you, their old age may make things difficult. Grace Lebow and Barbara Kane give a comprehensive view of how to manage this stage of your relationship in their book *Coping with Your Difficult Older Parent: A Guide for Stressed-Out Children*.[4]

Try sharing your knowledge of the twelve toxic beliefs with your family when a belief emerges as a problem. The third toxic belief (where you blame each other for failing to meet your expectations for being good family members) will be on everyone's list. It's not your parents' fault that they don't recognize expectations that are unreasonable any more than it's your fault for having the same problem. As you learn, you can try to lead your family to a more reasonable, kind and fair system. If you can admit you had an unreasonable expectation, perhaps your kid or parent can laugh and admit to one as well. My son had to laugh a lot at me when I suggested my ideas for what to wear to a job interview as a 3-D graphic artist. I had to laugh at my thinking I knew more than my thirty-five-year-old son did about his field just because I'm his parent.

Kids are often more willing to tolerate their parents' inappropriate intrusions than parents are to accept their kids' ideas. I've seen how teenagers, even while still chafing at their parents' attempts to manage them, can begin to apply some reason to their expectations. They begin to see their parents as people struggling to cope with their lives. I'm often impressed by how well young people can describe their parents' probable feelings when the parents exhibit annoying or even hurtful behaviors. Often they just need to be encouraged to engage their budding Adult and think about it. If you want to be friends with your adult kids, bite your tongue more often or at least laugh at yourself when you don't.

If either the parents or the kids in your family get caught up in an addiction, Adult-to-Adult sharing about beliefs and expectations will be stunted. Alcohol, drugs, gambling or computer addictions knock out Adult functioning and prevent Wise-Parent growth. If addiction is involved, friendship will be curtailed and even acquaintance connections will be strained. You can only prevent your own addiction but you do have some influence in your family. Get help and use it thoughtfully. With your children, of course, you have the most influence through your own example of coping with life sober.

How can you reboot your connection to your kids or parents? Adopt acquaintance-level behavior until it becomes clear whether a real friendship is possible. You can do this at any time in your life, if you wish. Even if your parents or kids are as dreadful as the neighbors who sent their dogs over to poop on my lawn, you can find ways to stop feeding the overcharged exchange. You may need to grieve thoroughly the loss of the parents or kids you wish you had to accept the ones you have. You may need to install loving friends in their place to support you. If you find yourself getting upset, ask yourself, "Am I really still *surprised* that my parent/kid is behaving this way?" Then laugh at your human folly in always embracing the idealized family. That will calm you down, allowing you to remain civil and cooperative.

Sibling Relationships

You're brought up to expect that you'll be lifelong friends with your brothers and sisters. Families with kids who share unselfishly and empathically from a young age are idealized on television and the movies. Some people do enjoy close connections with their siblings, and this is a wonderful support for their mental fitness. When parents function pretty well, kids can get most of their needs met. When parents are stressed, kids have to compete for affection, support and validation that are in short supply. This, along with parental modeling of stress-driven harsh discipline, can create a Darwinian environment where kids become abusive towards each other in their efforts to grab what they need.

Whatever the kids' family dynamics were growing up, they need not carry their attitudes and grievances into their adult relationships with each other. Ideally parents would teach their kids how to treat each other kindly and with respect. When parents can't do that, kids often blame each other for what happened as they grew up together. You may need to grieve the childhood you should have had in order to accept your siblings as an adult. Then you can approach your grown-up siblings without residual anger, which could prevent civility and smooth cooperation. For friendship to unfold, you'll both need to spend time together and build trust, just as with any other prospective friend.

The same twelve toxic beliefs that impact your other relationships are at work here. Consider the second toxic belief, where you can't feel worthwhile if you aren't the best at something. When your sister excels in math and your brother is great at football while you're just enjoying your friends and doing OK in school, you need wise parents to help you appreciate your worth. Your parents don't need to compare you to your siblings and scold you for not being as outstanding. If that happens, you may resent your parents and your siblings and doubt yourself. Cathy Jo Cress and Kali Cress Peterson offer ideas for how to find new ways of relating to your siblings as an adult in their book *Mom Loves You Best: Forgiving and Forging Sibling Relationships.*[5] Stephen Bank and Michael Kahn explore how to understand and develop your relationship with your siblings in their book *The Sibling Bond.*[6]

Other beliefs play a similar divisive role. If you feel you must have your parents' approval to be happy (the first toxic belief), you may try to get more recognition than your siblings to feel more worthy. You may even try to undermine a sibling's relationship with your parents to ensure your supply of this desperately needed approval. Of course, you don't need anyone else's approval to feel worthy; you just need a strong Wise Parent within yourself to stay comfortable.

You may disapprove of choices your siblings make and forget what positive things could help you stay connected. The third toxic belief feeds your tendencies to be upset with your parents and siblings for not measuring up in some way. When directed at you, it eats away at your personal confidence, making your Child insecure and more likely to crave your family's approval. Mental fitness allows you to feel good in your own skin and improves family relationships.

Civility and smooth cooperation can keep you connected long enough to allow you and your siblings to evolve your relationship and possibly become friends, if you weren't before. If your siblings need help, you'll most often want to offer it, to a reasonable degree, just because they're family. How to determine what's reasonable depends on many factors. Your sibling may treat you like a parent, approaching you with the same Indulgent-Parent-inspired expectations. A therapist can help you sort out what you can do and where you need to set some limits with siblings who threaten to drain your resources. Elisa Albert edited the book *Freud's Blind Spot: 23 Original Essays on Cherished, Estranged, Lost, Hurtful, Hopeful, Complicated Siblings*, which may give you more insight into your sibling relationships.[7]

Extended Family Relationships

With most of your own and your spouse's relatives, if you're married, you have acquaintance-level relationships. You may have some who are friends, but even with them it's good to remember acquaintance rules. You should keep your Adult tuned for civility and smooth cooperation, just like you do at work. This is because you're in some sense stuck with your relatives too. You can cut your ties with an abusive relative, but often at some cost to the feelings of others in the family. The fact that abuse can destroy family ties is a major reason why families try to deny it.

Short of abuse, you'll likely have some relatives who don't know about boundaries or trying to walk in anyone else's shoes. Underestimate how much you can change about a relative and be pleasantly surprised if someone uses a carefully phrased suggestion of yours. Mostly, you should pray for the serenity to accept what you can't change. As with neighbors, all you have to do with most relatives is get along for short periods of time.

In extended family relationships, people also may want to expect more from family than from other acquaintances. Because you're my cousin, I can ask you to let my son stay the summer with you. Because you're my niece, you should babysit for my kids and give me a discount. Because you're our daughter-in-law, you should have us over for a nice Sunday dinner a couple times a month. We expect you to bring gifts and your kids all dressed up to Christmas, Thanksgiving and Easter and to bring gifts for all the cousins too.

You may want to believe that your family cares about you just because you're related. But they often don't know you very well. They may not share your values or wisdom about friendship. Over the years you may develop deep caring for them anyway. Maintain a comfortable connection by offering dependable civility and smooth cooperation. Encourage them to talk to you, be thoughtful about what you share of yourself and remain positive or quietly retreat if they become negative. What works with neighbors and coworkers can help you stay comfortable with your family over the years.

You may feel like having big angry confrontations at times, but these rarely have the desired effect of straightening out the self-centered, insensitive boor you couldn't take one more time. He is not likely to change, and people will still invite him to the next holiday dinner. You'll be all anxious about it beforehand, but you'll want to visit with your cousin Joe, so you'll have to go. Save yourself the grief and just leave the room quietly if you need a break.

There are still limits you should set on what you agree to do with your relatives. You have a boundary around your marriage and your immediate family. You're responsible for them first. You need to be assertive with relatives who try to get more of your time and attention than you can reasonably give. If you're single, you still have this right. Try to find a compromise and express love as you set your limits. If they sulk or manipulate, don't give in. Unless they're of a mind-set to be bullies and abusive, they'll adjust because they do want a relationship with you. If they won't, you'll have a limited relationship or none at all, and that might be the best for you and your kids.

From your end as well, it's important to be mindful of what you're expecting of your favorite aunt, your generous grandparents or your cousin with the cozy cabin on the lake. Be a good acquaintance or friend and don't assume, for example, that they can offer this Christmas what they did in the past. They also must consider first their immediate family or personal concerns. Be considerate and discuss the needs on both sides before you make your plans. If they can't accommodate you, don't complain; just accept them with serenity.

In-Law Relationships

Acquaintance skills are essential in relating to the relatives of your spouse, kids or stepparents. Get along with them because you want to support your loved ones in getting what they need. Like neighbors or coworkers, these people will include some who may become friends and some you simply tolerate. The difference with these relatives is that they may expect more from you because you are now family. You may also do that with them if your Adult isn't paying attention. Even more than with your own relatives, you usually don't know each other. Your mother-in-law may take awhile to warm up to you. A sister-in-law may be threatened in some way. Your new son-in-law may lack social graces. So be a great acquaintance and let the relationships unfold.

Meanwhile, as you connect with in-laws on both sides, always keep in mind the words offered frequently by newspaper advice columnists: let the blood relative deal with her own family when there's a problem. This advice is often very difficult to heed. However, consider the reality that families prefer to deny problems as long as they can. In most cases, the more serious the problem, the more insistent the denial. Nothing unites a combative family like a common outside enemy.

You don't want to be in that spot. So don't call your daughter-in-law's mother to ask her to correct her daughter's manners at the table. Don't scold your husband's uncle for his drunken misbehavior at the last memorial service. Don't tell your mother-in-law your husband is too busy to help her fix the leak in the bathroom. Don't tell your sister's husband he needs to help with the dishes. If you can't persuade your spouse, child or sibling to speak firmly to his or her relative, try to find a way to avoid letting that person's behavior bother you.

This will not always be possible, or there may be times when both you and your close family member will need to confront a relative together, because the behavior is too harmful. Just be prepared, and prepare your family, for the in-law's blaming the whole problem on you. This is especially difficult when, for example, a husband is avoidant of conflict and won't stand up to his parents, who love to drop in for dinner unannounced. If your daughter is being mistreated by her husband but is afraid to stand up to him, you may risk your relationship with her if you confront him and could endanger her as well. If your sister confides that her new in-laws treat her like a doormat, encourage her to work with her husband to deal with them. By no means should you mention the problem when you see her mother-in-law at the next church function. Recognize the boundaries of your relationship with those who confide in you, as well as the possibility you may be the scapegoat in these situations with in-laws.

If you can't quite let go of the third toxic belief (that people who don't behave well should be blamed or punished) or the feeling that you *can't stand it* when a loved one is hurt, the best solution is a referral to a family counselor. Let the counselor sort out the crazy in-laws or the nonassertive spouse. Let the counselor somehow engage the family in working on the problem, if that's possible. It's cheaper than divorce or moving to New Zealand and better for your health than antidepressants or high blood pressure medicine. But don't expect them to go to the counselor you recommend, even if they asked you for the referral.

The third toxic belief is the main problem when you can't find serenity or acceptance with family members. After you've summoned the courage to try to change what you really feel you must, your Wise Parent should help you feel serene. But if a relative doesn't respond as you'd hoped, you may just be angry. They not only upset you, they shake up the whole family connection. This is hard to accept if you're close to your family. Ironically, your anger and that of others who embrace the third toxic belief give this abusive or selfish relative more power than his ugly behavior. Seek counseling for *yourself* to discover less confrontational ways to handle difficult relatives. Susan Forward offers good suggestions for how to cope with in-laws in her book *Toxic In-Laws: Loving Strategies for Protecting Your Marriage*.[8]

Wise-Parent Protection from Toxic Families

Many clients come in struggling to manage problems with their families of origin. We explore how they can try to maintain good acquaintance relationships with their family, and they consider whether friendship could be possible with any of them. After they've tried new approaches for a while, some conclude that they must keep considerable distance from their family. This leaves them feeling like there's something wrong with them because they can't be friends with people in their family. Some are confused by the fifth toxic belief, which is that their past experience with their family dooms them to fail in relationships.

The fifth belief is false for these reasons:

- Your Adult can become capable of defining what is fair for you in relating to your family.

- Your Wise Parent can comfort and support your Child without them.

- Your Critical Parent can be taught not to echo their disapproval of you.

- Your Child can thus be freed of unreasonable guilt and energy-sapping anger.

- Mentally fit friends can offer you the loving and fair feedback you need to grow.

- With this, your Adult can help your Wise Parent guide your Child into feeling good about itself, peaceful and happy.

- Your Adult can update your beliefs and put your past expectations of your family behind you.

Notes

1. Susan Forward with Craig Buck, *Toxic Parents: Overcoming Their Hurtful Legacy and Reclaiming Your Life* (New York: Bantam Books, 1989).
2. Karyl McBride, *Will I Ever Be Good Enough? Healing the Daughters of Narcissistic Mothers* (New York: Free Press, 2009).
3. Eleanor Cade, *Taking Care of Parents Who Didn't Take Care of You: Making Peace with Aging Parents* (Center City: The Cade Group, 2002).
4. Grace Lebow and Barbara Kane, *Coping with Your Difficult Older Parent: A Guide for Stressed-Out Children* (New York: Avon Books, 1999).
5. Cathy Jo Cress and Kali Cress Peterson, *Mom Loves You Best: Forgiving and Forging Sibling Relationships* (Far Hills: New Horizon Press, 2010).
6. Stephen Bank and Michael Kahn, *The Sibling Bond* (1982; rev. ed., New York: Basic Books, 1997).
7. Elisa Albert, *Freud's Blind Spot: 23 Original Essays on Cherished, Estranged, Lost, Hurtful, Hopeful, Complicated Siblings* (New York: The Free Press, 2010).
8. Susan Forward with Donna Frazier, *Toxic In-Laws: Loving Strategies for Protecting Your Marriage* (New York: HarperCollins, 2001).

III:4

Dating Fantasies and Realities

You might say it's unsporting to engage in dating with your Adult in charge. Isn't it supposed to be fun and spontaneous? Do you want to be that girl with the list of questions for every guy you meet? How can you find your soul mate when your Adult is controlling everything? Don't you believe in love at first sight? It seems everyone is thoroughly confused about what dating is about and how to do it, including therapists who are supposed to help people avoid the worst choices. This chapter will help you identify goals to direct your search for the right match. We'll explore how problems seem to arise as you make your choices, though science doesn't have dependable answers for how to overcome these. Then I'll describe the process of how to date to improve your chances of finding someone suitable. This is a task requiring skill, perseverance, self-confidence, commitment and, unfortunately, a hefty dose of good luck.

What Are You Looking For?

When I was in eighth grade, my English teacher, had the class write a description of the perfect mate. I still keep that essay to remind me of how ill-prepared a person can be for reality. You need to write that essay or make a list of what you require and what you want in a mate. Keep reviewing and revising it as you go through your experience of dating. You eventually may arrive at something that's both possible and desirable for an outcome. Don't just toss it out because you're afraid that if you're too fussy you'll never find anyone. This listing technique will help your self-observing Adult stay involved despite the excitement and pressure of your adolescent Child when you meet someone attractive.

Let's look at both short- and long-term goals. Patricia Love describes the first stage of a relationship very well in her book *The Truth about Love: The Highs, the Lows, and How You Can Make It Last Forever.*[1] Read this to learn what crazy things happen to your brain when you start to fall in love with someone; forewarned is forearmed. You will want to have these feelings about Mr. Right. It's perfectly sound to want chemistry with the person you hope you'll feel attracted to for decades. While you're meeting new people, this will be one of your first criteria for whether you have more than one or two dates. Your Adult and Parent parts should have no problem with this. What you must keep in mind is that now and for the rest of your life, you're likely to feel some of this chemistry with many people; there isn't just one person who can turn you on.

Therefore, chemistry is necessary but not sufficient for determining whom you should date. Much harder to determine is what kind of life partner this new acquaintance would make. Match.com, eHarmony and other Internet dating sites try to help people sort this out but often don't succeed. Work with your own list of qualities and interests. Add to that some questions that will give you insight into the person's functioning. What have you been working on to make yourself into a strong person who copes gracefully with stress and adversity? Your partner should be working on these things too. He should not be easily overwhelmed or quickly angered. He should not rely on addictions to fill time or handle stress. Those two requirements eliminate a lot of candidates.

Your prospect should have the genuine confidence that allows her to appreciate and comment positively about your strengths. Remember, that's how you build new behaviors—with positive feedback. If you want to keep growing, choose a partner who will encourage this in the small ways that count. If she accepts your positive feedback too, she's open to a good kind of equality in the relationship. This is one sign she may be adequately trusting and not too controlling for genuine intimacy. You'll want to see other signs of this.

Of course, you'll expect to have a guy treat you with respect by listening to what you say thoughtfully, making good eye contact and keeping his remarks positive and relevant. Can he talk about his concerns in a simple, respectful manner? Does he expect you to work things out with him verbally? Or do you find yourself trying to guess what he likes or wants because he won't communicate? Imagine how that would play out over the course of a couple of decades.

How does your prospect talk about other people? Her parents and siblings? Previous relationships? Friends? The people you both encounter? Do her comments reveal thoughtfulness and insight? Is she judgmental, critical, bitter or angry? Which of the twelve toxic beliefs do you think she might hold without knowing it? Does her Wise Parent offer new insights for you? Does her Adult lead when you problem-solve together? Can her Child play, or is she dominated by a harsh Critical Parent? Is her Child fair, or does she seek to be put first because of a strong Indulgent Parent? You have these concepts now; don't suspend them just because you want to find your soul mate.

How does your prospect interact with others? Review the skills needed to have positive acquaintance relationships. Does he maintain civility and smooth cooperation? Does he demonstrate a genuine interest in others and enjoy a wide variety of people? He doesn't have to like a crowd; he may be a highly sensitive person who needs a quieter venue. But if he can't handle himself in a way that will make your family and friends comfortable and keep himself comfortable too, there will be continual pressure for you to stay home alone with him. Some people in relationships like this go by themselves or just take their kids to their families to visit. Sometimes these isolated relationships become abusive. Is this how you want to proceed into your future?

What kind of friendships does your prospect have? If she doesn't know how to have and be a friend, she's not likely to be a competent partner. Does she connect with a few close friends or family? Are these long-term, supportive relationships? Does she want to introduce you after a few dates? Review the guidelines for friendship to be sure you aren't making an exception just because you have chemistry with someone. Your prospect must be capable of friendship, or she won't prove to be a real friend to you.

Some questions reveal whether your prospect is taking a responsible approach to managing his life. You can't do that for both of you, no matter how charming he may be. What skills has he developed to equip himself for adequate employment? Is he thinking about the long-term for his work and preparing in some manner to keep his skills growing? It's wise to *expect* job instability and the need to upgrade one's skills throughout one's working life. Marriage is painful with a partner who's unhappy with his work situation but unwilling to get additional training to change it. How does he manage his finances? How does he care for his things? How does he manage his time? Does he think about how he does these things and try to become more effective?

What can you discern about your prospect's family background? Does she have respect for both her parents, and they for her? Does she love them and attend to family needs? Do her parents love each other? If there was a divorce or her parents have problems in their relationship, has she worked to understand what went wrong? Is she compassionate about them or judgmental and angry? How does she get along with her siblings? Does she show empathy for their problems and try to be a supportive sister, without letting them take advantage of her? Does she think about these things and try to find a good balance? If she's estranged from her family, has she gotten counseling or otherwise come to peace with it?

Consider individual differences that will impact your relationship. Does your prospect have to cope with any of the obstacles described in Part II? What obstacles do you face? How do these work together? If you both have attention deficit disorder, for example, how will you make sure you can handle your finances or keep your schedule manageable? You may find lots of quick understanding but long-term difficulty with a life together unless you both work hard to compensate. Daniel Amen's book *ADD in Intimate Relationships* describes the problems ADD can cause that can occur when you marry, along with some solutions. What if you're both subject to depression, alcoholism, extreme anxiety or bipolar disorder? How could you work together to protect your family from the impact of these traits that can overwhelm Adult functioning? What are the genetic implications for your kids?

Is there mental illness, alcoholism or other serious disability in your prospect's family? Can he discuss these issues with you? How do you really feel about involving yourself with the particular problems his family has? How does he respond when he hears about any problems in your family? These issues have implications for your children and what you would have to cope with together. Look at what physical problems run in your families, as well. One client of mine decided that she didn't want to continue dating a man who had the same severe type 1 diabetes her mother had, even though they had a great connection.

It's common to see couples where the idea that opposites attract is in effect. These couples can work well together, balancing out their weaknesses. His optimism may know no bounds, while her realism counteracts his potential extravagances. He may find her stifling, and she may feel overwhelmed by his impulsivity. Outgoing and more private, introverted people often find each other. If the differences aren't too extreme, compromise and acceptance will be possible. If they can respect and value what they each bring to the table even as they chafe under the continual efforts to meet halfway, the relationship will help grow each partner's mental fitness enormously. And the genetic contribution to their kids may be more diverse and healthy, at least for these traits.

You may be feeling like you'll never find someone who could have a positive answer for all of these questions. But look at what you've been working on and how it's making you feel. Hopefully you're feeling more confident that you can have a good life because of your work to become mentally fit. That confidence will be very sorely tried if you choose a mate who's not willing to work for becoming a fully functional, confident person too. She should be working on the same things you're working to build in yourself. She should not be so proud, ignorant and stubborn that she won't do this. How could you understand or respect each other? The goals you have in finding a mate overlap greatly with your goals in finding your strongest self.

Problems You May Encounter

You may find you have chemistry over and over with people who don't come even close to matching the partner requirements described above. There's probably not just one factor playing into this. But one likely cause of your attraction to these inappropriate types is that you have unresolved issues with one or more of your parents. Do get into therapy and try to identify what allows you to stay with a person who's deficient in these ways. The best way to ruin your life and the lives of your children is to marry someone you don't really respect or who doesn't really respect you.

One reason people may choose a mate who will never be a good partner is that they have fears about real intimacy with another person. For example, if you keep dating people who don't really inspire your love, look at what you'd fear if you actually found someone you could love deeply. Your frightened Child may have you believing you couldn't survive losing this person. As a child you may have seen a parent devastated by a divorce. You may have lost a parent yourself and suffered terribly. Your Child needs reassurance from your Wise Parent that you could now endure such a loss better. You may not need to pull away from your promising prospect.

Remember that the tenth toxic belief (that adults must have one particular person they can depend on) is false. This belief and other fears about intimacy are very powerful, because they trigger your fight-or-flight reactions without your awareness. Elaine Aron describes intimacy issues very well in her book *The Highly Sensitive Person in Love: Understanding and Managing Relationships When the World Overwhelms You*.[2] Her book is helpful for anyone in close relationships, though it also offers special tips for highly sensitive people. I've observed that HSPs tend to overthink their interactions and get very intense in relationships, often too quickly. They need especially good insight into themselves and expert self-care to have comfortable, mentally fit close connections with others.

Anxiety when intimacy develops happens because you don't simply *lose* the Child sense of reality from when you were little. In Part I, chapter 4, I discussed how young children have simplified and self-focused ways of interpreting their experience. Appendix A summarizes these Child brain habits. When a child doesn't get what he needs, he often ends up feeling he was at fault, because developmentally young children tend to assume they cause what happens around them. If your parents blamed you for many family problems, they reinforced this tendency in you. Wise parents work to make sure their kids don't feel at fault for what happens to them because of parental difficulties. Leftover guilt could make you seek an intimate partner who seems to give you a chance to finally please and care for someone like your problem parent.

I've seen clients finally be able to recognize that their elation at having their abusive partner be kind to them for a while is not a healthy response. With difficulty they begin to see that they're in a desperate game of trying to get from this person the same responses they couldn't get from their hurtful parent. Their Child still believes they aren't good enough until someone like their parents say they're good and deserve to be treated with love. A kind and caring prospect doesn't offer this opportunity, so there may be less chemistry. Paul Coleman offers a comprehensive guide to intimacy both before and during marriage in his book *The Complete Idiot's Guide to Intimacy: Creative Ways to Get on the Pathway to Genuine Intimacy*.[3] Despite its unfortunate title, this easy-to-read book gives an excellent and comprehensive view of how to have good close relationships.

How to Find Appropriate People to Date

If lengthy questionnaires about values and interests would work to match people up, they wouldn't continue to have so much confusion in the dating situation. Yet Internet dating sites can still offer a good place to start. My brother Jay commented that since you're looking for a needle in a haystack, you'll need a very powerful magnet; the Internet sites provide that tool. Why not look among people who have similar interests and professed values? You'll have more to work with in ten years, when you're trying to keep the romance alive. A major advantage of Internet dating is that you are continually reminded that there are lots of people you can encounter. You don't have to try to make something work with a prospect just because you might not meet another one for six months, as was true fifteen years ago. You can risk ending the communication with someone who might *eventually* look OK, because you can easily encounter a new person who's closer to what you seek.

Expect you may take a couple of years to find your life partner. You may—and probably should—date a lot of people before you find one who's really right for you. If the two of you start moving for closure very quickly, this is a red flag. You don't have to back away but should slow down and give the relationship some time. People who have character flaws or other deficiencies won't always reveal them in the first few months. I've seen a few people who report that their partner's attitude changed for the worse as soon as they got married. Don't shut off your Adult, unbiased evaluations. If you feel like doing that, you're about to go into denial about the qualities you don't want to see. If this person will make a good life partner, denial won't ever be necessary.

There's a simple exercise you might try to sharpen your skills for spotting red flags. Try to remember the very first time you encountered someone you've dated. Replay in as much detail as you can how the interaction went. Even if you believe you're a poor judge of others, you can identify key issues when you engage your Adult away from your prospect. Note body language; did he seem comfortable and keep you comfortable nonverbally? Did he ask you questions and listen thoughtfully? How did he respond to your questions? What topics did he think were appropriate to bring up? I've found that many people are surprised at how well their initial experience with a prospect predicted what problems would unfold. Evaluate thoroughly your first experience before you start making excuses for your prospect or begin to feel too connected to question yourself.

One frequent problem encountered early in a dating relationship is how to read each other's readiness to engage in sexual intimacy. Women in particular can be taken aback when a guy assumes she's signaling interest. How can you (male or female) signal that you aren't ready for that without creating discomfort between you and an otherwise promising prospect? At first don't even ride in the same car together; meet where you plan to go. Then recognize that going into each other's places alone invites sexual behavior. Don't do that if you don't want to have sex and don't know your prospect very well.

Even if you know your prospect fairly well, don't go one-on-one if you've both been drinking. That cuts down your Adult functioning and dulls down your Wise Parent. If the impaired man is stronger than his prospect, very painful consequences may unfold. On an even more subtle level, manage your eye contact to communicate your level of interest. Note in movies how interest in another person is signaled. They hold their eye contact longer than usual. Don't hold eye contact for long periods if you need more time before you decide whether to be close with your prospect. Just break your gaze briefly as you talk together, and a sensitive prospect will get the message without words. With a less sensitive prospect, words don't help much. They'll read your behavior, eye contact, touch or going to their place alone as a "yes," no matter what they verbally agree to. You can't date as many prospects as you should, even one at a time, if you can't keep intimacy at comfortable levels.

There's one red flag you must recognize quickly when you encounter a prospect online or in person. Does she put you down as she talks to you initially or as the relationship develops? Whether she intends to do it or not, this behavior portends misery for you. You may find yourself doubting your own sense of how you come across and buy into your prospect's view of you. This may prevent you from confidently ending the relationship. There's a phenomenon you need to consider in these situations. It's called projection and occurs when the other person accuses you of attitudes and behaviors that really describe her. You won't be able to get her to recognize this, because her Adult is not strong enough to allow much monitoring or honest self-observation. Need I say more?

Verbal abusers minimize how bad their tirades are, just as physical abusers do. A good reference to help protect you from this kind of verbal entanglement is Susan Elgin's *You Can't Say That to Me! Stopping the Pain of Verbal Abuse: An 8 Step Program*.[4] Elgin's book offers ways to cope if you're in a verbally abusive relationship, but when you're dating, you're free to leave. Don't minimize the difficulty a verbal abuser will have with stopping his behavior. I've observed for many years how hard it is to get one to stop. It seems likely that verbal tirades offer a reward to some part of the abusers' brains; they are so persistent in maintaining both the abuse and their right to do it to you. It's also hard to teach the recipient of abuse to be firm and consistent enough to teach an abuser he must not do it anymore.

Another common problem area is when you or your prospect focus too much on your physical attributes. Remember that chemistry is necessary but not sufficient for a good relationship. If chemistry can only happen for you or your prospect when you're both young, perfectly fit and admired by others, what's going to happen in ten or twenty years? Does your guy check out other women when you're out together? He might not stop that behavior, and you'll really feel hurt when you no longer look much like that twenty-year-old he's ogling. Focus on the physical is also a red flag because it often indicates the prospect's incapacity for real intimacy. If he won't respond quickly and consistently to your complaints out of empathy for you, he's probably one you should throw back into the sea.

Read, talk with friends, introduce your prospect to your friends and family and meet hers. Spend time with her in a wide variety of situations. There's no rush to close the deal. Gavin de Becker's book *The Gift of Fear and Other Survival Signals That Protect Us from Violence* describes the kinds of behavior you should note with caution when you meet new people.[5] Albert Bernstein describes how to identify people who most likely have the personality disorders described in Part II, chapter 1 in his book *Emotional Vampires: Dealing with People Who Drain You Dry*.[6] Both these writers list specific red-flag behaviors you can look for. Why should you suspend your intelligence and Adult functioning when you're making such a life-changing decision? Romantic feelings come easily in the early part of a relationship. You want to be able to feel them in the later parts too.

If You Need to End the Relationship

You must emotionally injure others at times when you pull back from a relationship. You don't also have to insult them by letting them down easy because you believe they can't get along without you. One belief that prevents assertive behavior when you decide to end a relationship is that if your care about the other person, you must get very upset when they are hurt (the sixth toxic belief). Since you're the one who is going to hurt them, your guilt can make you be dishonest in damaging ways. It's helpful to consider the old expression "don't add insult to injury."

In fact, the lies and evasions people employ often cause much more pain than the rejection itself. I've observed that people can cope quite well when they know a relationship is over. They experience most of their anguish and symptoms when they're waiting to see what will happen. People waiting "on the fence" can get very sick if the confusion lasts too long. Sometimes they can't face letting go of their hope that the relationship will recover until the rejecting person makes his feelings clear. Have the courage to say it's over, and don't let guilt make you hurt someone more than necessary.

When you're ending things with a person you haven't been dating for very long, you don't have to give reasons at all. It's best if you meet online and e-mail each other for a while to be sure you even need to meet in person. This allows you to encounter many prospects in a relatively short amount of time to find some who meet your criteria. It's easier to break it off when you haven't met. If you decide you're not interested, you can stop responding to the person's e-mails or you can say you don't feel you have enough in common. If someone demands to meet you quickly, he's probably too focused on physical attractiveness. But do both of you a favor, and don't post a picture of yourself ten years younger and twenty pounds lighter. It's a real red flag when your prospect lies about himself to draw you in. In your early encounters, it's unkind to share your negative thoughts about the prospect.

Once you're in a relationship, it's appropriate to give your prospect (or partner) negative feedback to let her know when you're not getting what you need. If you want mentally fit relationships, you should definitely practice giving and receiving both negative and positive feedback. If you've both been honest along the way, then neither of you should be very surprised when the other wants to end it, though one of you may be hurt and argue to try to stay together.

When you're ready to end it, listing all your prospect's mistakes or faults is unnecessarily hurtful. You could remind her that you've tried resolving issues together without success, but don't enumerate the issues. A final hostile confrontation may result in intense long-term anger for one or both of you and won't help the two of you get along in the future. It may also result in your prospect trying to persuade you to give her another chance. Don't lay out your prospect's faults, even if you're prodded to tell her why.

When you must tell someone you need to end the relationship, plan to keep it short, firm and simple. Just say you feel there's no future in the relationship; you're not going to change your mind and you can't explain exactly why. And no, you won't go to lunch with her sometime. Remind her of all the love songs that say love can't be explained. If she verbally attacks you, say, "You've just noted another reason it's not working between us."

Consider using your phone to tell a prospect who has an ugly temper it's over. You don't deserve a final thrashing verbally or physically. This will allow you to hang up if necessary and will give the other person time to collect himself and preserve his dignity. Let him think you're crazy, if that's his reaction; it will help him let go of you. If violence from your prospect is a possibility, involve your family or friends to help ensure your safety. Just having them available signals to your prospect that you're serious and may help prevent him from becoming violent.

Reality Trumps Fantasy

Throughout your experience looking for an intimate partner, you'll maintain your Adult and inner-family balance better if you remember that, with patience, you can eventually find your match. Monitor to identify the fight-or-flight reactions in your gut before you act on them if you sense rejection. In the vast majority of situations, there's no need for desperate feelings of fight-or-flight when you're dating. Strengthen your Wise Parent to combat romantic mythology like the two of you being "meant for each other." Lots of people could be good intimate partners for you if you're both maintaining good mental fitness and working wisely on your relationship.

Be yourself for your prospects; don't try to project some fantasy ideal to draw them in, or you'll be wasting your time and theirs. If they like you just the way you are, they'll at least become a good acquaintance. If the relationship doesn't work out, friendship can occur once you can both be happy to see each other in love with someone else and fully accept that the romantic relationship is over.

With your Wise Parent, combat the beliefs that could lead you to a toxic relationship:

- I deserve someone who doesn't remind me of a hurtful parent.

- I don't need to struggle with someone to make them love me and treat me well.

- I can step back and evaluate whether a prospect is even capable of being a friend to me.

- I want a partner who has acquaintance skills and gets along well with others.

- I can give our relationship time to see how my prospect reacts to many situations and how time together affects her treatment of me.

- I have the right to end a relationship that doesn't feel right for me for the long run.

- I can have the courage to avoid adding insult to injury when I break it off with someone.

- I don't have to get the approval of my prospect or anyone else to end our relationship.

- My Adult can manage my inner family to keep me safe and comfortable when I date.

- My Adult can help me wait until a mentally fit prospect comes along.

- My Adult will keep monitoring to keep my Child secure through rejection and patient when I must reject others who charm it.

Notes

1. Patricia Love, *The Truth about Love: The Highs, the Lows, and How You Can Make It Last Forever* (New York: Fireside, 2001).
2. Daniel G. Amen, *ADD in Intimate Relationships* (Newport Beach: Mindworks Press, 2005).

3. Elaine Aron, *The Highly Sensitive Person in Love: Understanding and Managing Relationships When the World Overwhelms You* (New York: Broadway Books, 2000).

4. Paul Coleman, *The Complete Idiot's Guide to Intimacy: Creative Ways to Get on the Pathway to Genuine Intimacy* (New York: Penguin Group, 2005).

5. Susan H. Elgin, *You Can't Say That to Me! Stopping the Pain of Verbal Abuse: An 8-Step Program* (New York: John Wiley, 1995).

6. Gavin de Becker, *The Gift of Fear and Other Survival Signals That Protect Us from Violence* (New York: Random House, 1997).

7. Albert J. Bernstein, *Emotional Vampires: Dealing with People Who Drain You Dry* (New York: McGraw-Hill, 2001).

III:5

Marriage for Intimacy and Partnership

Janice and Brad met after dating several prospects and immediately felt a strong attraction. They had both built their inner family for a fair Critical Parent, a warm and ready Wise Parent, an alert Adult and a Child open to trust, love, laughter and intimate cuddling. They gradually got to know each other's friends and families. They worked earnestly to solve any problems between them with respect and creative compromise. After a couple of years of deepening their understanding and trust, they decided to marry. The ceremony was a joyful event. They drove off in a shiny car trailing cans tied on by their many well-wishers and lived happily ever after. Who knows a couple like this? Our fuzzy-thinking society doesn't promote this approach to marriage. This seems just too good to be true, devoid of the mystery and risk that spark romance.

You must deprogram yourself from childhood-based beliefs that risk and mystery equal romance before you can begin to find a viable partner for marriage. Risks that play out for forty or fifty years, tainting the lives of your children, aren't romantic; they're recklessly indulgent. Romance that warms your family through decades comes from thoughtful application of what you've learned while building your own mental fitness. It can only happen if you have a partner who's also committed to mental fitness. Whether you're reading this chapter with a prospect in mind or you've been married for many years, you need to know the ingredients for a healthy marriage.

The focus here is to apply what you've already learned while building personal mental fitness to the complex conditions of marriage. This chapter will define what commitment and intimacy actually require from each partner. It will then cover what marriage is and what it requires to be sustained. We'll explore the issues that cause problems in a marriage: lack of understanding, unfair distribution of the work, lack of problem-solving skills, abuse, jealousy and balancing the demands of family, friends and children. Finally, I'll describe how to create the opportunity emotionally for intimacy throughout your marriage. Mental fitness prepares you to develop the new skills marriage requires and to recognize when your own inner family confusion is preventing healthy cooperation between you and your spouse.

Commitment and Intimacy

Marriage differs from friendship because you bring to it special expectations of commitment and intimacy. You may expect that the intense longing for your intimate, exclusive relationship will carry you through the rough places in the life ahead. You agree to give up this closest form of intimacy with everyone else for as long as you live. You commit to forming a union in which your future is merged and your financial, health-care, relationship and residency decisions must be shared. This commitment in itself can lead either to a sense of security or creeping fight-or-flight reactions. How you manage to navigate all the choices you must make together impacts how secure you and your partner feel. With each decision partners must consider how to make sure that being committed doesn't morph into being trapped for either person. Friendship can make a person feel emotionally stifled but doesn't involve all the other limits marriage includes.

When dating, consider whether a prospective partner is actually open to marriage-type commitment or just thinks she is. People whose Child feels too vulnerable due to unwise Parent parts or a weak Adult put up barriers to intimacy they don't recognize. These barriers often prevent them from engaging constructively in the problem-solving a marriage requires. Examples of these will be addressed in each section below. Expect that you'll have some fight-or-flight reactions when you've committed to a marriage. You can't always keep on top of your frustrations at having to compromise so much in all areas of your life. How do you sustain yourself through the tough times while you wait to find out whether your partner will meet you halfway?

Hone your Adult self-management skills and strengthen your Wise Parent for dealing with yourself and your partner. Then develop some new skills for connecting in this unique, challenging and potentially very rewarding relationship. Control your extreme responses by remembering that unless there's life-threatening abuse, nothing about being married creates the immediate threat to your life that should trigger your body into fight-or-flight. This gives you time for calm, Adult functioning. Find ways to help your partner do the same, sharing some of your own Wise Parent messages. Gradually you can build the trust that supports you both in talking through all your new situations with respect and reason.

Protect Your Vision of Marriage

Aside from a slip of paper at the courthouse, your marriage is entirely a creation in the minds of you and your partner. Your family, friends and surrounding culture will press their ideas about what married people should be doing. But you and your partner are the only ones who can keep your own vision of marriage alive for you. When you think of it, all your other responsibilities have their own voices—your kids, parents, employers, creditors, neighbors, baseball team, etc. They pull on you constantly in several directions, sucking up your time and energy. It's all too easy for your marriage to be stomped out. You and your partner must commit to setting aside time and energy to renew your vision and keep it strong.

In fact, the only way to ensure that you maintain this special pact is to put your marriage ahead of everything else. Parents often say to me, "My kids come first." And I tell them that they're putting their kids first when they put their marriage first. I haven't met a kid in thirty-five years whose deepest wish isn't to have his parents love each other. Your kids are willing to participate in fewer activities or attend a less costly school in order to have family time with parents who bring love and harmony into their home. Parents will say, "I have to work overtime to pay the bills or keep my job." Below I'll discuss how you and your partner can learn to prioritize and problem-solve so you can live within your means and keep that sacred time for your marriage.

Friends and family who love and respect you will support your putting time with your family and partner first. It's a continual effort for both partners to hold on to this commitment for a quality marriage. You won't manage it all the time. Your parents may have a health crisis, one of your kids may require a lot of time and money for a special need, your hot water heater may flood your house, your employer may make unreasonable demands on your time for an indefinite period or you may have a serious financial problem. How do you put your marriage first through these things?

Begin by realizing that you want to keep your marriage first, and talk together about ways to do this. Find little ways to let your partner know you're thinking of him or her with love. My husband often leaves me a little note on a sticky pad saying "miss you" or "love you." I don't need flowers, jewelry or hours of his time that day to feel warm and cherished. Let each other know when one of you has found a good, simple way of giving love and keep doing it. Breakfast out on Saturday, a walk together in the afternoon or time to visit after the evening meal can allow you to share about your days and how you're each feeling in your lives.

Plan for larger blocks of time to spend together and practice taking some of that time just to share about each other. You'll need time to problem-solve about all the responsibilities in your life together, but you don't want all your time together to be about problems. Your marriage then becomes tainted with the moldy odor of burdens. Find ways to play together that aren't expensive or very time-consuming. Weekly evenings out over a quiet dinner or leisurely drives on a Sunday afternoon can work wonders. With as few as four interrupted hours a week to talk out problems and share happy moments, the problems will begin to diminish; six hours would be even better but aren't necessary every week.

How do you find this block of time to express the vision of your marriage? From the age of five, most kids can be taught to respect a private conversation between their parents. It's great for developing their self-control and offers a good example for their own marriages someday. Intense problem-solving or closer sharing requires time away from the kids. Your marriage will need both kinds of space, but you must both be open to find this time together. Unresolved problems often lead partners to avoid time alone together, hiding behind their many other time-sinks. Below are some tips for how to reduce the tension in marriage. When both partners want to find time together and recognize this is critical for their marriage, it's amazing how resourceful they can be. Too many people manage to find time for an affair, an addiction or their friends instead.

The Third Toxic Belief and Marital Harmony: Acceptance Trumps Understanding

The belief that people should be more virtuous, thoughtful, sensitive, helpful and capable than they usually are and that they should be blamed or punished when they don't measure up is blindly expressed in most marriages. The second part of this belief, that you should blame and punish *yourself* when you don't meet all the expectations in marriage, feeds your own feelings of being trapped and overwhelmed. How do you know what's fair to expect of yourself and your partner in marriage? It's relatively easy to be compassionate with friends who let you down but is very trying with your marriage partner. You tend to interpret your partner's failings as indications that he doesn't care so much about you or the marriage. Sometimes this does prove to be the case. How can you evaluate this ongoing issue over many years of marriage?

First, it's a good idea to consider what traits your partner brings to your relationship. Consider whether you or your partner struggle with any of the individual differences that can create problems in functioning. Consider also whether either of you might be participating too much in an addictive pastime. Try to discuss these issues together and reach some compromises that allow for your differences and help reduce tendencies to hide out in an addiction. If you can't reach an agreement, professional counseling can often help you find your balance together. You may find insight from a couples' group, available in many churches and through local counselors. These encounters can also help you appreciate the gender differences that color your communication and how to bridge across them. Patricia Love discusses these and many other important aspects of keeping your marriage strong in her book *The Truth About Love: The Ups, the Downs and How You Can Make It Last Forever.*[1]

Remember that your partner is first your friend and that you need to form expectations based on a good understanding of her. You won't take personally the behaviors of someone who has to work very hard to cope in some situations. You'll forgive yourself and feel less defensive when you know your own challenges. But for marriage even more than friendship, *acceptance trumps understanding.* Consider any couple you know who've been happily married for thirty or forty years. Ask either one of them why their partner does any of a number of peculiar things. Often they'll just laugh and tell you they don't know.

The trust in a mentally fit marriage leads to genuine acceptance of many things. If you believe your wife is generally truthful with you and she tells you she just likes to do things this way or arrange things that way, or she's too tired to make dinner or too busy to mend your pants, believe her. If your husband tells you he needs you to request fewer home remodeling chores or help him pay the bills, believe him. Give each other the benefit of the doubt and look for what your partner *is* doing to show that he or she loves you. Then, without blaming each other, work together to find the balance that works for both of you.

Consider the marital advice of a couple who celebrated sixty years of marriage with four kids. My husband's Aunt June and Uncle Rognar clearly loved each other deeply. Aunt June told the younger people gathered for their anniversary, "Remember the song, 'Let It Snow, Let It Snow, Let It Snow?' Just let it go, let it go, let it go." Uncle Rognar told us the most important thing to remember in marriage is to have patience with each other. When you let something go, you usually haven't achieved full understanding with your partner. If you have to be patient, you're watching your partner struggle with something that you have less trouble with, at least for the moment. These wise people had learned that accepting each other was what gave them their happiness together. Their acceptance gave them serenity, and their courage in challenging the third toxic belief allowed them to grow together.

Think about how you each prefer to express and receive love. Gary Chapman's book *The 5 Love Languages: The Secret to Love That Lasts* describes how a difference in these preferences can lead to relationships where both partners feel they're giving a lot but not getting much in return.[2] Both parties believe that they are putting the marriage and family first and that their partner is being insensitive, lazy or selfish. Chapman identifies five different ways of showing love: spending quality time together, offering positive feedback, serving each other, providing thoughtful gifts and touching, including sex. Problems arise when partners differ greatly in which language "counts" for them as love. Share with your partner how you'd each rate these five love languages and have a good conversation. Refrain from claiming that your love language is "real love" and theirs is just doing what they like. These love languages are deeply rooted in a person's family experience growing up and matter to each of you. They're how you feel loved.

Most often I see a gender difference where the wife complains that her husband *just* wants sex, while she wants love through positive time and conversation. Husbands may not listen well when their wives *just* want to talk and may complain that their wives deny them the sexual intimacy that most makes them feel loved. When your partner tells you how he feels, believe him. Listen and find a way to give and receive love so that both of you feel the glow. For lifelong mental fitness, there's nothing more powerful than to challenge yourself to grow continually in your capacity to give and receive love in all five of the love languages in your marriage and with others you encounter along the way.

In marriage even very compassionate people often bump up against the reality that empathy can give them a false reading. You have to consider how you'd feel in your partner's shoes and then make the adjustment for the fact that your partner differs from you because of how she's wired, family experiences, gender differences or anything else she tells you makes her different. If your partner is honest with you and knows herself at all, just believe her and make the adjustment.

If your husband tells you he doesn't need the home-cooked meal to feel loved, order in and share some quality time. If your wife tells you she doesn't need the new brooch but would really like you to help more with the kids, take turns putting the kids to bed and spend the money on a dinner out. When partners begin to do this, they will see the walls dissolve very quickly. I've even seen this happen for couples who came in after years of hurt and anger due to feeling unloved, unheard and unappreciated.

When Acceptance and Trust Are Not Possible: Abuse in Marriage

There are unfortunately too many marriages where the kind of acceptance and trust described above is not possible. Even with counseling, some people aren't capable of offering the benefit of the doubt. These people suffered childhoods in which they couldn't trust the family environment to nurture them; instead they experienced neglect, abusive language or even physical abuse. Many have witnessed years of abuse directed at their siblings or a parent. Many have watched their parental role models turn to alcohol or other addictions to cope. When these people enter a close relationship, all sorts of cues trigger memories of living in their original family situation. These are held in their Child and Parent parts and are not readily available to their Adult.

People whose parents lacked adequate Adult functioning generally end up with a weak self-observing Adult. Instead of looking at their own behavior, these partners are extremely aware of anything you do that could be interpreted as offensive. Growing up they lived with blame and punishment, not fairness and compassion, and that's what they expect in their new close relationships. But their weak Adult doesn't allow them to know this. They truly believe you intend to hurt them when you don't do or say what they want. This leads them into fight-or-flight anger very quickly. When you try to talk through this with them, they won't hear you and may even get angrier at you for denying what they believe to be your real intent. They treat you like they were treated or the way they saw another family member treated. They can't offer trust and acceptance.

The dynamics of abusive relationships are puzzling on the surface. Why don't these people decide to make it better for their own families? Often they think their new family has it good because they aren't as abusive as their own parent was. They can even resent their own kids as "spoiled" when their partner offers better than what they got as a child. Why do abused partners (most often women, when the abuse is physical) stay with men who might even kill them? Even when the abuser limits himself to verbal attacks, the victim often tends to stay too long. How many times has a woman come in to counseling week after week describing terrible verbal abuse and asked me if she was crazy? Men can also be victimized this way and often have trouble asking for help. I've come to think of long-term verbal abuse as a form of brainwashing that leads to something like a spell. The victim comes to believe deeply what the abuser says about him or her and loses the confidence to leave.

How do we understand this? The abuser has a powerful Critical Parent that is similar to her own parent's Critical Parent. She has an extremely weak Wise Parent and no idea how to calm or comfort herself. Her Child believes that her survival depends upon the attention and service of her partner and therefore is put into fight-or-flight the moment her partner fails to respond as she believes he must. Adult functioning is almost nonexistent in the close relationship due to this triggering of the Child to feel as she did when she was young and more vulnerable.

These partners can often function better in acquaintance relationships and at work, where they aren't triggered in this way. However, there will be occasional times when they react as though in a close relationship and get in trouble away from home, especially if they drink. Why do they seem fairly reasonable when they're dating? They aren't in the situation that triggers them and they want to make a good impression to lure in this key to their salvation. Very quickly most of them try to form an exclusive attachment due to their Child's deep belief they can't handle life on their own. This early pressure to attach was noted as a red flag in the previous chapter on dating.

The victim also usually has impaired Adult and Wise-Parent functioning and a harsh Critical Parent that she's more likely to turn on herself than others. In her family of origin, she learned that taking care of herself is selfish and that to be a good person, she always has to put the other family members, especially her husband, first. Sometimes the victim can also attack as she watched others do, but then she feels terrible guilt and believes the abuser when he says she's the one who's mean and unreasonable. The tenth toxic belief is a frequent problem, as it makes her feel she's unloving if she doesn't totally sacrifice herself. This same dynamic happens when a husband feels it's selfish to insist on decent treatment because he believes he must submerge himself in caring for his wife.

To heal a very abusive relationship, both partners need counseling separately and together, and their individual counselors should be free to talk to their couples counselor. Due to the distrust an abuser brings to all his relationships, this permission is often not granted to the individual therapists. The abuser doesn't share what he's doing at home with his individual therapist. He denies it as long as possible with the couples therapist. In couples therapy he works to persuade the therapist that his wife has all the problems, while the wife struggles to communicate what he's really like at home. The abuser is so well defended that he may not even remember accurately what happened in many cases and offers a convincing appeal.

Too many couples therapists subscribe to the belief that in all couples the fault lies equally with both partners. Some won't even diagnose or refer untreated and abusive bipolar clients for appropriate medication and individual work. They may continue for months to focus on how the victim is creating the problems. Competent couples therapists recognize the need to address mental illness and addiction before beginning couples work, according to Michael Ceo.[3]

Work with victims, usually the most willing participants in couples' therapy, is often frustrating and slow. Victims become isolated, which suits their abusive partner's agenda well, as it makes the brainwashing strategy more effective. Victims' friends and family grow tired of hearing their complaints and burn out with watching them and often their kids suffer. Other couples don't want to get together with a couple where one partner puts the other down and there's unpleasant tension cropping up unpredictably. Victims may avoid inviting friends to their home because their partner does things that embarrass them. It's hard for an already depressed victim to accept kindness from others, as this only makes him feel more inadequate. Thus, the abuser succeeds in having almost complete control over input to her spouse about who he is.

A paradox with these couples is that the abuser, who tears his partner down as ugly, incompetent, cold, mean and unlovable by everyone except him, does so to keep her from leaving him. He fears that if she has confidence and support, she will certainly leave him, because he deeply believes what his family told him about his own worthlessness. When he does briefly recognize his abusive treatment, his shame intensifies his low self-esteem. He often won't be able to express this or even know it for a long time in individual therapy with a gentle and unchallenging therapist. Abusers have little capacity to hear any negative feedback.

Trying to counter the intense and continual stream of abuse by a victim's spouse in a weekly therapy session is very difficult. The victim must be taught about his Wise Parent over and over, as it is crushed between every session. He tends to believe his Critical Parent, because its messages are reinforced by the abuser. When the victim tries to speak from his Adult, the abusive wife may accuse him of talking down to her. Since the abuser's Adult usually can't self-observe, the victim often can't calm the abuser's inner family. This is especially true when the abuser is angry and truly believes *she's* the victim at the same time she's aggressively attacking her spouse.

Victims desperately need friends in addition to their therapist to develop their Adult ability to trust what *they* observe in themselves and others. This support is available for spouses of alcoholics, gamblers and drug addicts in the companion groups for each of these addictions. Addictions are very much to be expected in abusers and eventually in their spouses, if they don't get help. Who wouldn't want to block out this continual barrage of abuse from a Critical Parent and/or spouse? A good reference to identify and cope with verbal abuse is *You Can't Say That to Me! Stopping the Pain of Verbal Abuse* by Susan Elgin.[4]

Why am I spelling out in such detail the dynamics of abusers and victims in this discussion about marriage? Because victims (and soon-to-be-victims when dating) have so much trouble understanding why they can't heal these terribly wounded abusers with their love. Abusers can't receive love because they don't believe they deserve it, they've never felt safe when close with anyone and they're very well armed to destroy anyone who tries to break through their armor. They're confusing because they desperately want to believe they can find love and get their hopes up, just like their victims do in the early rush of a relationship. Abusers are very persuasive that they *must have* and that their partners *can give* the love they've never had. Victims are quick to feel that they've betrayed their fragile partners when their partners are disappointed in them, and they try even harder. Victims feel both guilt and fear when they consider leaving their abusers.

It is hoped that this discussion will help you or your abused friend or grown child grasp what you're up against with these abusers. If even a skilled, caring therapist often can't win their trust, why do you think you can? You must face this fact sooner if you have children witnessing and building their beliefs from these abusive interactions. You can't change your abuser, and he isn't going to change unless he's fully committed to change. Only believe him if he demonstrates this by allowing appropriate disclosure in counseling and by ceasing any addictive behaviors that prevent his growth beyond where he is.

Abusers are famous for promising anything when you get to the point of actually leaving them. I'm sure you've read articles in the newspaper about people who have killed a spouse for trying to leave. The sooner you disentangle yourself from a very damaged abuser, the sooner you can begin to find healthy relationships and the less likely your abuser will try very hard to hold on to you. As noted in the previous chapter, be careful to protect yourself and your children, pets and home if your partner might become violent when you decide to end your marriage.

Jealousy in Marriage

Feeling jealous is most often an indicator that your Wise Parent is not taking good care of your Child, as discussed in Part III, chapter 1 on friendship. In marriage, jealousy can arise either from a partner's low self-esteem or from a partner's inappropriate attention to others of the opposite sex. Abusive partners frequently get most aggressive when they think their partner has shown interest in someone else, often without cause. As noted, they have deep feelings that they are unlovable and expect to be betrayed. However, many people who aren't abusive also suffer from jealousy during the course of a marriage. This stems from their belief that they must receive outside validation to feel good about themselves, which is a variation of the fifth toxic belief that happiness is controlled by outside circumstances. They need to discover that everyone must learn how to maintain a good level of confidence from within to be mentally fit and competent partners (Part I, chapter 5).

Partners can reduce each other's human tendencies to feel inse-cure by giving each other positive comments about appearance, accomplishments and contributions to the family. But if your partner still can't feel secure, he needs to work on reducing Critical-Parent messages that cause self-doubt and strengthening Wise-Parent mes-sages that support feeling confident. It's especially helpful if you can learn what kinds of compliments your partner most needs to encour-age him to feel good about himself. Talk about this together to clarify how you each feel. Once again, believe your partner if he tells you he wants some recognition about some aspect of himself or his activities. Then make an effort to notice these things and comment honestly and positively for the rest of your time together.

Through acceptance and trust, you support each other's Wise-Parent messages about your worth in being the person that you are. You could do this outside marriage, but it's easier with the continual loving encouragement from your spouse. On the other hand, if your spouse doesn't offer this support and also criticizes you, especially in your most vulnerable areas, you'll have trouble maintaining your feelings of worth. When this happens even non-abusive people with fairly normal Critical Parents can become jealous. In these marriages a partner can easily be hurt when her spouse makes any positive com-ment about a friend, neighbor or TV personality. A parent can even be jealous of the attention her partner gives to her children. To prevent this breakdown of support, partners need to be generous with their appreciation and sparse with their criticism.

Recognize Gender Differences

Gender differences create serious problems in many marriages. Men are often brought up to feel uncomfortable complimenting others or receiving compliments in some areas. Some say they feel exchang-ing compliments puts them at a disadvantage with others. With trust and acceptance in the marriage, men shouldn't have these concerns about their wives. Women are usually raised to give compliments thoughtfully and freely and feel hurt if their partner shrugs off their compliments. They feel lonely and neglected when they don't get them in return and become more vulnerable to depression and withdrawal.

Jonathan Kramer and Diane Dunaway describe this and other gender problems in marriage in their book *Why Men Don't Get Enough Sex and Women Don't Get Enough Love.*[5]

Our society is cruel to women in what it holds up to be the ideal female body. Few can achieve this very thin body with large breasts naturally. Black culture is much more reasonable than white about appreciating a wide variety of female bodies. By the time they're four-teen, most white females don't like their bodies and have to struggle to accept themselves throughout their lives. This means their husbands must not make any disparaging comments about their bodies and very much need to offer positive comments, assuring their wives that they find them attractive just the way they are. Men simply have to accept this about their wives. Since men rarely feel the same level of concern about their own appearance, they can't understand the inten-sity of their wife's feelings. They may be able to joke about their little pot belly or their balding head, but they'd better not joke about their wife's rounder curves.

Some men are driven to criticize their wives' appearance by their feeling that they must have better "arm candy" for other men to envy. This expression of the second toxic belief (that we must be better than someone else to be worthwhile) is terrible for a marriage and must be cast aside. Wives don't forgive careless negative comments about their bodies or helpful hints for how to lose weight. They carry each of these like knives in their hearts until they die. They also begin to pull away from sex because they feel self-conscious exposing their imper-fect bodies, especially to a man who's criticized them. I encourage women who are dating to be sure they find a man who has no inter-est in managing their bodies and finds a wide range of female bodies, including theirs at the time, attractive.

Men are more vulnerable in the area of career and financial achievement. Men are most often the ones who get upset when they see other men who make more money or who have a bigger house, better vacations and more "grown-up" toys. They often feel inade-quate if they can't provide for their families as well as they'd hoped. Women have more flexibility in this area and less of their self-worth tied up in their careers, especially if they have children. Gail Sheehy describes these differences in her book *Passages: Predictable Crises in Adult Development.*[6] Women need to accept that their men may feel less worthy when there are financial problems in the family. Women feel anxious about paying the bills, but they don't feel unworthy because of it very often, even if they've overspent. Women need to work as understanding partners with their husbands to live within their means and comment positively about how they appreciate their husband's work to support the family. Men should offer these comments, too, when their wife works outside the home.

Women will even express the belief that their husband would do his work anyway, even if he didn't have his family. While that may be true for some men, in most cases doing their job, even if it is unrewarding or stressful, is the way they feel they show their love for their families the best. Women also need to let their husbands know that they're worthwhile for much more than their work and that they are appreciated as fathers, companions and members of the community. Wives must be clear that they don't think less of their hard-working husbands because other men have a higher income. Paul Coleman discusses gender differences along with many other important issues for intimacy in his book *The Complete Idiot's Guide to Intimacy : Creative Ways to Get on the Pathway to Genuine Intimacy.*[7]

Infidelity and Marriage

When you and your partner develop a vision of your marriage, it will probably not include permission for infidelity. In a 2010 article in *Psychotherapy Networker,*[8] Tammy Nelson indicates that couples therapists who encounter infidelity should not judge their clients. They should consider alternative couple lifestyles with an open mind, because they are the new "normal." She states that therapists should support clients' efforts to explore sharing sex outside their marriage in a variety of ways with open communication between the marriage partners.

When couples openly embark on nontraditional marriages, one improvement on the usual partner-trading situation is that there's potentially less blame and not so much lying. However, I'm afraid that in most cases the human tendency to avoid unpleasant confrontations (the ninth toxic belief) will make these relationships even less honest than a traditional marriage. More people can get hurt or feel betrayed. Some of the parties may lack the ability to communicate well about these complex situations. There's increased opportunity for people's Adult to get swept aside when sex and intimacy include several people. How can children in these situations get models for resolving significant differences or a sense of what commitment feels like?

It's likely most people who pledge their marriage vows plan to be faithful and sexually intimate with just one person. A person who's committed to building a relationship of deep trust and acceptance won't be unfaithful or try to swap partners. In my experience, people who are unfaithful often don't understand what's possible in a marriage of commitment or how to get there. They're often unwilling to risk being honest with their spouse about their negative feelings or unskilled at working through a problem to a satisfactory resolution. They don't have good skills or habits for observing or maintaining themselves through a well-developed Adult and have a Child who's built up feelings of deprivation. Their Wise Parents are inadequate, their Indulgent Parents are powerful and their Critical Parents offer confusing messages about right and wrong.

These people may have grown up in families where there was poor communication and the parents were unhappy in their relationship, even if they loved their kids. They'll say, "I'm not going to put up with what my dad (or mom) did." Or they may have had parents who were unfaithful. They rarely look thoughtfully at what their own role was in the breaking down of their marriage. Many do cruel things to their spouse as they move in with someone they believe offers real love. They may feel no guilt, because they're convinced it was their spouse's uncaring behavior that forced them into infidelity. They often try to force their children to accept their new partner too soon after they separate and blame their former spouse for any reluctance the kids express.

Since we are but struggling human beings, our Adults don't always manage our minds adequately. Sometimes you get overwhelmed in your life together and fall out of love without realizing it, until you meet someone who seems more able to meet your needs. Then you may realize you haven't been as happy as you'd wished and choose to end your marriage. You fear that your spouse will be vindictive and turn your children and friends against you, take an unfair share of the money and make your life miserable. That is certainly possible but is much more likely if your spouse finds out you've been lying for months and having an affair while you leave her to cope with the family responsibilities. If you put her down, you certainly deserve her anger.

Instead, admit your failure to keep track of your own feelings and tell your husband the truth. If you can be discreet about the other person, that is wise. But don't lie about it if you get caught. Sometimes in relationships you have to hurt another person, but you don't need to add insult to injury. That's what lying does—insults your injured spouse with the message that you believe he can't get along without you or that you believe he will become a monster if you tell him the truth. With a very abusive spouse, that is a risk; with most spouses, it is not. If your spouse is very abusive, you'd best leave before you find someone else or you'll risk serious consequences for all concerned.

When a partner has an affair, trust and acceptance are shattered. Lying degrades trust, and the preference for another person for intimacy (even in "affairs of the heart") communicates rejection, rather than loving acceptance. A very damaging situation I often see is when a partner cools off to her spouse and tells him she's just not in love with him anymore but there's no one else. When he senses her distance and notices her increased absences, she tells him he's too jealous and insecure and gets very angry when he questions her or tries to check on her. She may even recommend he get counseling for his insecurity or go to counseling with him and complain about this, while she continues her affair. Counselors often pick up on the deception.

I strongly urge everyone in a relationship or contemplating one to read Patricia Love's *The Truth About Love,* mentioned above.[9] She describes what you can expect during the stages of a committed marriage between two people. She explains the intensity of the first stage of marriage, which she calls the infatuation stage, along with its powerful biological components. She also takes you into the creative later stages, during which you grow a love that is not easily shaken by the temptations of a new infatuation with someone outside your marriage. In a committed marriage, you have the best chance to develop your balanced Adult, Parent and Child parts and experience your fullest interpersonal self-expression.

Divorce and Mental Fitness

For those whose marriage seems to be near its end, counseling is helpful to understand what happened and how to cope better the next time. Sometimes you'll be surprised in counseling and discover new possibilities for your marriage. If not, it's best that you end your marriage before you take up with someone else. Develop your self-observing Adult enough to be honest with yourself that you no longer want to stay committed to your spouse and tell him or her as kindly and fairly as you can. Don't wait to face your marital problems until someone comes along to tempt you.

Take responsibility for your own failings in the relationship and don't try to salve your conscience by blaming your spouse. Instead, work on your own Critical Parent's messages about your human failings and revise unrealistic social expectations about marriage. Divorce is certainly a not-so-new normal, and it's unkind to criticize couples who find themselves going through this. Our society still creates beliefs which leave people going through divorce with damaged self-esteem, the need to prove it's their partner's fault and vindictive behavior that damages their children.

Many marriages won't last a lifetime. You aren't a failure if yours doesn't, and neither is your spouse. Call it a success if you enjoyed some happy years together, were decent and kind to each other and coped responsibly with any children you had. Then both of you can part with your heads held high and move on to new relationships with more confidence. Perhaps our marriage vows should state that we'll be committed as long as we can and that if we change our minds, our spouse will be the first to know.

You can teach your kids that you and your spouse worked hard to build a relationship but that marriage is one of the hardest things people try to do and you couldn't quite get it right. Help your kids understand that you both consider your time together to have been positive in many ways. Teach them that honesty and Adult responsibility are what make for good relationships by being honest (though discreet) as you end yours.

Even if you are very hurt and angry, your kids still must feel free to love both their parents. Explain that their relationship with your spouse is for life, because your spouse will always be their parent. Since spouses don't have that same connection, you can't feel the way they do. Your kids don't have to share your feelings to please you or support you by turning against their father or mother. Consider counseling for them to provide impartial guidance. Mary Hannibal offers proven guidance in her book *Good Parenting through Your Divorce: The Essential Guidebook to Helping Your Children Adjust and Thrive—Based on the Leading National Program.*[10]

Counseling to Heal Your Marriage

It's actually a testimony to people's desire to hold on to their marriage commitments that many couples overcome the distrust and hurt of an affair to build an even stronger relationship, often with the help of counseling. Other bruises to a couple's feelings in a marriage come through their inability to resolve problems in their life together. Many can forgive a partner a brief affair when they discover ways to prevent the communication breakdown and painful distance that developed between them. They find a new level of trust based upon improved skills in working things out together. They actually feel a change in the quality of the relationship and in the attitudes of their partner. This improved quality is what makes greater trust possible.

Whatever problems bring a couple to counseling, at first one or both are often very distrustful, frequently thinking about and threatening divorce. I often tell them I would have had an easier job if they'd come in several years earlier. People value their marriages so much that they often wait until they feel nearly hopeless before they risk taking their issues to a stranger who might make things worse. There are lots of things counselors can do to make things worse, like telling you that they recommend you get a divorce after just two or three sessions. They can side with one partner and blame the other. They can fail to insist on treatment for partners with serious mental health or substance abuse problems that would prevent them from using their Adult for couples counseling. Try to get referrals from someone you trust and then interview a few counselors until you find one both of you like. The therapist you choose should encourage you to have hope for your marriage if you and your spouse want to work on it.

To endure the first few weeks or even months of counseling, when all the problems are aired and solutions may feel slow to come, it's crucial to engage your Adult to manage your Child and help it to wait. I recommend a three-month plan. Think of yourself as having two inner Children, one who wants to quit the marriage and one who wants to stay. Mark a date on your calendar three months out and promise the Child who's pressing to leave that you'll consider its objections thoroughly on that day. Until then, that Child is to be quiet while you focus your energy on trying what the counselor suggests to make the marriage better. The hopeless Child won't actually keep quiet, but you'll have to keep insisting that this impatient Child wait as you keep refocusing with your Adult.

This will create a space for you and your partner to try new things together. It's very disruptive to be thinking off and on about packing your bags, moving to another place and all the financial and family-related issues that a divorce would raise. Threatening to leave each time your partner does one of his offensive behaviors escalates conflict and prevents new efforts to get along.

Counseling has little chance of turning the tide with this kind of between-session anguish. Keep setting aside your doubts and frustrations, even writing them down if you must, and then tackle them alone or with your individual counselor when the three months end. Your hopeless Child part needs you to be honest with yourself about your negative feelings at this time of reckoning and decision. Then you can consider if you've seen enough improvement to give it another three months.

The counselor's first task is to help each of you enlist your Adult to address the problems in your marriage. She must evaluate whether either of you have obstacles to doing this, like severe depression, anxiety, addiction or any of the other things described in Part II that prevent consistent Adult control. She may refer you for individual counseling, a psychiatric evaluation or a substance abuse evaluation before beginning. Some couples need a period of individual counseling prior to, or along with, the first few months of couples counseling. Until you have good access to your Adult, your counselor may work with you to establish some good roommate rules to reduce conflict. You'll try to behave like good acquaintances, with civility and smooth cooperation, as you prepare to begin the more difficult work of building friendship and intimacy with marital trust and acceptance.

Beliefs and Fears that Prevent Positive Change

Once he determines that each of you have Adult capacity, your counselor should help you to examine any beliefs that prevent you from trying his suggestions. Your work on these in Part I will make this stage of counseling easier. There are specific beliefs (related to the twelve toxic beliefs) that occur with great frequency in couples having marital problems. The first is a partner's expectation that a loving partner doesn't need to be told what she needs or wants and that true love gives insight and answers without verbal communication. You may believe that if you have to *ask* your spouse to do a certain loving behavior, it can't be sincere. Your counselor will have to work hard to challenge this one, because you may be quick to dismiss your spouse's efforts; anything the counselor suggests that your spouse do would be rejected by you as insincere or unlikely to last after counseling.

This belief is promoted by romance propagandists in our popular music, movies and novels. It has no foundation in reality, because people can't read each other's minds. You can make a good guess if you're not too wrapped up in your own worries and concerns. But in marriage you're often overwhelmed, overbooked and not able to focus on guessing what your partner would like. You can, however, respond as soon as possible to her request for help or affection. Even in the first blush of love, it's unreasonable to expect your new partner to guess what you want. Healthy, self-respecting dates will see this expectation as a red flag, a warning of problems sure to come.

A second belief that can prevent you from really investing in counseling is the belief that your partner won't sustain his positive changes once counseling is over. There are techniques similar to the thematic prompts that can help you get past this (Part I, chapter 4). Change is more stable if both partners have things they've agreed to say to each other to help stay on track. When the counselor coaches Brad to speak differently to his wife as they're discussing a problem, what does he tell the wife to say to keep Brad on track? She can learn to say something like, "Is that how you really want to say that?" to remind him and give him a chance to correct himself, instead of yelling at him or withdrawing in stony silence. If Janet takes on too many home duties and gets irritable, Brad can take her aside and ask her whether she really wants to do this by herself and what he can help her with. He doesn't need to slouch away to his computer, dreading what she'll say to him later.

Another issue that can interfere with your confidence that counseling could help is when your spouse gives the counselor more credibility than you. You may ask "Why will he listen when you tell him, but won't respect what I say? I've been telling him that for years." This happens so often that I've searched for a serious answer for these frustrated spouses. The first reason may be that spouses instinctively seek to keep the relationship equal to keep it healthy. If Bob lets Louise teach him how to discipline the kids, he may start to see her more as a mother than a wife. If Louise lets Bob tell her how to budget her household expenses, she may begin to see him as a father. This is deadly for romance. The counselor can be allowed to feel like a benevolent parent.

The second reason spouses may respond better in the counseling setting than at home is that having the counselor in the observer-manager Adult role helps both spouses engage their own Adult to look at how they're coping in their marriage. In this enhanced Adult mode couples can make great progress to resolve issues that their inner families could disrupt at home. A spouse may be more willing to follow the counselor's suggestion because her Adult can now recognize its merit. Once they try these new approaches the dynamic between them improves and their Child parts relax, allowing for continued Adult function at a higher level.

Another factor that will help you stay on track after counseling is that you'll feel so much better with the new atmosphere in your home. Like the pigeon in Skinner's box, you'll keep moving toward the goal because you'll keep getting rewarded all along the way. Punishment in the form of a partner's disapproval and hostile behavior just makes you quit trying to get the rewards of the relationship, much like the pigeon getting his feet shocked. If you both work to maintain your own mental fitness and kindly help your partner remember to practice the new habits, change will endure. Gradually, the new habits will replace the old and become almost automatic. You will never reach the point where you can assume your Adult will just maintain itself without determined and constant effort; your Adult must monitor and keep peddling to keep you balanced.

Give your partner the benefit of the doubt and assume he'll be glad to respond to your requests if he can. He doesn't have to think of it first himself. He may be willing to compromise in good faith so both of you can get your needs met. When you remember to put your marriage first, the goal of every discussion must be for each partner to feel heard and respected. The particulars of the compromise each time don't matter. What matters is that each of you feels that your partner wants to be fair and generous. If you find just talking to each other is difficult, take a look at *The Relationship Cure: A 5 Step Guide to Strengthening Your Marriage, Family and Friendships* by John Gottman and Joan DeClare.[11]

Resolving Your Differences

In the day-to-day life of a marriage, there are many opportunities to disagree. You can disagree about who's going to do what household chores when. You can argue about which friends or family will get your time and attention for what activities or holidays. You can struggle with how to split up all the tasks of caring for your children and pets. You can battle over how to spend your money and who should contribute what. You can want different types of vacations and weekend outings. You can have different priorities about what repairs or renovations should be done when and how much they should cost. The list is as long as your life. During the first stage of your relationship as you talk together, you'll usually believe you have seamless agreement about what's important in these things. You'll also feel like your love will carry you easily into resolving any differences.

There's another belief that sabotages growth in marriage. You believe you *can't stand it* when your partner disagrees with you. Remember that we humans have a brain that tends to interpret any difficulty as a threat to our lives. What couple hasn't had intense bodily reactions when they argue about almost any of these non-life-threatening issues? You must work very hard to keep your Adult in charge when you try to find a compromise with your partner, especially when you really care about getting your way in a situation. Too easily you go into fight-or-flight when your partner won't go along with you. You may forget your work on the twelve beliefs and begin to blame her for being the way she is, rather than accepting the differences between you. You may quickly stop trusting that your partner really wants to participate and do her fair share. You get angry and want to get away.

It's utterly false that love will make it easy to resolve your differences. It can help you stick it out through the tough negotiating, however. To promote full Adult participation, there are some essential ground rules for discussion. There should already be a ground rule for your relationship that if at any time either of you feels one of you is getting too heated for productive discussion, a brief separation to different rooms is called for. This should last until both parties feel calm enough for Adult functioning but should not last so long that there can be no discussion. Say, "Let's take a break for a few minutes" or "I need to take a break," not "You're yelling" or "\You're being too emotional."

Here are suggestions for how to have a positive, marriage-affirming discussion:

1. Observe your own state of mind. Are you feeling rushed, anxious, angry, tired or buzzed from a drink of alcohol? Are you mentally exhausted from dealing with a problem with your kids, a parent or someone at work? Schedule your times to talk early in the day on a weekend, when you're fresh and your Adult is fully available to consider your partner's ideas.

2. Identify a focus for the discussion. Have ready a calendar and a pad of paper to record your concerns and how you'll follow up after your discussion. If you each have paper, it may help you not interrupt, which can cause unnecessary irritation. One of you can begin by laying out what topics you want to discuss, and then your partner can add any on his mind. Decide which one or two most need your attention, then focus on one problem at a time, planning another time for additional topics.

3. Take turns in describing how you each see the problem and any ideas for a solution. For example, a bathroom has been torn apart for two months, the kids both have soccer games all weekend and your sister's family is coming over for dinner

Saturday night. Who can get the kids to their games or arrange transportation? How much can realistically get done on the bathroom, and why is it taking so long? And how will the house get cleaned and dinner made for Sunday? Plan what can be done this weekend, what could be done another time and how you can prevent this kind of pileup in the future. Define what each of you will do.

4. Discuss how you each feel about this plan. Try to problem-solve about the bathroom project without blaming anyone. Find ways to share as much as possible. Keep your Adult perspective by reminding yourselves that these problems involve inconveniences, not life-threatening issues. And remember that what's most important is to put your marriage, not your work priorities, first by making sure your partner feels heard and respected as you talk and when you finish. Finally, consider how you can also fit in some time for each other and adequate rest despite the pressing responsibilities.

There's a simple technique for prioritizing when you find yourself faced with too many projects. For example, you may be overwhelmed by this house you didn't know was a fixer. Each of you can list on a separate pad all the things you're aware need to be done, from tightening a doorknob to replanting a garden bed. Then separately go through your list and put "1" by the things you think need to be done first, "2" by the things that can wait a few months and "3" by things that don't need to be done until much later in the year or even next year. Compare lists and see if your partner has thought of some projects you'd forgotten or weren't aware of. Discuss any differences in how you've prioritized.

Next, go through the lists together and discuss the order of importance of any task that either of you marked with a "1." Put your initials next to the ones you'd be willing to do. Compare lists, discuss and make a final prioritized list with names assigned. Take turns with the tasks neither of you want to do or decide who will explore hiring someone to help. Then plan with the calendar a tentative schedule for getting these done. You may break some of these into smaller pieces in order to plan and allow both of you to contribute to finishing them. This approach ensures that each of you supports the timing of the projects being worked on. Then you won't get into arguments about why something one of you wanted to get done is waiting while the other is struggling to do the work and would really like some appreciation. You can use this process for any time you both feel overwhelmed with too many "have-tos."

Create the Conditions for Enduring Friendship and Love in Your Marriage

It can be very helpful for partners to work together through the goal-defining exercise described in Part II, chapter 7 and illustrated in figure 4. When you develop a shared plan for your immediate and long-term future that takes all these areas into account, you create a solid basis for understanding and support. Let's look at some of these goal areas to see how you could collaborate with your spouse for greater fulfillment. Write out your own goals in each area and then share them with your partner. Set some short- and long-term goals for the two of you to work on together. Write these down and plan to have occasional meetings to discuss them and how you're doing. Find ways to encourage each other to keep working on the goals and redefine them as needed.

Goals involving friends and extended family: You may want to make some new friends or find friends to help you accomplish some of your personal goals. Since couples often include one outgoing partner and one who is less comfortable socially, it's helpful for the outgoing partner to find some couples where all four of you enjoy each other. You can start with your same-sex friends and include your spouses sometimes. Friendship can then unfold, enhancing the mental fitness of all involved with improved support and positive time together. A great way to begin is to invite another couple out to breakfast, when everyone is rested, no one has to cook, it doesn't cost much, no one is drinking or having to pay for drinks and the time involved is limited. See how you all like each other and go from there.

Goals for improved health or recreational or community activities: Friends who'll support you and be buddies can make these goals fun, whether both spouses choose to participate in an activity or not. It causes unnecessary tension in a couple to try to force each other to share in all these areas for personal growth. People need to have freedom to cope in their own way, and partners may have different talents and interests. Of course, it's good to have some activities you share, as this allows for enough time together to maintain your marriage.

Goals for personal growth or spiritual development: These goals are intensely personal and must be individually determined. It's a bonding experience to discuss these together, as long as neither partner tries to pressure the other into believing as he does. You'll discover how you come together around your values for marriage and family and how you each understand your own journey and direction in life. It's a sign of good mental fitness when you can enjoy another person's differences without any need to convert them to your way of thinking or anxiety that you should change to theirs.

Goals for the family: You share a home, a future and financial responsibilities. What are some short- and long-term concerns you worry about separately and perhaps talk about off and on? Do you have a will? Are you saving enough? How will you manage an older parent's last few years or a disabled child's move into adulthood? Setting goals together gives you an opportunity to identify such issues and begin to plan how to address them. Who could advise you in areas where you don't have the expertise to plan? How could you find a common plan if you disagree about where you'd like to be in five years? List your questions and plan to keep meeting to find ways to address these issues, which can undermine your feelings of security and well-being if not addressed.

Leadership, Teamwork and Intimacy

As you work together, embrace the concept of leadership in the different areas you each must manage. For example, if Anna manages most of the household chores, she can express the attitudes of a leader instead of a resentful victim. A good leader inspires her followers by example and positive guidance. Anna can lead her husband and kids into making the house run smoothly by offering a list of chores to be done and inviting them to choose which they'd like (or not hate) to do on a permanent or rotating basis.

Family meetings can be held regularly to give members a chance to evaluate how everyone's doing and exchange tasks if they wish. These meetings should encourage further effort by recognizing the tasks completed well and the helpful attitudes expressed. Specific requirements about particular chores can be determined, such as when the deadline for completion should be. The dishes need to be taken out of the dishwasher before when? The vacuuming needs to be done by when? What's included in cleaning up the kitchen? With her Wise Parent shining, Anna can lead the meeting to a productive end.

Likewise, if Bill manages home maintenance and remodeling tasks, he can also call meetings, first with Anna to prioritize and plan what needs to be done, then with the kids to enlist their cooperation and understanding. Bill can teach some skills to Anna and the kids or arrange for them to attend a local workshop to learn a skill to help with a project. The kids may know someone who could help or suggest a friend they could visit overnight if things get messy. The family can feel closer through helping in the project if Bill leads them well. If he just tears out a bathroom without this support, he's likely to experience resentment and interference when the project impacts the daily activities of his family, instead of the appreciation he'd like. He can feel like a hero if his family has participated in the planning and he's enlisted them with respect.

You've been working to improve the quality of your marriage. You can set goals together for developing skill at sharing responsibilities, sharing more quality times together and finding more creative solutions to having the family lifestyle that you both want. Defining these helps you feel a shared commitment to achieving them, improving your motivation to keep focused on new changes. Although you probably don't need to have all of this in place before you can feel close enough for occasional comfortable intimacy, having these issues settled will bring you into a harmony that allows more consistent marital connection.

After you've read Patricia Love's *The Truth About Love* and accomplished the work you've explored here, you'll be ready for the passionate intimacy you can especially enjoy in a loving marriage. Check out Love's book with Jo Robinson, *Hot Monogamy: Essential Steps to More*

Passionate, Intimate Lovemaking[12] to improve your love life. Terry Real also offers excellent guidance in his book *The New Rules of Marriage: What You Need to Make Love Work.*[13] He uses similar concepts to those discussed in this book for understanding your inner workings as you strive for a good marriage.

Trust and acceptance grow deeper as the capacity to problem-solve effectively and without disrespect develops in a couple. Gradually you come to know you'll be together "till death do you part" because you can't imagine it any other way. You know you'll meet the new challenges as partners and that they'll be easier to bear because you can count on each other. Your daily courage in facing your own Indulgent and Critical Parents will help you find serenity in accepting your partner with the special trust that comes with a mentally fit marriage. As your marriage grows into a loving partnership, you can lead your children into becoming positive family members and ultimately the mentally fit adults you hope they will become.

Here are some reminders to help you stay on track with your Adult:

- Will my choice put my spouse into fight-or-flight?

- Am I treating my spouse as I'd like to be treated?

- What should I just accept about my partner? What does he have to accept about me?

- What annoying things that I do is my partner patiently enduring?

- Am I guessing what she thinks or wants when I should just ask her?

- Am I considering how he's different from me when I give to him?

- Am I competing with my spouse or cooperating?

- What's my part in this argument?

- What's within my power to change to make things better?

- What fun or encouraging moments can I bring to my partner today?

- What's a new idea for time together?

- Am I maintaining good self-care and keeping up with friends?

- How would I cope today if I weren't reacting to her?

- Blaming or punishing my spouse or myself for problems doesn't solve them.

- I can monitor to remain free to be myself and not feel stifled in my marriage.

- If I keep my Adult in charge, I may be able to help lead us to a calmer, more positive place.

Notes

1. Patricia Love, *The Truth About Love: The Ups, the Downs and How to Make It Last Forever* (New York: Fireside Books, 2001).
2. Gary D. Chapman, *The 5 Love Languages: The Secret to Love That Lasts* (Chicago: Northfield Publishing, 2010).
3. Michael Ceo, "Couples and Affairs: Managing the Clinical Challenges," Seminar by Cross Country Education, 2011.
4. Susan H. Elgin, *You Can't Say That to Me! Stopping the Pain of Verbal Abuse: An 8-Step Program* (New York: John Wiley, 2011).
5. Jonathan Kramer and Diane Dunaway, *Why Men Don't Get Enough Sex and Women Don't Get Enough Love* (New York: Simon & Schuster, 1990).

6. Gail Sheehy, *Passages: Predictable Crises in Adult Development* (1977; repr., New York: Ballantine Books, 2006).

7. Paul Coleman, *The Complete Idiot's Guide to Intimacy: Creative Ways to Get on the Pathway to Genuine Intimacy* (New York: Penguin Group, 2005).

8. Tammy Nelson, "The New Monogamy," *Psychotherapy Networker*, Vol. 34, Issue 4 (July/August 2010), 20–27, 60.

9. Love, *The Truth About Love.*

10. Mary Ellen Hannibal, *Good Parenting Through Your Divorce: The Essential Guidebook to Helping Your Children Adjust and Thrive—Based on the National Program* (2002; rev. ed., Cambridge: DeCapo Press, 2007).

11. John M. Gottman and Joan DeClare, *The Relationship Cure: A 5 Step Guide to Strengthening Your Marriage, Family and Friendships* (New York: Three Rivers Press, 2001).

12. Patricia Love and Jo Robinson, *Hot Monogamy: Essential Steps to More Passionate, Intimate Lovemaking* (New York: Penguin Books, 1995).

13. Terry Real, *The New Rules of Marriage: What You Need to Make Love Work* (New York: Ballantine Books, 2007).

III : 6

Adult and Wise Parenting for Mentally Fit Children

It takes a Wise Parent and a strong Adult to design an environment that guides your child with positive feedback instead of shocks to his feet. A majority of parents I've worked with guess that the pigeon in Skinner's box who gets shocks to his feet learns faster than the one who gets kernels of corn for a move in the right direction. The shock seems more powerful to the parent who yells or grounds a kid for two months. But as these parents who seek help have discovered, it doesn't teach the kids new behavior. Small rewards, like an encouraging word or some extra attention, may seem inadequate to turn a stubbornly resistant child into a cooperative one. But they helped Skinner's pigeon, who can't be as smart as your kids, learn very quickly.

Of course, children are much more complicated than Skinner's pigeons. But, like Skinner, your Adult must identify the core elements your kids need to flourish in your care. You don't have a cage for them but you must contain them in a gradually expanding environment until they're ready to function on their own. Your container must provide ways to teach using kernels of corn much more often than shocks to your children's feet. When punishments are needed to stop certain behaviors, they need to be focused and appropriate for each situation. This balance provides an environment where you can keep your kids energized to learn and give them direction as well. The container you create will also reduce the power of your Critical and Indulgent Parents to demoralize you and your kids.

273

This discussion will focus on how you can design your interactions with your kids at home to contain them wisely. As you find your own way to implement these designs, you'll discover that your Adult gets sharper and your Wise Parent develops in ways you wouldn't have imagined. Every new success of your child is a kernel of corn that will keep you motivated. You can learn how to turn their failures into new opportunities for both of you to grow. As you find new ways to inspire them to persevere despite frustration, you can learn how to inspire yourself too. Many clients who seek individual counseling because they lack confidence and aren't taking good care of themselves have a shortcut if they're doing well as parents. They can just ask themselves, "What would I tell my kids?" and begin talking to themselves with the same loving Wise-Parent care.

Keep the Twelve Toxic Beliefs Out of Your Container

Let's look at examples of how each of the twelve toxic beliefs could prevent your Adult and Wise Parent from guiding your family well. The beliefs are reprinted in appendix A.

1. The first toxic belief would allow your need for approval from a grandparent, your spouse or other adults you know to interfere with following your own wisdom with your kids. If you feel you must have your kids like or approve of you all the time, you're likely to create in them powerful Indulgent Parents and weak Wise Parents. You need to be wise and not overindulgent to build their Wise Parents.

2. The second toxic belief would have you compare your kids with the children of your siblings, neighbors or friends as a way to measure your success as a parent. Learning more about kids from other parents is positive; competing with them to prove you're a capable parent takes you off course. When you engage in this competition, you are ignoring the differences between each of your kids and other parents' kids. This is a sign that your Critical or Indulgent Parent is overwhelming your Wise Parent. Your Adult must guide your parenting decisions to

reflect the values you've chosen for your family. This will help your kids have a clear sense of what you believe is important for them and allow them to absorb your nourishing beliefs.

3. The third toxic belief would have your Critical Parent blame or punish your kids when they don't follow your rules or meet your expectations. It would also have you torment yourself and possibly your spouse if you felt you made an error in parenting. You also may blame your kids' teachers or friends if you buy into this belief. To avoid unfairly blaming your kids, your Wise Parent should learn what children at each stage of development can do. I'll discuss this in general terms, but it would be wise for you to study a book or take a class on parenting kids at different ages for a more thorough understanding.

    Parent training can help you be fair to yourself and give you ideas for managing your kids effectively. When you blame your kids' teachers, coaches or friends, you risk letting your kids off the hook for taking responsibility themselves. This is another way your Indulgent Parent can teach your kids to expect too little of themselves. Of course, in some cases your Adult may determine that your child does need to be protected from hurtful outside influences.

4. The fourth toxic belief would have you worry needlessly about present or future danger to your kids. It results from a weak Wise Parent and Adult who can't reassure you about your own ability to cope. This belief would affect your kids in two ways. First, you'd be instilling the idea that people can't relax with the confidence that they can somehow manage problems in their lives. Second, it would make you be overprotective and deny them opportunities to develop their own ability to handle stress in life.

5. 5. The fifth toxic belief would have you limit your expectations for your children because of problems in their history or in your family history. Johnny is not immature like Uncle Ted, though Uncle Ted may be immature like Johnny. Susie is

not necessarily fragile because she was premature. Tommy's problems in math may not be due to your divorce when he was four. Kids need to be free to explore their own challenges without your Critical or Indulgent Parent biasing their view of themselves. Be wise and use your Adult to find ways to support them as they stretch to grow up.

6. The sixth toxic belief would encourage your Child to get upset every time your kids have problems, because you believe that's how best to love them. But joining in their pain will only grow their Indulgent Parent. It's best for your Adult to stay in charge and evaluate what would be the best ways to help them learn from their experience. Your Wise Parent should encourage your kids to believe they have the strength to solve any problems they encounter and to know that you are always there to help, if necessary. If they've really gotten themselves into trouble, employ your Adult and Wise Parent to help them find solutions. Try to curb your Critical Parent and refrain from telling them "I told you so." They already know that. You want them to see you as an ally, not a rejecting person who only cares about their performance.

7. The seventh toxic belief would have your Indulgent Parent support your kids when they complain that it's terribly unfair when they try hard and don't get the grades, the spot on a team or the response from a friend that they'd hoped for. These situations offer your Wise Parent an opportunity to prepare your kids to persevere appropriately in the face of disappointment, rather than giving up and blaming others or even themselves. Your Adult can help them evaluate what they can reasonably expect from themselves, based on their own strengths and weaknesses and the realities of the situation.

    Your Wise Parent can teach your child that great performance and great discoveries only happen after many failed efforts. If your kids play to their strengths, keep learning and keep trying, they can eventually have a good life. If they quit easily, all the talents in the world won't give them that. And finally, your Wise Parent should help your kids realize that they will experience unfair treatment in life. Each of us needs to discover how to cope with unfair situations and people without getting bound up in debilitating anger.

8. The eighth toxic belief would have your Indulgent Parent blame your kids' problems on things that happen to them. The Indulgent Parent teaches you that it's useless to try to overcome life's hurts and disappointments. It says you shouldn't expect to be happy because of the injury in a car accident, the flood that wiped out your house, the friend who lied about you or the financial problems since you lost your job. You shouldn't expect to celebrate these things, but you should expect you can find ways to comfort yourself and your kids through them. Share with your kids inspiring true stories about people who overcame very tough circumstances and felt deep pride in themselves as a result. Consider Tootle, the little engine noted in Part II, chapter 2.

9. The ninth toxic belief would have your Indulgent Parent allow your kids to feel comfortable avoiding problems and procrastinating about doing chores or homework. It may allow you to function poorly as well. In this way your weak Wise Parent allows avoidance and denial to prevail in your family. As I noted earlier, this belief is the root of addiction and many persistent emotional problems. You want a strong Wise Parent to teach your kids how to face and manage the big and little challenges that come to them. Though you may have lacked sufficient inspiration before having kids, you may find that concern for your kids now motivates you to change. This is one instance of how parenting can help you grow.

    If you have trouble with this belief, it's wise to get professional help to keep your parenting strong. When you lack a strong Wise Parent, your Critical and Indulgent Parents fight for control. You and your kids relax too much, and then your Critical Parent bruises your Child and you go after your kids. The impact of the ninth toxic belief is serious. Your confusing treatment can lead your kids to avoid talking openly with you. They may find you too defensive when they criticize you and too punitive if they tell you about a mistake they've made. Who else do they have to guide them? Who else cares about them as much as you do?

10. The tenth toxic belief would have your Critical Parent demand that your kids seek your help, your company and your approval as a sign that they really love you. Your Indulgent Parent feels that as a loving parent, you should offer any help they seek. But a Wise Parent realizes that mature love allows people to develop independent coping skills that give them self-esteem. Too much help interferes with kids' ability to learn from their own mistakes. It robs them of the chance to discover their unique talents and abilities as they struggle to solve a problem. Parents who demand that their kids be overly dependent risk alienating them when kids' natural drive to become separate individuals emerges in adolescence. This hurts both the parents, who are then shut out of their kids' lives, and the kids, who still need Wise-Parent guidance as they venture out on their own.

11. The eleventh toxic belief would have your Indulgent Parent shower your children with feedback that they are unusually gifted, attractive or special. It would teach them to expect that others will also recognize their unusual status and give them special accommodation. Your kids then develop an Indulgent Parent that endorses several toxic beliefs and permits them to feel entitled to work less, receive more recognition or be spared most unfairness in life. Clearly this is a cruel thing to do to any child. They need a Wise Parent to help them understand the give-and-take required in all relationships. No friend, coworker or spouse wants to endure the preening and whining of someone who feels entitled to what others know they have to work for.

12. The twelfth toxic belief would also have your Indulgent Parent encourage your kids to feel better than other people, this time because they're smarter or more clever. This belief leads to

kids who feel they don't have to follow the same rules as other people because they deserve to go first. They'll grow up to feel like they can speed or cut into traffic, cheat on tests or their taxes, or shoplift or lie to get what they want. They haven't had a Wise Parent challenge them to consider what it would be like if everyone did what they are doing; they feel entitled to look out only for themselves.

This discussion illustrates why you as a parent must recognize your own toxic beliefs and practice combating them. Your kids will imitate you without knowing it and will have to overcome many of the same beliefs that make your own life more difficult. There's no guarantee your kids will overcome your example, even if they're given the opportunity. For example, maybe you're a conscientious highly sensitive person, and your child has attention deficit disorder with hyperactivity. Beliefs that make you uncomfortable may cripple him. Maybe you procrastinate until things pile up (the ninth toxic belief) but then knuckle down and do what's necessary for the laundry to get done, the bills to be paid and getting your job done at work. Your ADHD kid can easily follow your example in putting things off but won't be able to knuckle down and catch up. Your kids' needs thus can motivate you to correct beliefs you might never have challenged if you hadn't been a parent.

The Crib and Playpen Years

The container you'll create for your child from birth to age three must first of all ensure his physical safety and comfort. Plan to begin extra self-care to handle the increased stress on your physical health that an infant and toddler will bring. Next your Adult should determine how to arrange your home and your schedule for safety and support for bonding with your child. In these early years, your presence, your hugs, your smiles and your praise are the most powerful kernels of corn for your kids. They'll need you to set limits to teach them not to hit, break things, bite or scream. You'll need to insist that they mind you so they'll eat what they should, go to sleep in their own beds or take turns with another child.

There are numerous books to guide you with techniques to manage all these tasks in a positive way for your toddler. *Toddler 411: Clear Answers and Smart Advice for Your Toddler,* by Denise Fields, Alan Fields and Ari Brown, offers comprehensive guidance.[1] *Positive Discipline, The First Three Years: From Infant to Toddler—Laying the Foundation for Raising a Capable, Confident Child,* by Jane Nelsen, Cheryl Erwin and Roslyn Duffy, will help you lead with your Adult as you begin your parenting journey.[2]

Adjust Your Container as Your Child Grows

Your child will let you know when his container must stretch to allow him more opportunity to grow. He'll throw his toys out of his playpen and crib for a while to let you know he needs to explore. Then he'll just climb out. It's important for you to respond to these signals from your child about his developing needs with encouragement, not efforts to keep him restricted too long. The books noted above give some guidelines for what generally to expect about the timing of developmental changes for this age-group. These can help you know when to allow your child more room to grow.

One common problem for parents in today's fragmented communities is to provide kids access to other children their own age. For instance, two very devoted parents brought their three-year old daughter Emma into counseling because she expressed negative feelings about herself and seemed defeated before she began an activity. She lost her temper and cried too often. They lived in a lovely home out in the country and mom stayed home to care for her daughter with lots of positive attention. For three years Emma had experienced almost no time with other children and none with children her age. She had learned to compare her ability to do things with her parents' ability. They played with her often and thought their company was all she needed. Three afternoons a week at a daycare with kids about her age turned her around quickly into a confident, cheerful little girl.

Consistency Weaves Your Child's Container

The second principle your Adult needs is another gift from Skinner's pigeon. Skinner studied whether it made a difference in his pigeon's pecking efforts if he varied how he dispensed the kernels of corn.[3] He found that it made a lot of difference. His work on this led to the idea that parents must be consistent when they use consequences to teach their kids. Parents often dismiss the importance of this, because it's difficult to accomplish and they don't realize what their inconsistency creates for them and their kids. Some may have too strong an Indulgent Parent. Some complain that their child was always strong-willed and hard to manage.

Despite individual differences between kids here, it's important to recognize that parents' inconsistency creates most of this problem. Robert MacKenzie's book, *Setting Limits with Your Strong-Willed Child: Eliminating Conflict by Establishing CLEAR, Firm and Respectful Boundaries,* focuses on how to be consistent, beginning with your toddler.[4]

Skinner found that he could easily teach his pigeon to peck on the circle if he rewarded it every time with a kernel of corn. He wanted to find out how to get the pigeon to keep pecking with the least amount of corn rewards. He discovered that his pigeon would peck almost indefinitely if he gradually gave it fewer and fewer kernels. The number of pecks between rewards also had to be varied to keep the pigeon pecking.[5] How does this relate to parenting?

Say you want your child to obey you without having to be rewarded with praise or a treat every time. You begin during the early years to teach her, for example, to come when you call her. As she learns the new skill, you praise her with excitement every time. Gradually you both get used to this new accomplishment, and you stop praising her. She begins to come when you call only if she feels like it. But you expect her to come right away every time and you sometimes—but not always—scold her if she doesn't. She is not contained; she doesn't know when you expect her to mind you and when you don't.

How do you get her to come when you call her again without being too harsh? You need to begin praising her for coming when you call every time for a while and then gradually less often, until you only praise her occasionally. When she doesn't come at first, you scold her gently and remind her of what you expect. You make sure that she always obeys you by using what small rewards or mild punishments you need to get *consistent obedience*. Otherwise, your child learns that she only has to obey you occasionally to keep your rewarding parental attentions coming her way and you turn into the pigeon, *trained to complain consistently* by her occasional obedience. Kids are natural behavior-modification experts for their parents' behavior.

Very consistent parenting is especially important for your child from birth until age four. During this time you're teaching your child to trust you to take care of him dependably. He will install this trust in his Child as a sense of security that he's a good child and that he can get fair treatment from you. His developing Parent internalizes your parental words and behavior like a sponge. When you're consistent, he won't keep trying to get away with things you don't want him to do. He'll go to bed when you tell him to, he'll eat three bites of his green beans, he'll stop hitting his baby brother and he'll stop when you tell him not to chase his ball into the street.

You won't have to try to punish your child into minding you, which won't work long-term. The frustration expressed by your Critical Parent would be internalized by your kid as her own Critical Parent telling her she's bad. Very young children have simplified, black-and-white ways of sorting their experience and can't easily separate one naughty behavior from themselves as a whole, especially if you're expressing a lot of anger about it. Use your Adult to educate yourself about what you should expect from your child at each age and consult a child counselor if you have questions. Then be consistent in requiring her to mind your age-appropriate directions.

Parenting Four- to Eleven-Year-Old Kids with Your Adult and Wise Parent

By age four a child is beginning to observe himself, reflect on things, organize and plan. His Adult is beginning to express itself. Now it becomes much more difficult to be consistent with all the things you must guide your child to do. You need even more to have your kids cooperate with you and obey you most of the time. There isn't time or energy enough to negotiate over every issue that comes up. Kids in this age group often can't understand why parents would expect them to do many of the things required of them. It's normal for your kids to resist you when you try to require them to practice certain habits, like picking up their toys or taking a bath. They may not want to stop what they're doing or they may just not like to do the chore itself.

During these years children still look mostly to their parents for their feelings of worth, their understanding of how they should behave and for learning how to meet their social needs. They learn habits for how to care for themselves and their things and how to participate as part of a family. They begin to discover how to get along with other kids, including their siblings. They find out about some of their unique abilities, talents and weaknesses. Since children's brains change faster in the previous infant and toddler years and then later during adolescence, this is the most stable time of childhood. This eight-year period gives parents a chance to guide their children into family relationships that create in them a Wise Parent and alert Adult.

Children this age are still impulsive and tend to express themselves according to what's appealing at the moment. How can you manage them to keep interactions positive and still require them to learn new and often difficult habits? In many families parents can just keep after their kids and gradually get them to adolescence with pretty healthy inner families. This is more possible if both parents don't work full-time and their kids don't have significant problems with schoolwork or friends. Both parents must also avoid getting involved with an addiction, which would pull them away from parenting as a team.

Managing well is only possible if both parents (when there are two) have adequate Adults and Wise Parents. They can't use their Indulgent or Critical Parents much of the time. They must also work together in parenting to maintain a low level of stress for themselves and their kids. Foster Cline and Jim Fay offer comprehensive guidance in their book *Parenting with Love and Logic: Teaching Children Responsibility*.[6] Their colorful ideas for how your Adult can observe your parenting can help you learn how to manage your kids wisely. Thomas Phelan describes a creative system for managing kids in his book *1-2-3 Magic: Effective Discipline for Children 2–12*.[7] A DVD demonstrating his points is also available.

A new problem for parents in the past decade is the involvement of children at increasingly younger ages in electronic activities. As noted in Part II, chapter 2 on addiction, the younger a child is when he gets hooked on an addiction, the more likely he is to be addicted for life. Research is being conducted to determine the effects of electronic entertainment on this generation of kids, but you can see the effects yourself. What happens when you take your young son's video game away? What if you take away your ten-year-old daughter's phone? Do your kids quickly take up reading, playing ball outdoors or building with their Legos? Or do they lie around and complain for days that they're bored?

If you're paying attention and not partaking in an addictive activity yourself, you'll be able to regulate your children's access to activities that require too little of them. They need to learn how to give themselves a positive day. They need to develop their unique talents and adequate social skills beginning at least by age four. Video games or television don't challenge them in enough ways to discover what they can do themselves. Don't let them get sidetracked at this critical stage. Laura Kastner and Jennifer Wyatt offer guidelines for how to set limits on your kids' use of electronics in their book *Getting to Calm: Cool-Headed Strategies for Parenting Tweens & Teens*.[8]

Numerous websites for young kids encourage social networking and promise a safe experience. You may want to explore these to see if any would be good for your child and situation. Larry Rosen reported on research that led him to conclude Facebook can be either positive or negative for your child's development.[9] The effect depends on whether or not you set and enforce consistently firm guidelines limiting their use of such sites. Rosen also advised that parents monitor all their kids' activity online, guiding them in how to prevent or solve problems that occur. Facebook's policy is that kids must be at least thirteen to sign up, but this is subject to change and they can find ways around it. What age is best for your children to begin engaging in online activity remains in question. If you can't supervise kids from age four to eleven very closely, I'd urge you to make them wait.

What can you do if, at some point during this critical eight-year period, your family doesn't have the ideal conditions for you to manage your kids? What if your kids tell you by their oppositional behavior, fighting with each other, increased problems at school or expressions of anxiety and sadness that they aren't getting what they need from you? What if you're having marital problems that upset you and the kids?

How can you stabilize your kids and gain their cooperation? How can you create the structure at home that can help you be consistent? You need a containing environment where kernels of corn gently shape your child's behavior. Your Adult must stay in charge to keep your Critical Parent from trying to shock your child into compliance. Your Adult must keep your Indulgent Parent from letting your kids raise themselves.

Guidance to Get Your Kids and Your Parenting on Track

Let's consider a design for your home environment that has worked for hundreds of the parents I've counseled over thirty-five years. Appendix D offers figure 5, a drawing of a simple behavior chart and detailed instructions for using it. I developed it after trying others that specified particular behaviors and concrete rewards, like they use in school classrooms. They only worked for a brief time and didn't address the basic problems in the families. It turns out that kids would rather work for special attention from you than a treat.

Parents usually know what particular behaviors they want their kids to do and can guide them if their kids will just cooperate. Some parents need help to prioritize what behaviors to require, since kids can't change everything at once. And some need help with what they should expect of their particular child in the situation. Once parents are clear about what is appropriate to expect and are able to prioritize what changes should come first, they're ready to manage their kids' behavior. Here's a system that teaches kids under age twelve to obey their parents right away with a cooperative attitude.

This chart is designed to support your Adult when you have to manage children ages four to eleven. It allows you to engage and build your Wise Parent. It can help you avoid setting your children up to fail with your Indulgent Parent and then coming down on them with your Critical Parent. Some kids have commented that the chart was for their parents too. Parents report that their kids relax with this structure and find it a positive challenge to avoid "blue marks" for not obeying. The power struggles that exhausted and frustrated you will happen much less often. Kids this age like life better being on your side; they just need to find a way to do it.

You can understand why this system works by looking at what kids in this age group need from their parents. They still expect to be almost completely dependent on you. They instinctively seek your attention any way they can get it to gain input for their development. Early in their lives, many discover that they can get intense one-on-one attention from a parent when they do something wrong. They begin to seek negative attention, because it's easier to get than positive recognition. A parent will react when her child dumps grape juice on the floor, but when her child plays quietly on her own, she may just hold her breath, hoping it lasts.

This chart system is designed to restructure the interaction. The child is asked to give up seeking negative attention. This is why you don't give lots of warnings or engage in arguing very much; these behaviors reward his disobedience. Instead you give extra positive time at the end of the week and verbal encouragement every day. You don't take away any of the positive time you already have together. The chart helps ensure that you're teaching more with kernels of corn than with shocks to your children's feet. It helps keep your problem-solving Adult and kind Wise Parent in charge. It allows you to avoid more of the intense negative interactions with your kids that could bring out your Critical Parent.

When You Should Seek a Family Counselor

When you find your Critical Parent is emerging too often or when your child isn't responding to your efforts to improve your relationship, it's definitely time to seek a counselor. Your Adult should always make it clear that you're only criticizing a specific behavior, one that she actually can change. If you don't help her understand this because your Critical Parent has taken over, she'll feel like she's overall a bad child in your eyes. Remember that like toddlers, young kids continue to oversimplify and have black-and-white thinking. Her feelings about herself will be even worse if you really get mad and make global criticisms like "You never show any respect," "You don't appreciate anything I do," "You don't even love your sister," "You don't even try to take care of your things," etc. If you get so mad you call her names, like brat, lazy, mean or sneaky, you already know this is abusive.

Additional damage from repeated episodes like this happens because your kid absorbs your Critical-Parent messages and the toxic beliefs that fuel them. Then, under stress, her young Critical Parent will beat up her Child like you do and she may go on to do that to her kids. Your Critical Parent's shocks to her feet prevent the growth of her Wise Parent, leaving her Child anxious and filled with hurt and anger. This leaves your kid more prone to anxiety problems and depression in the future. It may cause her to distrust you and begin to protect herself by sharing less with you or even lying to keep out of trouble. It causes deep harm to her self-esteem and doesn't help yours much either. A counselor can help reset your interaction.

Be careful to select a counselor who will work with both you and your child. There are still counselors who believe a child client should be given the same confidentiality as an adult client. One family I see was severely harmed by a counselor who aggressively insisted their ten-year-old daughter required twice-weekly sessions indefinitely with-out any feedback to or from them. By the time she was twelve, she was verbally abusive to her parents and younger brother, failing in school and having prolonged tantrums when asked to help with a chore. The parents finally sought counseling for themselves and learned that this counseling approach was not appropriate. Family counseling has helped restore their ability to guide and manage their daughter.

A family counselor will use his Adult to look at your family's par-ticular needs. He'll help your Adult reassert itself to make things more positive at home. You may have questions about how to restructure difficult times for your kids or how to help them get along with each other and the friends they try to play with. You may be confused about how to manage your child's involvement in electronic activities. Your child may have special needs, like hyperactivity, learning problems or anxiety, which require extra parenting skill. Numerous books are available to help parent children with disabilities while maintaining good care for the rest of the family. Look online or ask your counselor for suggestions. Some are mentioned in Part II, chapter 1.

You and your spouse may need help to work together better in parenting. If your counselor doesn't have a structured system to help you be consistent and positive with your kids despite all the stress in your life, he may be willing to help you use the chart system described here, with modifications as needed for your child or situation. The behavior chart helps identify when problems with your child happen most often so you can restructure these difficult times. The chart helps parents work together better if both are willing to learn how to use it.

Parenting Through a Divorce

If you and your husband aren't able to stay together through your kids' childhood, you may need additional guidance to help you keep your kids on track. A counselor can help you and your kids if your Adult observes that emotions are escalating for any of you. Fight-or-flight won't help in this situation either, though it's a natural tendency for this broad a threat to your way of life. Mary Ellen Hannibal describes how to parent through this time in her book *Good Parenting through Your Divorce: The Essential Guide to Helping Your Children Adjust and Thrive—Based on the Leading Program.*[10] If you grow your Adult and Wise Parent to meet this challenge, your kids will have at least one parent they can trust to help them keep stable.

When the Behavior Chart Is Not Enough

When your child doesn't respond to your positive efforts to guide him with a chart system or a less structured approach, you may need to use a mild punishment to interrupt his pattern. You can take him to his room or put him in a chair away from you. This time alone for your child keeps him from interacting negatively with you when you've tried unsuccessfully to give him a direction. Originating in B. F. Skinner's labs, time-outs have been used widely to provide nonviolent guidance to children. They can help your child learn to seek kernels of corn from you, instead of shocks to his feet. In this case your attention is the reinforcing kernel of corn. A good, quick reference for how to use time-outs is available online at AskDrSears.com.[11] Like Skinner, Dr. Sears emphasizes that positive guidance and attention should dominate your interactions. Brief time out from these then serves as a mild punishment.

Time-outs are meant to be a mild shock, not an intense one. Therefore, they need to fit the situation and the age of your child. If your child doesn't respond to relatively short time-outs, you need to redesign her environment. It's up to you to create the container that will guide her in positive ways to learn what she needs to learn. Get help from a family counselor if your child indicates the containers you set up aren't working for her. Don't let your Critical Parent attack her for being a disappointment or attack your inner Child because you can't figure out what might work.

There's another simple technique you can use for behavior that's frequent but brief and more annoying than harmful. Your child may make a rude comment when you correct him, like "whatever!" He may say things or make noises that he knows will irritate you or a sibling. He may hog the air time with his talking, interrupting a sibling or you. You need to discourage this kind of negative-attention-seeking harassment with a consequence that's not too harsh but that will effectively stop the behavior; it should be more of a redirection than a shock to his feet. You need something that he can do by himself to cut off the negative attention from you that he's seeking. You want to be sure he understands what he should do instead of this negative behavior.

I've found that one page of sentences works from ages four to seventeen for these behaviors. Assign sentences like, "I will be respectful to my mother," "I will stop talking when I'm told to," "I will follow directions without talking back," "I will keep my hands to myself" or "I won't yell or throw things in the house." Give your child a lined sheet with the sentence you want her to copy and tell her she must return it to you before you'll do anything special for her. If the behavior happens at a time you can't institute this, tell her she'll owe you sentences later and be sure to follow through. Children from four to six can write fewer sentences while you spell the words for them as needed. My four-year-old grandson was crowing over his big sister's receiving sentences until I gave him some and made sure he could do them.

Avoid giving extra pages if your child argues or delays doing the sentences. If he acts up over having to do them, give him a chart warning or a time-out but not lots of negative attention. One page of sentences makes the point that your child must stop his behavior but doesn't cause a lot of resentment. It can be done several times a day if necessary and takes little effort from you. If your child gets too quick at one page, give him a one-page essay on why he should change his behavior. Your child can see that he can't just wear you down, because he's the one having to do the work. When your child steps aside from the interaction to do these sentences, it helps his immature Adult have time to reassert itself. Instead of a prolonged Critical Parent and angry Child interaction between the two of you, your Adult and Wise Parent are supporting your kid to build his own.

Time-outs and sentences both remove your child from social kernels of corn. They give her time for her developing Adult and Wise Parent to recover from fight-or-flight reactivity that's coming from her Child. Time-outs simply separate her; sentences help ensure she's focusing on new thinking and not entertaining herself in her room. It won't be effective if she learns to think, "I'll show them! I can have a good time anyway in here with all my toys, games, videos, etc." In some cases time-outs need to occur outside the child's room.

Time-outs and sentences shouldn't be increased to serve as punishment when your child acts out more severely. Other consequences should be used instead, like no dessert or missing a favorite television show or even a few days of television. They can be fitted to the situation; for example, when your kids yell or fight in the car, you can pull over and tell them they'll owe you sentences or a time-out when they get home. If you're in a store and they won't mind you or have a fit because you won't buy them something, you can simply take them home. Don't give them lots of warnings then, either. If you're struggling, a counselor can help you reorganize for more positive interactions.

The chart system can help ensure that you don't get into a relationship with your child in which most of the interaction is negative. After your family is back on track with your Adult and Wise Parent leading and your children mostly cooperating with you, you can stop using the behavior chart. Bring it back again if your kids start falling back into their old habits and your Adult notices more Critical-Parent pressure within you.

Once you don't need so much structure to get your child's cooperation, be sure to continue providing special one-on-one time to keep building a strong positive connection. Appendix D describes how to create this positive time. Your child wants this special time with you, just as you seek it with people closest to you. How can *you* most easily tell when people really value you? They want to spend time with you for fun and sharing. During the critical years before your child reaches puberty, you must build a relationship in which he knows that you deeply value him as a person. Through this he will come to value himself for the things you value in him. It's the best source of lifelong self-esteem and the simplest way to impart your values. Adele Faber and Elaine Mazlish offer specific dialogues to illustrate how you can keep your one-on-one reward time with your child positive in their book *How to Talk So Kids Will Listen and Listen So Kids Will Talk*.[12]

Parenting Your Adolescent (Ages Twelve to Seventeen) with Your Adult and Wise Parent

A 2011 article in *National Geographic* magazine by David Dobbs laid out the latest research about the extensive rewiring that the adolescent brain goes through until kids are about twenty-five.[13] Dobbs describes how during this period the brain allows the flexibility needed for a child to become an Adult at the same time it gradually stabilizes. The Adult brain area remains flexible for the longest period of time. This allows it to develop the capacity it will need to manage the inner family and outer world. Before it's fully formed, adolescents can be unpredictable, capricious, moody and dangerous to themselves or others. Their fledgling Adult can't see the whole picture yet; it sees things more narrowly from their own point of view about what they can handle.

As the parent of one of these amazing works in progress, how can you figure out how to manage your teen? There are some basic principles to guide your Adult, many of which we've already explored for parenting younger kids. Your child still needs and wants a strong connection with you. Having worked with adolescents in many settings for the past thirty-five years, I have continued to be impressed by how powerful one-on-one adult attention is for them. Abused teenage boys placed in group homes, behaviorally disordered youths in special classrooms and privileged teens coming for individual counseling all respond more to quality attention than anything else we adults can provide. The angriest complaints and the deepest sobs come from teens whose parents can't or won't treat them like valuable people by spending positive time with them.

For younger kids, positive time is easier to create. They're happy just to have fun with you. Adolescents define fun in more challenging terms. Their brains focus upon finding out who they are and what they can do well. They can be irritating as they try to let you know how they're different from you in dozens of ways. This helps them feel separate from you as they engage in self-exploration. They can get very upset with you when you try to insist they take your point of view about anything. Discussions about how to fold the laundry, do their homework, manage their things or prioritize their time all can lead to huge battles. Even if you maintain your Wise Parent and keep your Critical Parent in check, you may still be stymied by their exquisite adolescent sensitivity to any hint of an insult.

Of course, your teen may also have times when she's wise beyond her years, compassionate and empathically supportive. You may be tempted to think this could last if she wanted to maintain it. Recognize that she'll probably have more trouble sustaining her Adult-Wise-Parent dominance than you do. Kids differ greatly during these years in this capacity. Some seem to have very little control of it; others are much more able to keep their internal balance from an early age. The inherited traits discussed in Part II, chapter 1 play a big role in this. But there are some things you can do to help your teen learn how to keep stable through all the brain-remodeling disruption.

All that you've learned about how you can keep your Adult in charge applies as you try to help your adolescent develop his own strong Adult. How can you create an appropriate container for him to learn all these concepts? Your teen is beginning to form his own container to provide his own kernels of corn and even his own consequences for going in the wrong direction. You can't support his growth with a behavior chart, where all he must do is obey you to succeed. How can you design your relationship to be sure it stays constructive, despite all his rebellious tendencies?

Positive Contracting to Guide Your Adolescent

When you need to ask your teen to cooperate with you more, there's an appropriate alternative to the behavior chart for younger kids. This method allows more flexibility for your teen and for you. Anyone who's tried to form a contract for behavior change with his adolescent has probably emerged from the experience certain that his kid was born to be a lawyer. You can turn around negative situations, such as when you've grounded your teen for months at a time or yelled at her until you've embarrassed yourself when your Critical Parent took over. For lack of a more inspired term, I named this strategy positive contracting.

Here's how you institute this new approach. If you're married, include your spouse in this process. First determine what changes you'd like your teen to make. If there are many, prioritize them and select a few to present to her for consideration. Say to her, "I need more cooperation from you around these things. I realize it will be difficult for you to make these changes but I really need your help. If I see that you're making an effort, I want to let you know I appreciate it. I would like to take some special time next weekend for just the two of us to get together and do something fun. You can think about what you might like to do. Don't make it too expensive. I'll let you know as the week goes along how I think you're doing. We'll feel more like getting together if we have a good week." Ask your teen if she sees any problem with doing any of these things. Try to problem-solve with her, as long as she'll work with you.

You should choose changes that you know your teen can easily accomplish, especially at first. Some examples are talking more respectfully to you, being kinder to a sibling, feeding the dog more faithfully, clearing his things from the family areas every day, putting his dishes in the dishwasher, getting to bed on time, starting his homework earlier or getting off the phone or computer with less argument. Don't ask for more than about four of these at a time. Give him time to establish new habits before you add more requests. Acknowledge his efforts briefly and tactfully as the week goes by. He won't like it if you get pushy about how much better it is for him to do things your way. Emphasize how he's making things easier for *you*, rather than for himself, and say a brief "thanks."

When the weekend comes, don't take away a regular positive activity if your teen doesn't improve much. If she's shown more cooperation in some areas, even if it's not yet at the level you'd hope, do the special activity with her. Try to discuss your activity with her ahead of time, planning something she suggests, if possible. You can play a game together on the computer, bake something that she wants to make, take a bike ride, go for a hike, shoot baskets, go fishing, take a walk around a new area and have lunch, give each other pedicures or take in a ball game. Don't suggest going to a movie or any other activity that precludes conversation. Help her discover that you can be a pleasant person to hang out with.

Whatever else you do during this reward time, don't lecture or scold your teen. You have plenty of time for that, and he needs to experience you in a new way. He wants to feel like you find him to be an interesting and enjoyable companion. Then he'll feel like you see him for the person he is and you're not just interested in his performing according to your values. During this time encourage your teen to share about anything he wants to, whether it's a new CD he likes, what's happening socially, where he'd like to travel someday or what movie stars he admires. Avoid grilling him by asking too many questions. Review Adele Faber and Elaine Mazlish's work, noted above, for tips on having good conversations.[14]

Talk to your teen like you'd talk with a friend. Share your own musical favorites or social experiences (discreetly) with the give-and-take you'd have with a friend. For a while, especially if there's been a lot of distance between you and your kid, you may need to give more. Share information about yourself, even silly things. Even if it seems awkward for a while, your kids will recognize that you're trying to make them comfortable. They're grateful when you don't put them on the spot. Don't give up if it takes a few outings to have your teen open up a little. She'll recognize you're trying to show *her* more respect and consideration and she'll respond eventually. Remember that no matter what teens might say or do, they want very much to feel your love and respect.

Gradually you may be able to drop the contract format as your teen develops habits that make life better for both of you. Continue to schedule regularly your one-on-one special activities and build your relationship. You're cementing the basis for a lifelong friendship once your teen grows up. You're developing the trust and communication that will allow your teen to seek your guidance and help when he encounters problems he can't handle. If he knows you respect and trust him, he won't fear that you'll give him unfair or overly restrictive consequences when he makes a mistake. He'll call you for a ride if there's no one sober at the party to bring him home. He'll ask your advice about how to deal with a troubled friend. He'll tell you when he feels overwhelmed or depressed. He won't want to ask for your help if he believes you'll take over right away and try to enforce your solutions.

Consequences that Encourage Your Teen's Adult

Along with positive contracting, you'll have times when you have to provide your teen with punishment to redirect him or simply stop a negative behavior. The use of sentences for annoying and frequent behavior has been discussed. Many parents resist trying this technique because they believe it won't work. It was the only punishment we used in a class for behaviorally disordered teenage boys, except on the rare occasions when a couple of them became violent and we had to call on the Juvenile Justice Department. The class was very successful because the young, athletic teacher gave caring attention to his boys all day long. This was the only reward offered except for the reward the kids felt when they learned their school lessons. As parents you can offer similar caring attention, which will motivate your kids to want your approval. In this context kids respond well to mild punishments like sentences.

When parents do try using sentences, they're often amused or amazed at their teen's response. In one family, the very accomplished sixteen-year-old daughter had tyrannized her parents for years by talking nonstop. Her parents instituted sentences and targeted this excessive talking. She got sentences a few times a day at first and gradually became capable of normal conversation. When her fourteen-year-old brother finally got sentences assigned, he almost seemed to feel honored and asked his mother how she'd like the heading on the page. Try it; paper's cheap.

You may also need to limit your teen's access to activities he likes if he won't take on the responsibility of doing some he doesn't like. The rule for this is to take as little away as is needed for him to get the message. You'll trigger less rebellion and keep your relationship more positive. Teens are acutely aware of the fact that you have the power to "ruin their lives." Don't abuse it. Foster Cline and Jim Fay offer more Wise-Parent guidance in their book *Parenting Teens with Love and Logic: Preparing Adolescents for Responsible Adulthood.*[15]

If your teen is rude to you or refuses to do what you ask, take his phone, television show, computer time or car privileges away for a day or two, not a month. Remember that you can always take the privilege away again if needed, once you've given it back. Time goes by more slowly for kids than adults, and they don't need a heavy shock to their feet to learn what you expect of them. But consider what you tell them ahead of time, get coordinated with your spouse and follow through with the consequences you've promised.

Remember that you must be consistent to avoid teaching your kid to keep pecking at you for the same things indefinitely, just like Skinner's pigeon. If you give in occasionally, you're creating a very persistent and strong-willed teen. Then you have to crack down hard to get him to stop, which will hurt your relationship and your kid's self-esteem. Don't let your Indulgent Parent take over in these situations; it will build his Indulgent Parent. Laura Kastner and Jennifer Wyatt offer guidance for managing tough teen attitudes in their book *Getting to Calm: Cool-Headed Strategies for Parenting Tweens & Teens,*[16] mentioned earlier. Being cool-headed means keeping your Adult in charge.

Your rules for bedtime, homework, healthy eating, curfew and reporting on where your teen is form the container he needs at this age to manage his life and feel secure. Exceptions can be negotiated occasionally, but you need to be firm about what habits you expect in these areas that impact your teen's health and safety. Many parents get overwhelmed and let their teens develop poor eating and sleeping habits. Their exhausted and malnourished kids can't function normally and have more problems with depression, anxiety, concentration and Adult judgment.

Your teen learns to care for herself as you care for her and will adopt your Wise-Parent guidance. Watch the example you offer in how you take care of yourself. "Do what I say, not what I do" doesn't fly with adolescents. Amy Tiemann edits the articles of eleven women writing on how to grow through parenting in her book *Confident Parents, Confident Kids—Letting Go So You Both Can Grow.*[17]

Adult and Wise-Parent Coping with the Electronic World

Some of the privileges kids have take over their lives and leave parents feeling helpless. Relating to their friends by cell phone and on Facebook or the Xbox has become the norm for many kids by the time they're teenagers. Managing their time with these activities can be a nightmare for parents. I recommend to parents that they limit their kids' time on any electronic device from the very beginning, as noted above. Instead of allowing whole weekends and evenings to be spent this way, allow only a couple of hours a day. Insist that your kids invite friends over and go out to do non-sitting activities with them.

One of my most Xbox-addicted older teen clients looked forward to going places with friends when he was older and on his own but said he had no idea what they'd do or where they'd go. He had little interest in dating or even driving and barely got by in school, though he was very bright. He wouldn't eat properly or exercise and had little skill in expressing himself in conversation. Microsoft just keeps working to make Xbox even more consuming. I saw a fourteen-year-old who'd been on Xbox many hours a day since he was twelve. He refused to do any schoolwork. When I asked him what he planned to do after he got on his own, he said he'd just play on his Xbox. Substitute "drugs" for Xbox, and what would you as a parent do? There should be warning labels on these electronic devices.

Work with your child beginning with her first introduction to cell phones to recognize how they could be misused. Encourage her to use her phone to arrange times with others and have brief conversations. Discourage use of the phone to have continual contact with friends and no time for her own thoughts. She needs to develop herself alone as well as in connection with others. During your one-on-one time together, introduce her to activities she can do on her own, like crafts, reading, bicycling, gardening or cooking. She needs to develop the same independent sense of worth and comfort described for you in Part I, chapter 5.

There's strong social pressure today to allow kids as they get older to spend most of their spare time online. There's always been social pressure on teenagers to drink or have sex, and parents have stood against this effectively in many cases. Parents need to set limits with these new threats to their kids' development. The biggest problem is that parents often aren't home to enforce any limits for their kids' use of cell phones or computers.

Lock up the computer or video game or take it in your car if you need to separate your teen from it when you're at work. Total removal of the Xbox or particular games may be appropriate, especially for younger adolescents. It's too late if you try to take them away when your kid is almost an adult. He may run away or become self-destructive in order to assert his independence. However, you can temporarily limit the use of the Xbox or cell phone, even for older kids, as a consequence for not cooperating with chores or the routines you set for them to be healthy. Do this when you're home and can enforce your consequence.

As discussed in the chapter on addiction (Part II, chapter 2), the early use of drugs and alcohol leads to addiction for kids. Early excessive use of electronic stimulation may have a similar impact, as it deprives the youth of time to develop skills for relating to others and to explore a variety of interests. Our brains developed with the input of five senses, not just sight and hearing. What's the impact of reducing the kinds of stimulation our kids receive during this period of rapid brain development? The impact on school performance and social skill is already apparent in many cases. Their Indulgent Parent blossoms while their hooked up. Remember that your teen will notice your computer and phone behavior too. She'll resist your giving her limits if you don't manage your own involvement thoughtfully.

When School Problems Arise

Avoid creating a situation where your kid is receiving more shocks to his feet than kernels of corn from you because of school issues. By this age, if not before, kids want their schoolwork to be their business.

Their budding Adult wants to figure out how to manage it according to their young Wise-Parent priorities. If you get too involved, they often begin to believe that all you care about are their grades and performance. This feeling increases if you punish them with whole months of grounding until their grades improve. If your youth is well engaged with his school program and mostly getting his work done, let him take charge. Don't punish him for not getting all As and Bs.

What guidance should you offer? From ages twelve to fifteen, it's important to set a particular time well ahead of bedtime for homework to be done. The place your teen does it should be quiet and free of distractions. Your teen should be able to ask for your help but not have you stand over her while she does her work. You should be able to observe that she's not on the phone or playing on her computer during this time.

Your role is to ensure that your teen has the opportunity to do his homework, not to force him to do it at the level you choose for him. You can offer to look it over for him, but don't require that he share it with you. He has the power not to turn it in or perform on the next test; he has to want to do it. Ask for the serenity to let go in this situation. You may have the courage to fight with your teen, but the wisdom is in knowing that you can't change him much here. Avoid battles you can't win to help maintain your relationship with your child.

Allow kids sixteen and older to experiment with how they study, but continue to insist on their getting adequate sleep. Some kids are ambitious beyond what is healthy, trying to keep active socially, participate in extracurricular activities, get top grades and complete a college AA degree at the same time they complete their high school degree. Some parents push the double degree as a cost-saver for their family. Your Adult and Wise Parent must guide your youth to a level of activity that allows time to get eight or nine hours of sleep most nights. He needs to learn how eat for good health and cook basic wholesome foods. He needs time just to relax, enjoy fun with family and friends and experience contentment in his life.

You're guiding your teen in the self-care basics she must have for mental fitness. Youth may give her the energy to take on a lot at times, but she must find a basic level that she can maintain. I see kids whose efforts to excel at too many things for too long have left them burned out, depressed and feeling negative about themselves. They set unrealistic standards and attempt too much, but in the absence of parental insistence on some reasonable balance, they think they're failures if they can't keep it up. They often worry about disappointing their parents. Express pride when your kid is wisely balancing her life in ways that will allow her to maintain a good level of performance. Don't encourage overextension and unrealistic goals. When your youth goes off on her own to college or work from her own apartment, you'll be glad she has habits for taking good care of herself.

If your youth has trouble with his schoolwork, encourage him to explain how he sees the problem. If you maintain a positive relationship, your teen is more likely to want your help with this and any other problem he faces. Don't dictate solutions or threaten consequences. Use your Adult to help his Adult analyze where the problem is. Does he need extra help with some concepts in a class? Are his study skills adequate for his assignments? Is a particular teacher failing to provide the structure he needs for learning? Discuss with him how you can help him in each situation.

Your job is to help your teen learn not only her math but also how to navigate a complex system. If she prefers to talk with a teacher first herself, encourage this. But if she doesn't and the problems persist, take her along to talk with her teacher to get the teacher's view of the problem. Afterwards, try to help her see things from her teacher's point of view without taking the teacher's side. Remind her that teachers who see 150 students a day can't be there often for one student. If you find that the teacher isn't going to help her, take her to talk with a school counselor. Ask what support is available for extra help with a particular subject or with study skills.

If your youth is beginning to fail some classes or has lost his motivation to do schoolwork, don't try to punish him into functioning better; that just shuts behavior down and creates hostility. Your teen needs to develop some new coping skills if he's having this much trouble. You need to help him learn these skills by properly dispensing kernels of corn. Your Adult needs to explore your options if your youth can't or won't use his school opportunity to prepare him for independence.

Some kids will admit they don't want to grow up; they feel overwhelmed with what that requires. You can understand how they feel, so stay on their side and help them find another path. Some just need more time for their brains to develop. Some school districts have alternative school programs that provide more one-on-one time with teachers to help them individualize their program. Some will thrive in the less controlled, more adult environment of a community college.

Here's another situation where private counseling can really help. When you call for the appointment, check to be sure that the counselor has a policy of working both with you and your teen. You do need to be sure the counselor is getting an accurate picture of what's happening, but you want to allow space for your kid to form a relationship where she can openly discuss anything that's bothering her, including you. The counselor should have a special disclosure statement in which what is confidential and what will be shared with the parent is spelled out. A sample of one that's worked well for my clients is given in appendix E.

A Job Can Help Your Teen Grow Up

Some teens who won't use their time to study should be required to get a job .Their Indulgent Parent may be too strong. Most jobs available to kids give them an environment where they can succeed and get friendly treatment and recognition just for being dependable. If your teen isn't treated with respect, encourage him to look elsewhere. Older friends might be able to suggest a better job situation. A reasonable work experience can help a youth get more confidence rapidly. The low wages paid in these jobs, along with their lack of opportunity, can help motivate him to want more education. Encourage your teen to find work close to home or on a bus route to avoid just handing him a car.

While your teen copes with her new responsibilities, offer encouragement and prepare to let her make her own mistakes. She may need to discover for herself what happens when you're late to work or fail to go in, do a poor job, or act disrespectful to a boss. You just need to encourage her to try again and talk it out with you if she wants to. Be sure to refrain from talking down to her. It's okay if she blows some jobs while she learns. Keep in mind that it's her responsibility that needs development, not yours. And new behavior is built with kernels of corn, which in this case can be your recognition of what she *is* doing to learn about working. Don't try to hound her into doing it your way.

When to Encourage Your Teen to Drive

Examine carefully the pros and cons of having your teen begin driving or driving his own car. This is a serious issue and should be managed by your Adult and Wise Parent, not your Indulgent Parent. Just check the incidence of car accidents for kids in their first year of driving if you're considering rewarding your youth with a nice car he doesn't help pay for. Don't let your Indulgent Parent set your kid up to be a careless driver.

Consider how much time you have to drive with him before he goes on his own and be sure he has enough experience to develop the habits practice gives. Some kids are so committed to not growing up that they need encouragement to practice. Good driving habits will free your teen to focus on the special situations that require quick judgment. Practiced habits will allow him to handle the distractions of driving with other kids in the car or talking on the hands-free phone. Don't let him drive unless you are sure he's ready.

Try hard to be sure that you're making your decisions in the best interest of your adolescent. Some families find it helpful to get their teen get a car because she could drive younger kids to their activities while the parents work. Some families want their kids to drive to a job to earn money to help the family or cover some of their own expenses. If you've ever known parents who've lost their child in a car accident they could have prevented, you'll be careful not to move too fast to let your teen drive on his own.

You've invested years in trying to provide the environment for your teen to grow up to be safe and mentally fit. Don't rush to treat her like she's capable of coping with Adult judgment consistently. Consider how hard it is for you with your mature Adult brain to keep your Adult in charge. Share some of your struggles with your teen and discuss ways to improve Adult and Wise-Parent functioning. Let her know you're on her side, even as you set some limits. If you've built your connection over several years through good one-on-one times together and wise parenting, she'll trust you and cooperate.

Parenting Your Young Adult from Eighteen to Twenty-Five

Eighteen is the socially determined age for youths to be declared ready for adulthood; it is not a biologically based choice. As David Dobbs notes in his article described above, the brain is not fully developed until about age twenty-five. Kids this age seem like adults in some ways and young teens in others. Our social confusion about how to treat young people this age makes it worse for them. We make it illegal for them to drink but send them off to cope in war. Parents aren't legally required to provide for their needs, but most of the jobs available to them won't support them. These paradoxes create life-threatening possibilities for our young people to make mistakes without parental guidance. For example, they can move in with an abusive partner or go on a trip with a kid who uses drugs, and there's nothing a parent can do about it.

How can your Adult sort out this situation to help you maintain a constructive relationship with your not-quite-adult grown-up child? From age eighteen on, youths expect to be treated like equal adults. If you've been able to establish a mutually respectful and friendly rapport before this time, you and your kid will have an easier time navigating. If you have a more complicated relationship with less trust or respect on either side, you can still begin to forge a better situation between you.

This is the point in parenting where you really need to cling to Serenity Prayer wisdom. Let's review it again and then see how it can help maintain your mental fitness as you parent.

> God grant me the serenity
> To accept the things I cannot change,
> The courage to change the things I can,
> And the wisdom to know the difference.[18]

Let's start with the last line. Your Wise Parent has been preparing for this challenge as it has grown through the years that you've parented your child. You've studied the twelve toxic beliefs to learn what you can reasonably expect, rather than what you grew up thinking was possible. Your Adult has been working to stay aware of your kid's coping abilities as he's developed. Your knowledge of him and your understanding of what's normal for kids this age allow you to make educated guesses about what he can handle. The new wisdom for this time in his life is that he has the freedom to exercise a different opinion about that. To remain supportive and available if he does feel he needs your suggestions, you need to let go of your attachment to your ideas about what he can do.

Now consider the third line of the prayer. Instead of working on your kid, you must find the courage to change yourself and your worries that would limit her exploration. Kahlil Gibran conveys beautifully why you need to let go in *The Prophet*, in the section entitled "On Children."[19] Change your habit of thinking you have the answers for her and genuinely encourage her to discover her own answers. Become a dependable source of positive ways to look at her mistakes and learn from them. Don't be a master of "I told you so." Listen to her ideas and consider how they might be great, if only for an experiment that will teach her something.

And then when your beloved young adult does what he thinks he must, you need the serenity to let him have the experience with all its consequences. If he gets cited for drunk driving, don't make it easy for him. Be wise and try to feel serene, even if he's angry with you for this. If he lands a job that sounds too hard for him, don't pressure him with advice. Be wise and realize he'll be justifiably hurt and angry with you if you don't respect his right to handle it on his own. In each situation your Adult must consider how to support the growth of your kid's Adult and Wise Parent from a respectful distance.

Boundaries in Relating to Your Young Adult

Now it's time to review the chapters on friendship, acquaintance and relative relationships. You've studied them for your own understanding. Now look at them through the perspective of your young adult. Many of the things you're trying to offer her are the same things you'd offer a good friend. If she doesn't respond like a friend, try offering her the civility and smooth cooperation you'd offer an acquaintance as much as possible. Give her time to find a comfortable way to relate to you. Consider what boundaries are needed in your relationship with her. Try to set limits in a way that keeps the door open but requires respect for your rights to a reasonable life.

When your young adult has a lot of trouble assuming adult respon-sibilities, make adjustments based on your knowledge of him. Decide what cooperation you must have from him and make a contract he must follow if he wants your help. He wants to be respected as an adult, and you're no longer legally responsible for him. His Indulgent Parent must be curbed. Contracts wouldn't have been helpful or enforceable before he was eighteen. Now he must realize it's a privilege to live with you or receive financial support from you—a privilege he must earn by cooperating with your home rules.

This is another time when a family counselor can help you and your young adult find a way to get along while she still needs your support. A counselor can add the insights of her specially trained Adult to evaluate what your kid is actually capable of doing. She can help you find resources in the community for special help if needed. When your youth's Adult is impaired by any of the conditions described in Part II, like substance abuse, severe attention deficit disorder, anxiety or bipolar disorder, she usually won't be able to function like an adult as soon as other kids. These problems delay Adult development and could prevent the growth of a solid relationship between you and your kid. A counselor can help get both of you back on a positive footing to prepare for a later launch into adulthood.

Until recently our social confusion was reflected in the nearly total lack of books to guide parents through these years. The vast dif-ferences between youths this age seem to make any general recom-mendations nearly impossible. Yet some brave writers have tackled this challenge. Ruth Nemzoff gives solid guidance in her book *Don't Bite Your Tongue: How to Foster Rewarding Relationships with Your Adult Children.*[20] Fred Schloemer offers good suggestions in his book *Parenting Adult Children: Real Stories of Families Turning Challenges into Successes.*[21] Linda Herman provides unique insights for build-ing strong young adults in her book, *Parents to the End: How Baby Boomers Can Parent for Peace of Mind, Foster Responsibility in Their Adult Children, and Keep Their Hard-Earned Money.*[22]

Coming Full Circle

You may have noticed that during this discussion of parenting, I've referred back to chapters you read before to develop your own mental fitness. Let's review what would ideally happen if you could maintain your mental fitness throughout your parenting years. In the infant and toddler years, you'd need to embrace the lessons from Part I to take care of yourself while you provided the security your child needed. Your Adult would eliminate Critical-Parent and Indulgent-Parent beliefs and the fight-or-flight overreactions that could harm your vulnerable young child. Your Adult would provide consistent guidance based on what your child needed as he developed rapidly through those years.

From the ages of four to eleven, which is when your child's own Adult begins to emerge, your Adult and Wise Parent would provide the positive structure for her to grow new skills along with her own more capable Adult and supportive Wise Parent. This structure also would provide the stability to help you remain calm and function well as you parented. It would allow you and your child to form a bond where you could trust and enjoy each other. If you are working with a spouse, positive structure could help the two of you share similar parenting strategies to provide consistency and security to your child. This would also help you feel closer in your marriage as you shared comfortably in helping your child grow.

If you or your child had trouble, your Adult could refer to Part II (and a counselor if needed) to identify what inherited or acquired problem sabotaged either your Adult functioning or your child's attempts to manage herself. Your Adult would strengthen your Wise Parent through this to help you use kernels of corn for both yourself and your child to overcome these interfering influences. Seeing your child function better, thanks to your well-informed Adult, could inspire you to learn more about how to overcome particular weaknesses for both of you. Your own inner Child would feel better, because you're released from an addiction, less anxious or more accepting of an inherited tendency like learning disabilities or bipolar disorder. Feeling more confident, you'd have more energy for sharing in fun times with your child or being firm with her when she needed that.

Your Adult would recognize that the changes that come with adolescence require changes in your parenting strategy. You'd offer more flexible guidance, allowing your teen to negotiate with you and develop assertive skills he'll need. You'd improve your own self-care and friendship support system to ensure that you weren't relying on your teen to be more grown-up with you than would be good for him. You'd seek support from his school, a counselor or other community resources to provide the gradually expanding environment kids need to gain the skills that will equip them to take responsibility for themselves. You'd provide limits that would help him keep safe and focused on activities that help him grow.

Finally, you and your young adult would be ready for her to begin taking on adult responsibilities. She'd feel confident she could manage new and challenging situations. You'd feel secure that she'd take good care of herself and maintain a positive connection with you. And you'd have the relationships in your life that would help you let go of your kid when she needs you to manage your own anxieties about her. You or your teen might have special problems that cause difficulty along the way and limit how much either of you can handle on your own. But you could still have a respectful and mentally fit relationship if you've each developed the best Adult and Wise Parent you can.

Remain Mindful of the Third Toxic Belief

Hopefully by this point, your Adult and Wise Parent are recognizing that this ideal for creating the best mental fitness for yourself and your kids offers another opportunity to set you up for hurt, anger and disappointment. The third toxic belief would have you set an unrealistic standard by which to judge yourself and others and then blame yourself or them when you couldn't meet it. Having a vision of what you're trying to do in parenting is good for setting priorities. It shouldn't serve as a measuring stick for your Critical Parent to use on your Child or your kids. It's an illusion, not a real possibility for human beings. It's wise to remember on a continual basis that you can't expect yourself or others—including your kids—to maintain the Adult ability to observe and manage the human inner family all the time.

As parents you experience the hottest cauldron for honing your Adult to its highest level of functioning. It matters so much to you that you do a good job, and you have to manage your kids when you're tired, stressed out, sick or broke. You have to struggle mightily to keep your Adult in charge at least an adequate amount of time to raise your kids into mental fitness. Therefore, you must install into your Wise Parent and theirs the understanding that we are all works in progress. Your kids will prefer your company when they're grown up if you regularly acknowledge your own capacity for Adult blind spots.

You'll want to advise your kids at times, and they may ask your advice. My son and I found this formula. He talks to me at times about a challenge in his life, and I listen before venturing this: "I'm having some ideas about what you might do here; would you like to hear them?" My son, who's now grown up with two kids, still responds by saying, "Sure, if you won't get upset if I don't use them." This is also a good approach to use with your spouse or your friends when a discussion gets too heated. It invites an Adult-to-Adult exchange and reassures the Child in each person, reducing fight-or-flight tendencies.

You wouldn't always use this, of course, but it's a good strategy with your kids, as long as they seem to expect you're very invested in having them follow your advice. Eventually, you may not need this precautionary formula, but it's nice to have it when communication might otherwise be difficult. You are the most dependable lifelong mentor available to your kids. Keep your Adult and Wise Parent alert for times when *you're* making the give-and-take difficult and refocus. In good marriages it doesn't matter who's right in a conversation; it just matters that each person ends up feeling heard and respected. The same is true for friendship and for good relationships with your kids.

The Fruits of Your Mentally Fit Parenting

At the end of Part II, I discussed ways you could maintain your Adult and Wise-Parent growth for life, despite all the tendencies for your inner family to take over. I noted the Biblical guidance to "judge the tree by its fruits." As a parent you might be tempted to consider your children's successes as fruits that prove the validity of your belief system and guidance. Then when they have trouble, you may feel like you've failed as a parent and doubt the beliefs you tried to live by. Mental fitness is the fruit of your efforts to keep your Adult in charge; you can only help your children begin to find theirs.

There are many reasons why you should not see your children as in any way the fruits of your own journey. For one, if you adhere to this belief, you might tend to pressure your kids to succeed in the ways that reflect your definition of success. This alienates them and cuts you off as a mentor. They know they have begun to make a lot of their own choices by the time they're twelve. They don't even tell you all of them and they couldn't. These choices include which friends they choose to admire and hang out with, the amount of effort they put into their education, whether they get involved in an addiction and even whether they'll make use of any extra help you try to get for them.

Any of these choices can skew their response to what you're trying to teach them. When they're younger teens, you can put some limits on them, but ultimately they decide. If you try to pressure them to give up a friend, an interest or a career plan, you're likely to drive them away from you. They feel it is the ultimate disrespect for you to try to tell them who or what they should love. You wouldn't allow a friend to do this to you and still call them a friend, so don't do it to your kid. If your kid is in trouble at any point in his life, encourage him to get help from an impartial counselor. Get help yourself if you're confused about what's best for you to do, but avoid pulling out your Critical Parent. Your kids never get over wanting to believe that you value them as people, not just as evidence of your own competence as a parent.

You have continual challenges for keeping your Adult in charge and your Wise Parent strong. Part I covered how your ancient brain parts create fight-or-flight reactions over minor problems every day and prevent the full function of your more evolved Adult executive brain. Part II described many of the obstacles to Adult function that can occur in response to the stressors of everyday life. Inherited traits, anxiety, addiction and depression can potentially overwhelm your Adult for years. Part III explored what might interfere with your Adult during your various relationships with people.

The fruits of your journey to develop your mental fitness are within you. They reside in your Wise Parent and secure Child. As you look back upon any of your life experiences, you must not judge yourself based on your present wisdom. After all, some of that wisdom is the result of mistakes you made along the way. Your kids will get theirs the same way. That's how your friends, parents and neighbors learn, too. Your journey can take you full circle, and you can have empathy for everyone you meet, including your kids.

It's best to talk to yourself like this:

- I did the best I could, given the understanding I had at the time.

- I've learned to work smarter to improve my understanding before I act.

- I'll never be able to see myself as others see me.

- I must ask them how they see me from time to time.

- I can't really ever walk in another person's shoes, nor can they walk in mine.

- But I can listen to them and appreciate the effort they're making.

- I can also give myself credit for my own efforts to be honest and try my best.

- My best isn't possible all the time.

- My efforts are what I bring to my journey.

- Wisdom comes from reshaping my efforts after my mistakes.

- Gentle good humor over my mistakes is the gift of my Wise Parent to my Child.

- Laughing gently at myself is the best defense against anxiety, addiction, anger, grief and despair.

Notes

1. Denise Fields, Alan Fields and Ari Brown, *Toddler 411: Clear Answers and Smart Advice for Your Toddler*, 3rd ed. (Boulder: Windsor Peak Press, 2011).

2. Jane Nelsen, Cheryl Erwin and Roslyn Duffy, *Positive Discipline, The First Three Years: From Infant to Toddler—Laying the Foundation for Raising a Capable, Confident Child* (Roseville:: Prima Publishing, 1998).

3. B. F. Skinner, *Science and Human Behavior* (1953; repr., New York: The Free Press, 1965), 190–191.

4. Robert J. MacKenzie, *Setting Limits with Your Strong-Willed Child: Eliminating Conflict by Establishing CLEAR, Firm and Respectful Boundaries* (Roseville, CA: Prima Publishing, 2001).

5. Skinner, *Science and Human Behavior*, 99–100.

6. Foster Cline and Jim Fay, *Parenting with Love and Logic: Teaching Children Responsibility* (1990; rev. ed., Colorado Springs: Nav Press, 2006).

7. Thomas Phelan, *1-2-3 Magic: Effective Discipline for Children 2–12* (Glen Ellyn: ParentMagic, Inc., 2010).

8. Laura S. Kastner and Jennifer Wyatt, *Getting to Calm: Cool-Headed Strategies for Parenting Tweens and Teens* (Seattle: ParentMap, 2009).

9. Jamie Chamberlin, "Facebook: Friend or Foe?," *Monitor on Psychology*, Vol. 42, (October 2011).

10. Mary Ellen Hannibal, *Good Parenting through Your Divorce: The Essential Guide to Helping Your Children Adjust and Thrive* (2002; rev. ed., Cambridge: DeCapo Press, 2007).

11. AskDrSears, http://www.AskDrSears.com, 2011. Last accessed May 27, 2012.

12. Adele Faber and Elaine Mazlish, *How to Talk So Kids Will Listen and Listen So Kids Will Talk* (1980; rev. ed., New York: Scribner, 2012).

13. David Dobbs, "Beautiful Brains," *National Geographic*, Vol. 220 No. 4, (October 2011).

14. Faber and Mazlish, *How to Talk So Kids Will Listen.*

15. Foster Cline and Jim Fay, *Parenting Teens with Love and Logic: Preparing Adolescents for Responsible Adulthood* (1992; rev. ed., Colorado Springs: Pinon Press, 2006).

16. Kastner and Wyatt, *Getting to Calm.*

17. Amy Tiemann, *Courageous Parents, Confident Kids—Letting Go So You Both Can Grow* (Chapel Hill: Spark Press, 2010).

18. Reinhold Niebuhr, Serenity Prayer at AA History and Trivia online, http://www.aahistory.com. Last accessed May 27, 2012.
19. Kahlil Gibran, *The Prophet* (1926; repr., New York: Alfred A. Knopf, 2001).
20. Ruth Nemzoff, *Don't Bite Your Tongue: How to Foster Rewarding Relationships with Your Children* (New York: Palgrave Macmillan, 2008).
21. Fred Schloemer, *Parenting Adult Children: Real Stories of Families Turning Challenges into Successes* (Louisville: Butler Books, 2011).
22. Linda Herman, *Parents to the End: How Baby Boomers Can Parent for Peace of Mind, Foster Responsibility in Their Adult Children, and Keep Their Hard-Earned Money* (Chicago: NPI Upstream, 2013).

III:7

The Thirteenth Toxic Belief and Happy Endings

Years after I'd learned about cognitive-behavioral therapy, I discovered a thirteenth toxic belief. It's the idea that there always has to be a happy ending. I knew I was a romantic, raised on '50s movies, TV shows and books that had happy endings. I didn't know how fully hooked I was on this belief. One day as I drove up the hill toward my house, I had a little epiphany. I'd been obsessing, as highly sensitive people often do, about a relationship that had never really been more than an acquaintance relationship. Then my acquaintance, who had for many years pointedly kept her distance, began to request friendship-like services from me. Discussion led to no resolution.

I was frustrated and bored with my mental efforts to resolve the ending of this pseudo-friendship. I said to myself, "OK, you know when you repeat a behavior like this, there's probably some belief driving it." Some would add that the definition of insanity is repeating the same behavior and expecting a different outcome. But not wanting to go there, I just probed my inner family to find out what it might be. It wasn't one of the toxic twelve. Then it hit me: I couldn't find the serenity to accept that there was no way for me to resolve the problem by myself, no matter how many ways I tried to look at it. There couldn't be a happy ending, as I could only change *my* end of the relationship. Both parties must bring courage and commitment to make a real friendship happen.

You may wonder if this book has a happy ending. That depends on your courage and commitment to yourself to find your own mental fitness. It depends on how hard you work to grow a belief tree that nourishes you (see Part II, chapter 7). For me and my belief tree, the happy ending is that I don't have to know the ending. We may have beliefs about what happens at the end of our lives, but we don't know for sure. I think we need to have the serenity to accept this limit on our human understanding. What we believe happens at the end of our lives may influence what goals we choose along the way and whether we define a purpose for our lives or not. Religious wars are fought over such issues.

The purpose of this book is to help you develop the *how* of mental fitness. Then, with your Adult dependably in charge, you can take your time to explore and define the *why* of your life. You'll need to do this to avoid depression and some of the other obstacles to mental fitness. I suggest you focus on the process of how you live until you have good habits of self-observation and a stable inner family. To strengthen your Wise Parent, consider how the wise people you know find meaning in their lives.

As you identify wise people, you'll find that each one has flaws that could disappoint you. The third toxic belief (that people should be blamed and punished for their very human mistakes and blind spots) is the toughest one for most people. I think that's because we struggle to make sense of what being human really involves. We see the beautiful good that people can do and then the terrible wickedness. Within even the most conscientious people there are impulses to overreact from a self-focused point-of-view. No one can escape feeling like a frustrated four-year-old after being sleep deprived or overstressed for too long.

It's a lifelong, daily and at times minute-to-minute effort to keep you Adult engaged. No one can do it all the time. Some do it much less. But everyone deserves to be taught how to do it beginning at a young age, when the mind is most receptive. Life feels better with your Adult in charge. Your Child can play more freely without getting into trouble. Your Parents won't lead you into trying to control, blame or punish others.

You'll be able to accept wisdom from all kinds of sources to build your Wise Parent. You won't tend to dismiss the example of people you admire upon discovering incidents where their Wise Parent and Adult weren't fully engaged. Remember not to think in black and white; we live in the shades of gray between these extremes. It takes patience to sort out your understanding of another person with accuracy. You're not simple, and neither is anyone else.

The third toxic belief tempts you to think you know enough to judge someone else or yourself and turn loose your Critical Parent. Happy endings are only possible if you learn not to do that very often. In the New Testament of the Bible, Jesus Christ is quoted, as he dies a painful death on a cross, to say, "Father, forgive them, for they know not what they do" (Luke 23:34). He could certainly have invoked the third toxic belief and blamed the people responsible for killing him. I take his meaning to be broader, including all of us human beings. We so often don't know what we do. Hindsight's twenty-twenty, it's said. If we learn to keep our Adult in charge more of the time, we can have fewer regrets.

Violence and hate are rooted in the twelve toxic beliefs. They appear when you feel threatened—threatened for your life, your lifestyle, your job, your status, your self-esteem, etc. As you learn not to interpret most challenges to be life-threatening and body-engaging, you can become more tolerant and patient. Your personal Skinner box must keep you working for newly defined rewards and goals as you go through your life. You must keep energized for your journey through strategies like those discussed in this book. For many this effort would prove too discouraging without the belief that some power for good is pulling for them.

The Serenity Prayer begins, "God grant me..." It's a prayer to a "higher power," as the twelve-step groups (such as Alcoholics Anonymous) call it. A majority of people on Earth believe in some higher power. As a therapist I've found it easier to help people overcome the obstacles in Part II if they have some openness to the idea of a higher power that cares about them. If you find that you come to a point where you lack the optimism, energy or courage to keep trying to create a good life for yourself, I urge you to open your mind to new possibilities and new sources of wisdom.

Your frustration or even hopelessness may tempt you to think you have all the answers and that *you don't like them.* Actually your Child's telling you that it's time to strengthen your Wise Parent to cope with the new challenges you face. Don't let your Indulgent Parent keep you from taking responsibility for finding answers that work to keep you engaged with life. Read, question and search what others believe all around the world and in past times. Find a belief tree you can embrace or fertilize the one you've already planted. Then have a picnic under it as it grows and eat from its life-giving fruits for the rest of your life.

Appendix A

CBT Basics: Eight Steps, Twelve Toxic Beliefs and Three Child-Brain Habits

Eight Steps to Identify and Combat Toxic Beliefs

1. Monitor, every two hours. To monitor, choose a number between one and ten that reflects your general sense of well-being, with ten being the best and one being the worst you can feel.

2. Note dips in mood by comparing your numbers.

3. If your number drops, review the two-hour period for a disturbing event or thought.

4. Ask about the situation: "What did I believe it meant?" or "What expectations did I have?"

5. Challenge the beliefs or expectations. Substitute more realistic, comforting and valid concepts, reflecting what *your own* experience has taught you to expect, rather than what your programming says *should* happen.

6. Note especially tendencies to say "I can't stand it" or "Why me?" These set off the most painful episodes of despair, anger or anxiety with their fight-or-flight signals.

7. Practice and be alert for similar situations triggering unrealistic expectations and their associated hurt and disappointment. You'll find you have just a few tough ones. Study memories of your parents' beliefs and teachings for the roots of these.

8. Make time for this process; it often uses a lot of energy. Note even the smallest improvements and insights to build upon and avoid staying with discouraging thoughts when change comes slowly. Remember that some anger or disappointment is often appropriate. Your goal is just to reduce the intensity of reactions that disable you, not eliminate all negative feelings.

Twelve Toxic Beliefs

Here are common beliefs to memorize for quick recognition as you monitor:

1. You must have the approval or love of one particular person or most other people.

2. You can feel proud of your efforts only if you perform better than someone else.

3. People (including you) should be blamed or punished when they don't measure up to the standards you set.

4. If something threatening might happen, it's helpful to worry about it frequently.

5. Your past is responsible for most of your present behavior and emotional adjustment.

6. A kind and compassionate person must get very upset over other people's problems.

7. It's unbearable when you work hard for something and you don't get it.

8. Happiness depends on what life gives to you.

9. It's more comfortable to avoid than to face problems or responsibilities.

10. If you love others, you have a right to be very dependent upon them, and they on you.

11. If you're very talented or attractive, you're entitled to recognition and an easier path.

12. If you're very clever, you can find shortcuts around the frustrating rules in our society.

Three Child-Brain Habits

As your Adult monitors, you may notice habits of thinking that don't seem connected to a Parent belief. These may be carryovers from your smaller, simpler child brain that will remain until you reprogram them.

1. **Black-and-white thinking**: A young child's brain simplifies when it tries to organize its intake of data. Young children naturally think things are either bad or good, always or never, happy or sad, fun or boring, big or little, black or white. They need to be helped to see that there's a range of options in each case and have trouble even comprehending this until their brain matures.

2. **Overgeneralizing**: Again, the simpler child brain often fails to recognize or accept the difference between two similar situations. A child may get upset when an event doesn't unfold as it did a previous time when he enjoyed it, as when grandma comes to cook instead of playing with him. He may be fearful of a situation that reminds him of a traumatic experience, like going in the water if he got water up his nose once. Even when a parent tries to explain how the new situation is different, the child will still hold on to his original belief about it until his brain can contain the new concepts.

3. **Over-connection to others**: Young children naturally believe they are the center of attention and also feel like they cause what happens around them. They assume that others, especially their parents, can read their minds and that they know what their parent is thinking or feeling. A two-year-old can easily have a tantrum because his mother

didn't know what he needed and has to be helped as he develops to express himself so he can be understood. Young kids feel responsible if things go wrong and sometimes when things go well. Children born on the Fourth of July often think the fireworks are for them until they're four or five. It takes Wise-Parent guidance and years of experience for people to realize how little power they actually have over events and other people. And Adults frequently assume others can know their intention or their need without being told, especially when they're married.

Since people don't automatically outgrow these immature brain habits, such habits can remain to confuse your thinking indefinitely. Your Adult must identify these errors and work with the Wise Parent to retrain your Child part for more complex functioning. These mental habits represent only three of several that have been identified. They have been chosen because they seem to occur most often; the others usually get handled when CBT is practiced on the twelve beliefs.

Appendix B

Your Multifaceted Self-Esteem

Do you ever think you have low self-esteem? Do you think you have high self-esteem? For most people, it's likely their answer to both questions should be yes. Contrary to popular belief, self-esteem is not an either-or commodity. You can identify specific areas that are low and work on increasing your confidence in them. Please rate each area below:

Mind:

	Low	High
Nonverbal intelligence (math, spatial)	1 2 3 4 5 6 7 8 9 10	
Verbal intelligence (reading, speaking)	1 2 3 4 5 6 7 8 9 10	
Creativity	1 2 3 4 5 6 7 8 9 10	
Talents (specify_____)	1 2 3 4 5 6 7 8 9 10	

Body:

Facial appearance	1 2 3 4 5 6 7 8 9 10
Body shape	1 2 3 4 5 6 7 8 9 10
Body condition	1 2 3 4 5 6 7 8 9 10
Other (hands, feet, other features)	1 2 3 4 5 6 7 8 9 10

Interpersonal:

Intuitive	1 2 3 4 5 6 7 8 9 10
Empathic	1 2 3 4 5 6 7 8 9 10
Tolerant	1 2 3 4 5 6 7 8 9 10
Honest	1 2 3 4 5 6 7 8 9 10
Responsible	1 2 3 4 5 6 7 8 9 10
Thoughtful	1 2 3 4 5 6 7 8 9 10
Generous	1 2 3 4 5 6 7 8 9 10
Anger control	1 2 3 4 5 6 7 8 9 10
Boundaries	1 2 3 4 5 6 7 8 9 10
Communication	1 2 3 4 5 6 7 8 9 10
Other: _____	1 2 3 4 5 6 7 8 9 10
Particular relationships (brother, spouse, etc.)	1 2 3 4 5 6 7 8 9 10

Personal skills:

Organization	1 2 3 4 5 6 7 8 9 10
Mediator	1 2 3 4 5 6 7 8 9 10
Leader	1 2 3 4 5 6 7 8 9 10
Domestic arts (cooking, sewing)	1 2 3 4 5 6 7 8 9 10
Other: _____	1 2 3 4 5 6 7 8 9 10

Appendix C

How to Shut Down a Panic Attack or Other Extreme Fight-or-Flight Reaction

1. *Don't* take a deep breath.

2. Breathe out slowly as long as you can. Count if you wish.

3. Hold your breath awhile.

4. Take a very small breath.

5. Breathe out slowly again as long as you can.

6. Continue this pattern until you feel calm. As you reduce the oxygen going to your brain, tell your inner family to switch off your body by reminding yourself:

   - I'm safe right now.
   - My life is not in danger.
   - I can handle these feelings.
   - No need for fight-or-flight.

7. Don't say:

   - It's unbearable.
   - I can't stand it.
   - I can't take any more.
   - This is killing me.

8. You can say:

   - I hate this.
   - I don't want to stand it.
   - This is horrible.
   - I'm really upset over this.

If you can't do the above, count backwards by sevens from two hundred. The harder this is for you, the better it will work. Then practice the above techniques.

Appendix D

Behavior Chart and Guidelines

Behavior Chart

Name_____   Attitude___Cooperative_____

Date_____   Behavior___Obey parents_____

Time	Sun	Mon	Tues	Wed	Thurs	Fri	Sat
7:00 - 9:00 am							
9:00 - 11:00 am							
11:00 - 1:00 pm							
1:00 - 3:00 pm							
3:00 - 5:00 pm							
5:00 - 7:00 pm							
7:00 - 9:00 pm							

In the spaces:

Yellow - obeys 1st time.
Orange - obeys with one warning.
Blue - more than one warning.

Reward time with a parent if no more than 5 blue marks in a week:
Frisbee with Dad in park.
Cookies with Mom.
Monopoly with Dad.
Do a craft with Mom.

Figure 5 offers you a picture of a deceptively simple behavior chart that can help guide you and your child between the ages of four and eleven into mutual cooperation. Some parents have created their own spreadsheets, and others draw one with a ruler. Sitting with your child, fill in his name and the date. Explain that he gets a fresh chart and a fresh start every week. Then you fill in the word "cooperative" in the blank next to "Attitude." Describe examples of what cooperative would mean for your child. For instance, she would come to dinner right when you call her or pick up her toys before guests come over when you ask her, without arguing.

Next to "Behavior" you fill in the words "obey parents." Tell your child between the ages of four and six or seven that you're going to give her some directions to see if she knows how to do this chart. A small twinkle in your eye is OK here, but you should try to act serious. Tell her she needs to pretend she's in the army for a few minutes. Then tell her to do simple things like stand up, turn around twice, touch her toes, reach up high, go over and touch a lamp or sit down. If you have a very resistant young child or an older child who knows what "obey" means, this may not be useful to try. In that case, you should just proceed to the next step; your child will learn specifically what he has to do once you begin with the chart.

The body of the chart consists of spaces for each two-hour period of the day, seven days of the week. Here's how you fill it in:

- The two-hour spaces will be left blank for times when your child is not in your care, away at school or at a friend's house. Also leave them blank when your child is asleep at night.

- As the chart suggests, a space will be filled with orange if, during a two-hour period, the child just gets warnings. There should only be one warning for each different thing you ask him to do.

- If at any time during a two-hour period your child doesn't obey after one warning, you'll fill in the whole space for that period with blue. If he disobeys again, even several times, during the same two-hour period, he still gets just one blue mark. This allows a child to have a bad mood without blowing his whole week.

- Don't be tempted to get more detailed when you fill in the chart. It will be hard for you to maintain. Don't complicate the scoring. This simple system communicates well with your child, and that's all it needs to do.

- Fill all spaces when your child is in your care with yellow unless she's gotten a warning or a blue mark. This indicates to your child when she's cooperated with you, either because she obeyed when you asked her or she just followed your rules without being told. All these yellow spaces provide kernels of corn that keep the chart positive.

- You can use different colors, just keep them consistent.

- Keep your charts in a folder, not on the refrigerator. Your child can get them out to show people if she wants to. Some kids are really embarrassed to have their errors on display.

At first some kids may try to tear up their chart, but soon they will understand how it helps them. At the bottom of the chart are spaces where you fill in briefly what rewards your child can earn by obeying you and cooperating. Here's the list of guidelines for rewards that are effective.

1. Rewards should emphasize having *positive one-on-one time* between a child and a parent. They should not include both parents or another child. This is a precious time for you and your child to get to know each other better. How do you get to know a friend? Isn't it easier when just the two of you try to connect than when one or two others are also present to distract you? Kids will try hard to get this private time with you.

2. Rewards should take about *one and a half hours*. This gives enough time for an activity but doesn't require so much that you'll have trouble fitting it in to your weekend schedule. Don't go overboard at first by giving more time, only to have to withdraw to shorter activities as time goes on. That will set your child up to feel disappointed, not rewarded. Be consistent, especially until you've gotten the pattern established.

3. One of these rewards should happen *each weekend* if your child has earned them. Kids will give you only one or two passes before they stop believing you'll deliver the promised reward. Some kids will last

longer, but they'll be hurt when you don't keep your promise and may become less interested in minding and cooperating with you.

4. *Encourage your child to suggest activities he'd like to do with you.* Children react to this in a variety of ways. Some are full of ideas and need help in selecting ones that aren't expensive or too long. Some feel like they are being put on the spot and need time or possibly some positive experience with the chart and a reward you choose before they will suggest anything. A few kids are negative and need you to express your enthusiasm for having a happier time together at home and to find some new fun things to do together.

5. You should offer a few ideas for things you'd like to do with your child. These should be activities where you can relax and be playful and not have to teach or manage your child's behavior very much. Playing a fun game, doing a craft, going out for lunch, walking around an interesting area, picking out some books at the library and reading together, and baking something together are all activities that don't cost much and could happen easily again. Try to identify activities you don't usually do. Otherwise, if your child doesn't earn his reward one week, you'll be punishing him by withdrawing something. Keep doing the usual activities like soccer or family outings as you did before the chart. If your child doesn't earn the reward one week, express your hope that you'll get to try again together next week.

6. If you're married, include your spouse as much as possible in working with the chart. Especially be sure to take turns with your one-on-one rewards to help both parents connect better with your child. If you have more children under the age of twelve, they may need to have charts as well. Even if they don't have charts, they'll each expect the rewarding one-on-one time on weekends. With two kids, you and your spouse can each take one child during the same time period, alternating each week. With adolescent kids, there's a different system. They'll also want that one-on-one time with you but might prefer a longer activity twice a month or monthly, if they're doing well.

7. With four- and five-year-olds and some less mature older kids, waiting a week until there's a reward is too long. For them you should plan a fifteen-minute activity near the end of each day that they don't get a blue mark and offer a lot of verbal encouragement when they follow your directions. You can read to them from a special book they haven't had before or play a brief game together.

Here's how you begin using the chart with your child:

1. When you introduce the chart, briefly explain that your child will have yellow in the spaces when he obeys you the first time you tell him to do something for that period. He'll also get yellow if he just follows your rules without being told. He'll get an orange space if you have to give him a warning. Tell him you'll say, "If you don't do (what I asked) right now, you're going to get a blue mark." Explain that if he doesn't do it after the warning and you have to ask him a third time, he'll get a blue space. Explain that he's allowed to make some mistakes, as he can get five blue marks in a week and still get a reward.

2. When you first begin using the chart, tell your child something he must do. If he does it right away, praise him for cooperating with you. If he doesn't, remind him that now with the chart he must do what you tell him to do right away without arguing and give him just one extra chance.

3. Following this, if he doesn't mind you (he may argue or ignore you), he gets just one warning. Don't be tempted to give more warnings. It just confuses your child about what you expect, and he'll push for more warnings because he wants your attention. The sooner you're clear with him, the easier it will be on both of you.

4. If your child still doesn't mind you, tell him he's getting a blue mark.

5. If upon hearing this your child gets very upset (and many do at first), comfort him, reminding him that he doesn't have to be perfect; he can get up to five blue marks and still have his special time with you

on the weekend. But don't negotiate. One blue mark is a very mild consequence. Give him a time-out in his room if he's acting up too badly about it. Time-out guidelines are discussed in the parenting-chapter text.

6. If your child won't mind you after you've given him a blue mark, it's still important that you make him do what you asked. You can tell him he has to take a time-out until he's ready to do it. You can mention to him that he's lucky to have the chart as a warning system so he won't have you yelling at him or get so many time-outs or other consequences.

7. If your child gets a couple of blue marks, encourage him to cooperate more so you both can have that special time together the next weekend. Let him know you're really looking forward to it and that you hope he'll be more successful for the rest of the week.

8. You're in charge of deciding what is reasonable to ask your child to do at his age and must consider his temperament and the time of day. It's up to your Adult and Wise Parent to make it possible for him to succeed by considering all these factors. If you can see that he's trying but is still getting too many blue marks, don't give him more warnings or more punishments. Instead, scale back what you're asking of him. Note if blue marks happen at a particular time of day and restructure that time so there's less pressure on him and you.

    You should make it possible for your child to get through most weeks without more than five blue marks. Kids really prefer not to get them. Reconsider what you're expecting of him and reduce the number of things you're telling him to do. Perhaps you need to work with him to clean up all those toys. Maybe some toys should be rotated so he has fewer to manage. When you have more than one child, they'll fight with each other, and you may find a lot of blue marks occur when you try to intervene. Consider the whole situation and how you can change it to help your kids get along. What's the age difference? Do they have much in common in their play? How many hours and days must they play with each other without a break? Could other friends be included to offer some separation that's not a time-out? If you get stuck here, a counselor can help you figure out what changes could be made.

Appendix E

Adolescent Disclosure Statement

Adolescents who come for counseling with me have a right to understand from the beginning the way I will work with them and their parents. It is my belief that all youths benefit by having the best possible relationship with their parents. When they come in to talk with me, they also want to feel that in some sense what they say to me is confidential. Otherwise, they would simply talk directly with their parents. It is my goal to open up lines of communication between teens and their parents as much as possible. It is also important to realize that developmentally, adolescents need some privacy as they work to become independent.

In trying to balance all these issues and to maintain trust with both the parents and adolescents who come to me, I follow these guidelines:

1.   Information shared with me remains confidential unless the youth and I agree that it would be helpful to involve his or her parents in the particular issue. Often youths want help in communicating their needs to their parents.

2.   When a youth is doing something I consider dangerous, I will share it with his or her parents. I will discuss with the youth how and when the information will be shared with the parents (e.g., with or without the youth present, whether the youth or I will present it, etc.)

3.   Unless I feel there is imminent danger, I will schedule the next session to include at least one parent. If there is imminent danger, I will contact the parents at once.

At present, here is what I consider "dangerous":

- Sexual intercourse or pregnancy

- Frequent usage of marijuana, nicotine or alcohol

333

- Any usage of any other drug

- Deliberately going places where parents can't supervise

- Associating with people who are dealing drugs or carrying guns

- Riding in cars with intoxicated or unsafe people

- Suicide attempts or harm to one's body

- Anorexic or bulimic behavior

- Physical conflict with others

I am willing to modify this policy for each family. For example, if a parent considers something else dangerous (like *any* alcohol consumption), I will agree to report the activity, as long as the youth knows this before choosing to tell me about it.

Youths have the right to know that Washington State law provides that there is counseling available after age twelve in which their parents are not included. I have chosen not to offer counseling on this basis but will help youths find a reference to help them, if that's what they believe they need. Modifications for this family:

I have read and understood the above Disclosure Statement and agree to follow its guidelines:

Youth   _____   Date _____
Parent   _____   Date _____
Parent   _____   Date _____
Therapist   _____   Date _____

References

Adler, Bill Jr., *Outwitting the Neighbors: A Practical and Entertaining Guide to Achieving Peaceful Coexistence with the People Next Door* (New York: The Lion's Press, 1994).

Albert, Elisa, *Freud's Blind Spot: 23 Original Essays on Cherished, Estranged, Lost, Hurtful, Hopeful, Complicated Siblings* (New York: The Free Press, 2010).

Alcoholics Anonymous (New York: Alcoholics Anonymous World Services, 1976).

Amen, Daniel G., *ADD in Intimate Relationships* (Newport Beach: Mindworks Press, 2005).

Amen, Daniel G., *Change Your Brain, Change Your Life* (New York: Three Rivers Press, 1998).

Amen, Daniel G., *Healing ADD* (New York: Berkley Books, 2001).

Amen, Daniel G., and Lisa C. Routh, *Healing Anxiety and Depression* (New York: Penguin Books, 2003).

American Psychiatric Association, *Diagnostic and Statistical Manual of Mental Disorders,* DSMIV-TR (2000); see also http://www.Allpsych.com/disorders/dsm.

Arden, John B., *Rewire Your Brain: Think Your Way to a Better Life* (Hoboken: John Wiley, 2010).

Aron, Elaine N., *The Highly Sensitive Person: How to Thrive When the World Overwhelms You* (New York: Broadway Books, 1997); see also http://www.HSPerson.com, accessed June 7, 2012.

Aron, Elaine, *The Highly Sensitive Person in Love: Understanding and Managing Relationships When the World Overwhelms You* (New York: Broadway Books, 2000).

AskDrSears, http://www.AskDrSears.com, 2011, accessed May 27, 2012.

Attwood, Tony, *The Complete Guide to Asperger's Syndrome* (Philadelphia: Jessica Kingsley Publishers, 2007).

Bank, Stephen and Michael Kahn, *The Sibling Bond* (1982; rev. ed., New York: Basic Books, 1997)

Barth, Roland S., *Lessons Learned: Shaping Relationships and the Culture of the Workplace* (Thousand Oaks: Sage Publications, 2003).

Bassett, Lucinda, *From Panic to Power* (New York: HarperCollins, 1997).

Baumeister, Roy F. and John Tierney, *Willpower: Rediscovering the Greatest Human Strength* (New York: Penguin Press, 2011).

Beck, Judith, *The Beck Diet Solution: Train Your Brain to Think Like a Thin Person* (Birmingham: Oxmoor House, 2008).

Bennett, Charles A., *Volunteering: The Selfish Benefits* (Oak View: Committee Publications, 2001).

Benson, Herbert, *Beyond the Relaxation Response* (New York: Berkeley Books, 1985).

Benson, Herbert, *The Relaxation Response* (New York: William Morrow, 1975).

Berne, Eric, *Games People Play: The Psychology of Human Relationships* (1964; rev. ed., New York: Ballantine Books, 1992).

Bernstein, Albert J., *Emotional Vampires: Dealing with People Who Drain You Dry* (New York: McGraw-Hill, 2001).

Brantley, Jeffrey and Wendy Millstine, *Five Good Minutes in the Evening* (New York: MJF Books, 2006).

Breggin, Peter R. and David Cohen, *Your Drug May Be Your Problem: How and Why to Stop Taking Psychiatric Medications* (2000, rev. ed., Philadelphia: DaCapo Press, 2007).

Black, Claudia, *It Will Never Happen to Me* (Bainbridge Island: MAC Publishing, 2001).

Brown, Sandra A., Matthew McGue, Jennifer Maggs, John Schulenberg, Ralph Hingson, Scott Swartzwelder, Christopher Martin, Tammy Chung, Susan F. Tapert, Kenneth Sher, Ken C. Winters, Cherry Lowman, and Stacia Murphy, "A Developmental Perspective on Alcohol and Youths 16 to 20 Years of Age," *Pediatrics*, Vol. 121 Suppl. 4 (April 2008).

Brown, Thomas E. *Recognizing ADHD: Neurobiology, Symptoms and Treatment* (Chicago: Pragmaton, 2001).

Cade, Eleanor, *Taking Care of Parents Who Didn't Take Care of You: Making Peace with Aging Parents* (Center City: The Cade Group, 2002).

Camus, Albert and Philip Thody, *Return to Tipasa, Lyrical and Critical Essays* (New York: Vintage Books, 1970).

Carbonell, David, *Panic Attacks Workbook* (Berkeley: Ulysses Press, 2004).

Carnegie, Dale, *How to Stop Worrying and Start Living: Time-Tested Methods for Conquering Worry* (1944; rev. ed., New York: Simon & Schuster, 1984).

Carnegie, Dale, *How to Win Friends and Influence People* (1936; rev. ed., New York: Simon & Schuster, 1981).

Carnes, Patrick J., *Out of the Shadows: Understanding Sexual Addiction* (Center City: Hazelden, 2001); see also http://www.GentlePath.com, accessed on June 7, 2012.

Carter, Les and Frank Minirth, *The Anger Trap* (San Francisco: John Wiley, 2003).

Carter, Steven and Julie Sokol, *Help! I'm in Love with a Narcissist* (New York: Evans Publishing Group, 2005).

Ceo, Michael, "Couples and Affairs: Managing the Clinical Challenges," Seminar by Cross Country Education, 2011.

Chamberlin, Jamie, "Facebook: Friend or Foe?," *Monitor on Psychology*, Vol. 42, (October 2011).

Chapman, Gary D., *The 5 Love Languages: The Secret to Love That Lasts* (Chicago: Northfield Publishing, 2010).

Clark, David M., and Christopher G. Fairburn, *The Science and Practice of Cognitive-Behavioral Therapy* (New York: Oxford Press, 1997).

Cline, Foster and Jim Fay, *Parenting Teens with Love and Logic: Preparing Adolescents for Responsible Adulthood* (1992; rev. ed., Colorado Springs: Pinon Press, 2006).

Cline, Foster and Jim Fay, *Parenting with Love and Logic: Teaching Children Responsibility* (1990; rev. ed., Colorado Springs: Nav Press, 2006).

Coleman, Paul, *The Complete Idiot's Guide to Intimacy: Creative Ways to Get on the Pathway to Genuine Intimacy* (New York: Penguin Group, 2005).

Cozolino, Louis, "How Evolved Are We? The Triune Brain in the Consulting Room," *Psychotherapy Networker*, September/October 2008, 20-27.

Cress, Kathy Jo and Kali Cress Peterson, *Mom Loves You Best: Forgiving and Forging Sibling Relationships* (Far Hills: New Horizon Press, 2010).

de Becker, Gavin, *The Gift of Fear and Other Survival Signals That Protect Us from Violence* (New York: Random House, 1997).

Dobbs, David, "Beautiful Brains," *National Geographic*, Vol. 220 No. 4, (October 2011).

Dobbert, Duane L., *Understanding Personality Disorders: An Introduction* (Westport: Greenwood Publishing Group, 2007).

Dodes, Lance, *Breaking Addiction: A 7-Step Handbook for Ending Any Addiction* (New York: Harper Collins, 2011).

Donoghue, Paul J. and Mary E. Siegel, *Are You Really Listening? Keys to Successful Communication* (Notre Dame: Sorin Books, 2005).

Elgin, Susan H., *You Can't Say That to Me! Stopping the Pain of Verbal Abuse: An 8-Step Program* (New York: John Wiley, 1995).

Ellis, Albert and Robert Harper, *A Guide to Rational Living* (Hollywood: Wilshire Books Co., 1977).

Faber, Adele and Amy Tiemann, *Courageous Parents, Confident Kids—Letting Go So You Both Can Grow* (Chapel Hill: Spark Press, 2010).

Fields, Denise and Alan and Ari Brown, *Toddler 411: Clear Answers and Smart Advice for Your Toddler*, 3rd ed. (Boulder: Windsor Peak Press, 2011).

Finch, David, *The Journal of Best Practices: A Memoir of Marriage, Asperger Syndrome, and One Man's Quest to Be a Better Husband* (New York: Scribner, 2012).

Forward, Susan with Donna Frazier, *Toxic In-Laws: Loving Strategies for Protecting Your Marriage* (New York: HarperCollins, 2001).

Forward, Susan with Craig Buck, *Toxic Parents: Overcoming Their Hurtful Legacy and Reclaiming Your Life* (New York: Bantam Books, 1989).

Fox, Douglas, "The Private Life of the Brain," *New Scientist*, November 2008.

French, Gerald D. and Frank A. Gerbode, *The Traumatic Incident Reduction Workshop* (Menlo Park: IRM Press, 1992).

Freud, Sigmund, ed. Peter Gay, *The Freud Reader* (New York: W. W. Norton, 1989).

Gibran, Kahlil, *The Prophet* (1926; repr., New York: Alfred A. Knopf, 2001).

Gottman, John M. and Joan DeClare, *The Relationship Cure: A 5 Step Guide to Strengthening Your Marriage, Family and Friendships* (New York: Three Rivers Press, 2001).

Grand, David, http://www.BioLateral.com, accessed June 8, 2012.

Grandin, Temple and Ruth Sullivan, *The Way I See It: A Personal Look at Autism and Asperger's* (Arlington: Future Horizons, 2008).

Grandin, Temple (made-for-television biopic), Ruby Films, Gerson Saines Production, HBO Films (USA, 2010).

Grant, Jon E. and Marc N. Potenza, *Pathological Gambling: A Clinical Guide to Treatment* (Arlington: American Psychiatric Publishing, 2004).

Greek, Milt, *Schizophrenia: A Blueprint for Recovery* (Athens: Milt Greek, 2008, rev. ed., 2012).

Hallowell, Edward M. and John J. Ratey, *Delivered from Distraction: Getting the Most Out of Life with Attention Deficit Disorder* (New York: Ballantine Books, 2006).

Hannibal, Mary Ellen, *Good Parenting Through Your Divorce: The Essential Guidebook to Helping Your Children Adjust and Thrive—Based on the National Program* (2002; rev. ed., Cambridge: DeCapo Press, 2007).

Harper, James and Jayson Austin, *How to Get Off Psychoactive Drugs Safely: There Is Hope. There Is a Solution* (2005; rev. ed., Charleston: CreateSpace, 2011).

Harris, Gardiner, "Talk Therapy Doesn't Pay, So Psychiatry Turns Instead to Drugs," (*The New York Times* 5, 2011). See also http://nytimes.com/2011/03/06/ health policy/06doctors.html, accessed June 25, 2012.

Hazelden, http//hazelden.org., accessed May 25, 2012,

Herman, Linda, Linda Herman, *Parents to the End: How Baby Boomers Can Parent for Peace of Mind, Foster Responsibility in Their Adult Children, and Keep Their Hard-Earned Money* (Chicago: NPI Upstream, 2013).

Hickman, Martha Whitmore, *Healing after Loss* (New York: HarperCollins, 1994).

Hobbs, Carolyn, *Joy No Matter What* (York Beach: Conari Press, 2005).

Horchow, Roger & Sally, *The Art of Friendship: 70 Simple Rules for Making Meaningful Connections* (New York: Quirk Packaging, 2005).

Hyman, Bruce M. and Cherry Pedrick, *The OCD Workbook* (Oakland: New Harbinger, 2005).

James, John W. and Russell Friedman, *The Grief Recovery Handbook* (New York: HarperCollins, 2009).

Jones, Bliss, *Benzo-Wise: A Recovery Companion* (2009; rev. ed., Nichols: Campanile Publishing, 2010).

Kastner, Laura S. and Jennifer Wyatt, *Getting to Calm: Cool-Headed Strategies for Parenting Tweens and Teens* (Seattle: ParentMap, 2009).

King, Brian E., *Understanding Personality Disorders* (Haddonfield: Institute for Brain Potential, 2011).

Kramer, Jonathon and Diane Dunaway, *Why Men Don't Get Enough Sex and Women Don't Get Enough Love* (New York: Simon & Schuster, 1990).

Kübler-Ross, Elizabeth and David Kessler, *On Grief and Grieving* (New York: Simon & Schuster, 2005).

Lanius, Ulrich, "Dissociative Processes and EMDR: Staying Connected" (Workshop, Seattle, WA, October 5, 2001).

Lebow, Grace and Barbara Kane, *Coping with Your Difficult Older Parent: A Guide for Stressed-Out Children* (New York: Avon Books, 1999).

Lester, Gregory, *Personality Disorders in Social Work and Health Care* (Nashville: Cross Country Education, 2004).

Love, Patricia and Jo Robinson, *Hot Monogamy: Essential Steps to More Passionate, Intimate Lovemaking* (New York: Penguin Books, 1995).

Love, Patricia, *The Truth about Love: The Highs, the Lows, and How You Can Make It Last Forever* (New York: Fireside, 2001).

Lukeman, Alex, *Sleep Well, Sleep Deep: How Sleeping Well Can Change Your Life* (New York: M. Evans & Co., 1999).

Lurie, Steve, *Connect for Success: The Ultimate Guide to Workplace Relationships* (Lawrence: Empowered Work Publishing, 2009).

MacKenzie, Robert J., *Setting Limits with Your Strong-Willed Child: Eliminating Conflict by Establishing CLEAR, Firm and Respectful Boundaries* (Roseville: Prima Publishing, 2001).

Maskovitz, Richard, *Lost in the Mirror: An Inside Look at Borderline Personality Disorder* (New York: Taylor Trade Publishing, 2001).

Mason, Paul T., and Randi Kreger, *Stop Walking on Eggshells: Taking Your Life Back When Someone You Care About Has Borderline Personality Disorder* (Oakland: New Harbinger Publications, 1998).

Elaine Mazlish, *How to Talk So Kids Will Listen and Listen So Kids Will Talk* (1980; rev. ed., New York: Scribner, 2012).

McBride, Karyl, *Will I Ever Be Good Enough? Healing the Daughters of Narcissistic Mothers* (New York: Free Press, 2009).

McKay, Matthew and Peter Rogers, *The Anger Control Workbook* (Oakland: New Harbinger, 2000).

Motivation Store, http://www.getmotivation.com/store, accessed May 23, 2012,

Mueser, Kim T. and Susan Gingerich, *The Complete Family Guide to Schizophrenia: Helping Your Loved One Get the Most Out of Life* (New York: The Guilford Press, 2006).

Naiman, Rubin R., *Healing Night: The Science and Spirit of Sleeping, Dreaming and Awakening* (Minneapolis: Syren Book Co., 2006).

Nelsen, Jane, Cheryl Erwin and Roslyn Duffy, *Positive Discipline, The First Three Years: From Infant to Toddler—Laying the Foundation for Raising a Capable, Confident Child* (Roseville: Prima Publishing, 1998).

Nelson, Tammy, "The New Monogamy," *Psychotherapy Networker*, Vol. 34, Issue 4 (July/August 2010), 20–27, 60.

Nemzoff, Ruth, *Don't Bite Your Tongue: How to Foster Rewarding Relationships with Your Children* (New York: Palgrave Macmillan, 2008).

Newton, Michael, *Destiny of Souls: New Case Studies of Life Between Lives* (Woodbury: Llewellyn Worldwide, 2000).

Newton, Michael, ed., *Memories of the Afterlife: Life Between Lives: Stories of Personal Transformation* (Woodbury: Llewellyn Worldwide, 2009).

Newton, Michael, *Journey of Souls: Case Studies of Life Between Lives* (St. Paul: Llewellyn Worldwide, 1994).

Niebuhr, Reinhold, Serenity Prayer at AA History and Trivia online, http://www.aahistory.com, accessed May 27, 2012.

Novotny, Amy "Resilient Kids Learn Better," http//:monitor on psychology.com, Vol. 40, October 2009, accessed June 25, 2012.

Peele, Stanton, *7 Tools to Beat Addiction* (New York: Three Rivers Press, 2004); see also http://www.peele.net, accessed June 8, 2012.

Peele, Stanton with Archie Brodsky, *Love and Addiction* (New York: The Viking Press, 1980).

Phelan, Thomas, *1-2-3 Magic: Effective Discipline for Children 2–12* (Glen Ellyn: ParentMagic, Inc., 2010).

Piper, Watty, *The Little Engine that Could* (New York: Philomel Books, 2005).

Polster, Erving and Miriam, *Gestalt Therapy Integrated: Contours of Theory and Practice* (New York: Vintage Books, 1974).

Potter-Efron, Ronald T. and Patricia S., *Letting Go of Anger: The Eleven Most Common Anger Styles* (Oakland: New Harbinger, 2006).

Price, Michael, "More Compassion, Less Competition," http//:monitor on psychology.com, Vol. 40, December, 2009.

PubMed, http//www.ncbi.nlm.gov/pubmed, accessed on May 25, 2012.

Rando, Therese A., *How to Go on Living When Someone You Love Dies* (New York: Bantam, 1991).

Real, Terry, *The New Rules of Marriage: What You Need to Make Love Work* (New York: Ballantine Books, 2007).

Roland, Paul, *Meditation Solutions* (London: Octopus Publishing Group, 2002).

Ronson, Jon, *The Psychopath Test* (New York: Riverhead Books, 2011).

Sarkis, Stephanie Moulton, *Ten Simple Solutions to Adult ADD* (Oakland: New Harbinger, 2005).

Sartre, Jean-Paul, *Existentialism is a Humanism* (New Haven: Yale University Press, 2007).

Schiraldi, Glen R., *The Self-Esteem Workbook* (Oakland: New Harbinger, 2001).

Schiraldi, Glenn A., *The Post-Traumatic Stress Disorder Sourcebook* (New York: McGraw Hill, 2009).

Schloemer, Fred, *Parenting Adult Children: Real Stories of Families Turning Challenges into Successes* (Louisville: Butler Books, 2011).

Semmelroth, Carl and Donald E. P. Smith, *The Anger Habit in Relationships: A Communication Workbook for Relationships, Marriages and Partnerships* (New York: Writers' Showcase, 2000).

Shapiro, Francine, *Eye Movement Desensitization and Reprocessing: Basic Principles, Protocols and Procedures* (New York: The Guilford Press, 1995).

Sheehy, Gail, *Passages: Predictable Crises in Adult Life* (1976; repr., New York: Ballantine Books, 2006).

Siegel, Daniel J., *Mindsight: The New Science of Personal Transformation* (New York: Bantam Books, 2010).

Skinner, B. F., *Science and Human Behavior* (1953; repr., New York: The Free Press, 1965).

Skinner, B. F. *The Technology of Teaching* (New York: Appleton-Century-Crofts, 1968).

Smith, Brendan L., "Inappropriate Prescribing," *Monitor on Psychology* (June 2012).

Smith, Manuel, *When I Say No, I Feel Guilty* (New York: Bantam Books, 1975).

Stearn, Jess, *Yoga, Youth and Reincarnation* (New York: Bantam Books, 1965).

Stout, Martha, *The Sociopath Next Door* (New York: Broadway Books, 2005).

Strong Vocational Interest Inventory, https://www.cpp.com/products/strong/index.aspx, accessed November 10, 2012.

Trafton, Jodie A., William P. Gordon and Supriya Misra, *Training Your Brain to Adopt Healthful Habits: Mastering the Five Brain Challenges* (Los Altos: Institute for Brain Potential, 2011). See also http://www.brainpotentialinstitute.com, last accessed November 10, 2012.

van der Kolk, Bessell A., "New Frontiers in Trauma Treatment," workshop by The Institute for the Advancement of Human Behavior, 2007.

Weekes, Claire, *Hope and Help for Your Nerves* (1969: repr., New York: Signet, 1990).

Whitfield, Charles L., *Boundaries and Relationships: Knowing, Protecting and Enjoying the Self* (Deerfield Beach: Health Communications, Inc., 1993).

Yager, Jan, *Friendshifts: The Power of Friendship and How It Shapes Our Lives* (Stamford: Hannacroix Creek Books, 1999).

Yager, Jan *When Friendship Hurts: How to Deal with Friends Who Betray, Abandon or Wound You* (New York: Simon & Schuster, 2002).

Index